The Case against Afrocentrism

# The Case against Afrocentrism

Tunde Adeleke

University Press of Mississippi    Jackson

www.upress.state.ms.us

The University Press of Mississippi is a member of the Association of American University Presses.

I wish to acknowledge the following journals for permission to include versions of previously published articles: the *International Journal of African Historical Studies* for adaption of my 1998 article, "Black Americans and Africa: A Critique of the Pan-African and Identity Paradigms," in chapter 3; the *Canadian Review of American Studies* for the use of portions of my 1999 award-winning article, "Who Are We? Africa and the Problem of Black American Identity," in chapter 1; and the *Western Journal of Black Studies* for excerptions from my 2005 article, "Historical Problematic of Afrocentric Consciousness," in chapter 4.

First printing 2009
∞
Library of Congress Cataloging-in-Publication Data

Adeleke, Tunde.
  The case against Afrocentrism / Tunde Adeleke.
    p. cm.
  Includes bibliographical references and index.
  ISBN: 978-1-61703-331-5                    1. Afrocentrism. 2. Pan-Africanism. 3. African diaspora. 4. Africa—In popular culture. 5. African Americans—Race identity. 6. Blacks—Race identity. I. Title.
  DT15.A35 2009
  305.896—dc22                           2009008846

British Library Cataloging-in-Publication Data available

This book is dedicated, with love and affection, to my children Tosin, Toyin, and Chinyere, and with gratitude from the entire Adeleke clan, to James Ekere Usen, and Ayo Saddique, exemplars of true friendship, and finally, in loving memory of my senior brother, Raufu Bawa Alabi Adeleke "Bawan Allah," patriarch of the Adeleke family, Omo Mewu, Oroki, Sun re O

# Contents

# Preface

The decision to write this book was made, rather subconsciously, in 1992 at the Annual Symposium in the Humanities jointly organized and hosted by the College of Humanities, the Center for African Studies, the Department of Black Studies, and the Columbian Quincentenary Committee of the Ohio State University. The theme of that symposium was "The Black Diaspora: The African Experience in the Americas." The event—which attracted scholars from Africa, Great Britain, Canada, the West Indies, Europe, and Latin, Central and South America—was an occasion to reexamine the Diaspora in the five hundredth year of Columbus's "discovery," an epochal stage in the constellation of events and developments that were critical to the making of the black Diaspora. Among the delegates from Africa, Europe, North America, and the Caribbean was a euphoric undercurrent of satisfaction at what had been accomplished despite overwhelming odds and adversity. The dominant mood was one of celebration. I presented a paper titled "The Diaspora: Dialectics of Enduring Contradictions," which interrogated what I then saw as some of the ambivalences and contradictions that have characterized the relationship of continental Africans and blacks in the Diaspora.

I envisaged the conference as more than just an occasion to celebrate the Diaspora. In my judgment, it should go beyond celebrating the social, economic, political and cultural developments of blacks over these centuries and showcasing their intellectual worth and wealth, beyond interrogating the relations between Diaspora blacks and dominant groups in their respective locations. The conference should be an opportune moment for critical introspection, a time to reexamine Diaspora blacks and continental Africans in relation not only to the outside "Other" but also, more significantly, to the inner "Self." Therefore, I decided to focus my paper not on the traditional and popular binaries—Europeans versus Africans/Blacks, exploiter-exploited, and superior-subordinate— but on a completely differently and often invisible but unacknowledged binary: continental Africans versus black Americans. What kinds of contradictions and ambivalence have informed their relationship over these centuries? How have continental Africans and blacks in America, for example, dealt with, and conceptualized, each other through history? What forces, factors, and circumstances shaped the relationship? In other words, rather than embrace the progressive, triumphalist, and celebratory frame of analysis and mood that seemed to dominate discourse on the subject, and was pervasive at the conference, I chose to identify and interrogate instances of tension and contradiction in the relationship. These tensions and contradictions, in my judgment, belie the dominant, prevailing, and overarching ethos of mutuality and kinship. Bad judgment! In a conference where everyone seemed enamored to the theme of mutuality, cooperation, and highlighting of successes and triumphs, the introduction of a paper or discussion on issues of differences and contradictions was troubling and disturbing, and it unleashed a storm of angry rebuke and condemnation.

Within this context, and in hindsight, my paper was counterintuitive, for it introduced negativism and pessimism into an optimistic and celebratory context. It injected themes of contradiction and conflict into discourses meant to be overwhelmingly positive and celebratory. It was like striking a match into a powder keg. The explosion was deafening. Before I could conclude my presentation, several hands went up, and for the next half hour or so, I endured repeated verbal assaults. Critics questioned my intellectual credentials and judgment for daring to suggest that the relation between Africans and blacks in Diaspora was characterized historically by anything other than harmony and consensus. A keynote speaker, then president of a historically black institution, could barely restrain herself as she launched into verbal tirades. A fellow panelist, an African from Ghana, began his presentation with a public apology to the audience. I felt isolated. Not one voice came out in my defense. Shortly after the end of the session, however, several attendees approached me to say how much they agreed with me and proceeded to share corroborating experiences from their respective institutions and countries. I was at a loss for words to articulate my disgust at these intellectual cowards. But there was this remarkable young black American woman who introduced herself as the granddaughter of one of the black American leaders who had conspired against the Jamaican and Pan-Africanist Marcus Garvey in the 1920s. This was an issue I had discussed in my presentation. She proceeded to say how she desperately wanted to share her perspective but was scared by what she had just witnessed happen to me. This experience only emboldened me. To have been subjected to such vicious rebuke for daring to present an alternative viewpoint strengthened my resolve to pursue the theme further. But first, I had to reexamine my sources and ascertain for myself whether or not I had misread or misrepresented the sources. I hadn't. The entire episode convinced me that this cloak of hypocrisy, this homogenizing ethos and consciousness that seemed to dominate discourse on Africa and black Diaspora history and relationship had to be confronted and deconstructed. No credible understanding of history can come out of a paradigm that discourages critical discourses.

The experience of this conference and my determination never to be silenced resulted six years later in my critically acclaimed study *UnAfrican Americans: Nineteenth Century Black Nationalists and the Civilizing Mission* (University Press of Kentucky, 1998). This book, *The Case against Afrocentrism*, is a continuation of this critical discourse. The drive toward essentializing race and ethnicity, especially in the last two decades, has reinforced a culture of intellectual intolerance, the type that Molefi Asante underscored in his call for intellectual vigilance. As he pontificated in *Afrocentricity*, "Our collective consciousness must question writers who use symbols and objects which do not contribute meaningfully to our victory. How could a black writer be allowed to use symbols which contradict our existence and we not raise our voices? Afrocentric criticism must hold especially accountable the works of Africans, continental or diasporan . . . The times are surely different and we must now open the *floodgates of protest* against any non-Afrocentric stances taken by writers, authors, and other intellectuals or artists" (emphasis added).

This is a declaration designed not to facilitate critical discourses but to stifle opposing views and nurture a monolithic intellectual cult. That day, at the Columbus conference, I felt drowned in the *floodgates of protests* unleashed by the intellectual police. In the end, they failed. The African and black American experiences are too complex to be subsumed under a single intellectual rubric. The essays in this book further underscore this complexity. They illuminate deep and pervasive ambivalence and paradoxes in the relationships of continental Africans and Diaspora blacks, relationships defined concomitantly by claims and affirmations of affinity and consanguinity, within a problematic and subversive context characterized by undercurrents of historically and culturally mediated tension and dissonance. Consequently, *The Case against Afrocentrism* calls for reconceptualizing constructs and paradigms that have traditionally been the underpinnings of a unifying essentialist worldview.

# Acknowledgments

This book has benefited, directly and indirectly, from the contributions of many individuals, institutions, and organizations. Over the past decade and a half, I have had the opportunity to encounter scholars who shared their perspectives and engaged me in critical discourses that helped to refine the ideas and themes in this book. Chapter 1, "Africa and the Challenges of Constructing Identity," is a revised and expanded version of a paper I first presented at the 2005 Nordic Association for American Studies Conference hosted jointly by Vaxjo University, Vaxjo, and the Blekinge Institute of Technology, Karlskrona, Sweden. I am grateful to Gunlog Fur for the invitation and to the discussants at the conference for their insightful comments and suggestions. Chapter 3, "Essentialist Construction of Identity and Pan-Africanism," is also an expanded version of a paper titled "Pan-Africanism: A Call for Re-Conceptualizing," which I presented at the 2007 *AfriKanistentag* Conference in Vienne, Austria. Special thanks to Norbert Cyffer, my former colleague at the University of Maiduguri, Nigeria, now of the Center for African Studies, University of Vienna, for inviting me to speak at the conference, and also to all the commentators and discussants. I also want personally to acknowledge, with gratitude, Kwame Opoku for his stirring critique of my session at the Vienna conference and for challenging everyone to rethink racial categorization, especially the problematic use of the term "Black." Chapter 5, "Afrocentric Essentialism and Globalization," grew out of two papers presented at international conferences. The first was the 2002 "Cultural Citizenship: Challenges of Globalization" conference held at Deakin University in Melbourne, Australia, at which I presented a paper titled "Black Americans and the Global Context." Many thanks to Michael Leach for the invitation and to the commentators of my session, whose critical comments I found immensely helpful. The second was the 2004 special session of the Collegium for African American Research (CAAR) held at the Austrian Association for American Studies Conference in Salzburg, Austria. I am indebted to Christopher Mulvey and Hanna Wallinger, then CAAR president and secretary respectively, for inviting me to present my work on *Gloracialization*.

This work also benefited from my brief visit to the World History Institute of the Capital Normal University (CNU) in Beijing, China, in the spring of 2007. I had the privilege of meeting and exchanging ideas and perspectives with a wonderful group of historians who challenged me to rethink and refine the theoretical underpinnings of this study. I owe my visit to the initiatives of two individuals. First, my friend and colleague here at Iowa State University, Xiaoyuan Liu, who first suggested that I seriously consider visiting China, and then proceeded to put me in contact with his alma matter, CNU. Xiaoyuan not only facilitated my visit but also took time out of his busy research trip to China to introduce me to facets of Chinese hospitality and culture. The second was Professor Xu Lan, director of the World History Institute, who was very receptive to the idea of hosting a scholar in African American Studies and worked hard to secure an official invitation. I delivered a series of lectures to students and faculty of the Institute on the theme "Black Americans and the Challenges of Race, Ethnicity and Identity." I gained and learned much from the comments and perspectives of the students and faculty. The entire trip was intellectually rewarding and culturally enriching. I was overwhelmed by the generosity and hospitality of the entire faculty and students, especially Professors Xu Lan, Zhao Junxiu, Liang Zhanjun, and Zhou Gang. I would be remiss if I did not acknowledge the incredible and selfless efforts of the student hosts who sacrificed long hours to ensure that I had a most endearing visit and experience—Huang Minghua (Eileen), Li Jun (Vicky), Wang Fei, and Hou Zhongzhen. Eileen was simply incredible. I was both awed and humbled by her incredible encyclopedic attention to details of Chinese history and civilization, as we meandered through crowds of tourists in Tiananmen Square, the Forbidden City, the Summer Palace, Imperial Gardens, and, most unforgettably, as we breathlessly ascended the Great Wall. She never lost a beat.

I would also like to thank my good friend and compatriot Ikponwosa Ekunwe (aka Silver), political scientist and researcher at the University of Tampere, Finland, who has been a steady and reliable host during my numerous visits to Finland. He remains an invaluable intellectual resource. Silver has consistently challenged my thoughts about, and thereby enriched my understanding of, more recent developments and trends in the African Diaspora, especially in relations to recent African migrations to Scandinavia and the Nordic countries. To break the monotonous routine of academic conference, I could always count on Silver for sumptuous Nigerian dishes and critical African cultural reenactments. I have fond memories of watching a Finnish musical group, decked in African attire and led by a Nigerian, perform traditional Nigerian Igbo highlife music.

The Case against Afrocentrism

# Introduction

# Afrocentric Essentialism

In a lengthy presidential address delivered to the National Emigration Convention in Cleveland, Ohio, in August 1854, Martin R. Delany (1812–1885) emphasized the pervasiveness and virulence of racism in the United States and urged black Americans to consider immigrating to external locations such as Africa and the Caribbean, where they would have unfettered opportunities to develop and realize their full potentialities.[1] In Delany's judgment, race had become perhaps the single most critical factor in human relations, both within the United States and on the international scene. As he poignantly declared, "It would be duplicity longer to disguise the fact that the great issue, sooner or later, upon which must be disputed the world's destiny, will be a question of black and white, and every individual will be called upon for his identify with one or the other."[2] Accenting the color line, Delany proposed a Manichean construction of domestic and international relations—blacks against whites, Europeans against non-Europeans. Since, in his judgment, coexistence on the basis of equality and freedom appeared inconceivable, blacks needed their own domain of independence and nationality elsewhere, preferably in Africa. For Delany, the continued quest for integration in America had become a culturally destructive option that potentially could also jeopardize and possibly obliterate the African identity of blacks.[3]

To his nineteenth-century contemporaries, Delany was the quintessence of blackness. In Delany's makeup, according to a biographer, there was no compromise with whites. This reputation of Delany as uncompromisingly anti-white, and a consistent advocate of the color line is widespread and entrenched. Yet, Delany was not born and raised with this disposition. He started out a believer in the promises of the American Dream and fought fervently against separatism. By the early 1850s, however, he had come to a critical crossroads. Disillusioned with the lack of change and apparent invincibility of racism, he began to spearhead and galvanize the emigration movement. It was in this capacity as leader and president of the emigration movement that he convened the Cleveland convention of 1854. After the convention, he spent the next eight years crusading for emigration. In his writings and speeches, Delany drew attention to the ubiquitous nature of racism and to what he perceived as a more sinister and troubling reality: a conspiracy by American whites and those he referred to as their "Anglo-Saxon cousins" to subordinate, subjugate, and exploit Africans and blacks in the Diaspora ad infinitum.[4] Race became, in Delany's judgment, the engine dynamo of global development, with the white race occupying the top echelons of the societal ladder, a position that conferred benefits and privileges of immense proportion, while blacks, and people of color generally, were confined to a life of deprivation and degeneration. In Delany's judgment, the reality mandated racial solidarity on the part of oppressed blacks. In order to conquer oppression and escape perpetual subordination, blacks had to unite and forge a common front. He committed himself to the pursuit of black unity and separatism from 1852 until the outbreak of the Civil War in 1861 compelled him, once again, to reverse course and embrace integration.

Almost fifty years after Delany's speech, W. E. B. Du Bois published his seminal work *The Souls of Black Folk* (1903), in which he echoed Delany's racialized worldview by characterizing "the problem of the twentieth century" as "the problem of the color line, the relation of the darker to the lighter races of man in Asia and Africa, in America and the islands of the sea."[5] Du Bois's declaration proved prophetic. No issue dominated international relations in the twentieth century, and shaped the relationships between peoples in different parts of the globe, particularly in the regions he identified, as prominently as race. Many analysts have in fact ventured the prediction that, judging by the state of contemporary race relations, particularly the ascendance of ethnocentric and cultural jingoistic consciousness on a global scale, race and, ipso facto, the color line, would indeed become the substantive problems of the twenty-first century.[6] Although he too emphasized the color line, Du Bois cautioned against overemphasizing race, given his dualistic construction of the black American. He portrayed blacks as a people formed of the dual experiences and heritages of Africa and America, and constantly tormented by the conflicting values and ideals emanating from this duality. As he explained,

> One ever feels his two-ness,—an American, a Negro; two souls, two thoughts, two unreconciled strivings; two warring ideals in one dark body

. . . The history of the American Negro is the history of this strife,—this longing to attain self-conscious manhood, to merge his double self into a better and truer self. In this merging he wishes neither of the older selves to be lost. He would not Africanize America, for America has too much to teach the world and Africa. He would not bleach his Negro soul in a flood of white Americanism, for he knows that Negro blood has a message for the world. He simply wishes to make it possible for a man to be both a Negro and an American.[7]

Thus, Du Bois warned against sacrificing one identity and heritage for the other. Both possessed intrinsic essence and validity and should, therefore, be acknowledged and respected. Both Delany and Du Bois underscore the primacy of the color line as an essential dynamic of American history, but they had radically different considerations in mind. For Delany, separation was a major consideration: the creation of an independent black nationality in Africa. Du Bois was a little ambivalent. Although he too emphasized race and racial consciousness, the complexity and duality of the Negro was an equally compelling consideration. While race mattered to Du Bois, and he eventually became active in Pan-Africanism, his analysis took due cognizance of, and accented, the American dimension of the Negro identity.[8] Both Delany and Du Bois would go on to use their racial convictions to support paradigms that advanced Pan-African consciousness and movements designed to unify all blacks and peoples of African descent upon a platform of economic, social, and political struggle and regeneration.

The concept of the color line that Delany and Du Bois emphasized has a deep historical pedigree. Some scholars trace its origin back to the dawn of enslavement in the New World. In fact, color was the defining essence of the South's "peculiar institution" from its inception in the seventeenth century to its demise in the mid-nineteenth century. The color line defined and shaped the relationship between masters and slaves. It conferred human qualities and attributes to the former while depicting the latter as subhuman.[9] Despite its historical depth, the color line has, however, been conceived and understood essentially in terms of a demarcation paradigm, that is, a concept that validates racial boundaries. There have not been any serious attempts to probe its deeper ramifications. There are indeed critical but neglected dimensions and implications of the color line that significantly shaped the attitudes and orientations of those within the parameters of the line, especially in relation to others deemed external, and by implication hostile, to the racial group.

The concept of the color line implies the imperative of racial unity and consensus within the parameters of a distinctive racial category. Put differently, the color line is much more than acknowledging racial boundaries. It is also an affirmation of the pertinence of racial unity and consensus, of the need to further, within the racial group, mono- lithic and homogeneous values—a condition deemed fundamental to the struggles and survival of the race in what is perceived as a hostile world environment. Everyone within the racial group is therefore ex- pected to subscribe to a particular worldview, to remain faithful to what are perceived to be the needs, interests, and aspirations of the group. This mandates avoidance of actions or utterances that would seem to compromise or erode racial solidarity. At all times, members are expected to contribute positively to furthering the corporate in- terests of the racial group, and to be prepared and willing to defend the race regardless of the issues and circumstances. In essence, the color line is premised on absolute allegiance and devotion to one's racial group. This dictates an orientation to society and reality defined by alienation, racial and ethnic exclusivity, and an almost paranoid disposition that dichotomizes society and reality into conflicting and irreconcilable entities.

Delany boldly and more forcefully proclaimed and defended this broader dimension of the color line in his writings and speeches than did Du Bois. His analysis of American and global relations in the late 1850s and early 1860s underscored a rigid racial demarcation and con- struction of social, historical, and political realities. Delany discerned a global order in which whites/Europeans sought black subordination. To escape this fate, he called for emigration and the creation of an independent black nationality.[10] In a letter soliciting support for his emigration scheme addressed to Dr. James McCune Smith, Delany wrote,

> The present state of the political affairs of the world more than at any pe- riod since the establishment of international policies among Christian governments—which policies comprehend and imply all nations and peo- ples, whether civilized or heathen—call for and imperatively demand our attention as descendants of Africa in whole or part . . . One of the most prominent features in the present conflicts, struggles, and political move- ments among the nations of the world seems to be: Which can reduce us

to a condition the best adapted to promote their luxury, wealth, and ag-
grandizement, to which as a race, for centuries we have contributed more
than any other race."

Nothing was more important for Delany at this phase of his career
than to convince blacks of the supreme importance of, and imperative
for, constructing a countervailing platform of struggle based strictly
on racial demarcation. To him, race mattered more than anything else,
and he urged all blacks to unite in the spirit of his 1854 declaration.

The color line was, therefore, conceived not only to draw attention
to the potency of race as a factor in determining public policies but
also to underscore the necessity and establish modalities for racial solidarity. Equally significant, it was meant to affirm and defend a group's
corporate identity built upon race and ethnicity. This broader dimension of the color line has, however, proven to be more idealistic and
visionary. Though racism mandated the color line, its very essence and
existence depended on the attainment of balance or harmony within a racial group. In other words, the color line doctrine affirms the
indispensability of racial harmony and consensus to the sustenance,
strengthening, and survival of the racial group.

History, however, has shown a consistent muddling of the color
line. In order to sustain the line, its advocates suggest, blacks must
exhibit cohesiveness built on shared feelings of love and confraternity.
Some observers contend that the ascendance of racism and the problematic state of black America (measured by economic poverty, social
and political subordination and marginalization, problems of drug ad-
diction, teenage pregnancy, unemployment, the alarming rate of ho-
micide, and so forth) accord legitimacy to the color line. In essence,
these negative and destructive circumstances and factors have become
unifying elements that authenticate the color line. It becomes incum-
bent on all blacks to rally behind the line. Actions or movements that
seemed to efface the color line, or even compromise its authenticity,
were often frowned at and vociferously opposed. For many, therefore,
toeing the line, faithfully advancing, and defending, at all times and
under all circumstances, the interests and problems of blacks became
the litmus test of racial identity. It is this allegiance that establishes
one's authenticity as a black person. It is also what distinguishes an
authentic black person from an "Uncle Tom."[12]

The conviction of confraternity evokes anger and resentment toward those who, either through actions or utterances, appear to com-

promise or undermine the interests and aspirations of the race. Racism is presumed to be of such potency as to obviate any basis for disrupting or muddling of the color line. Intraracial problems and contradictions are expected to be kept within rather than made issues of public discourses that could potentially damage the image of the race and thereby provide the other group (that is, the racial enemy on the other side of the color line) ammunition with which to further malign and mistreat the race. The mandate of racial solidarity stands indissoluble, even in circumstances when the conditions and complexities of the racial group clearly demand critical introspection and self-criticism. In this respect, the color line accents racial censorship and discourages actions or comments that are critical of blacks, especially if such criticisms could become subjects of public discourse. Such self-criticisms, however justified, are discouraged because they present the outside world with the image of a black community in crisis and disarray, thus compromising the struggle at critical moments when the entire race was expected to stand together in harmony and unison. A good illustration is the responses of some black nationalists and scholars to the publication of Keith Richburg's *Out of America: A Black Man Confronts Africa*. Published in 1997, the book immediately provoked anger and resentment among black Americans and Africans. In radio and television talk shows and on network news, angry respondents lambasted Richburg, accusing him of maligning and misrepresenting Africa and of displaying ignorance of African history. Many called him a black racist, an Uncle Tom, someone who manifested profound self-hatred and confusion on identity.[13] Members of a group referred to as "mainstream African American middle class" dismissed Richburg as "a self-serving Uncle Tom looking to make good with his white bosses."[14] Former chair of the African American studies department, Temple University, Molefi K. Asante, found the book "offensive and obscene." He described Richburg as someone "caught in the spiral of psychic pain induced by . . . 'Internal inferiorization.'"[15]

Although today the color line is not officially proclaimed as vehemently as in the past, it nonetheless remains a defining characteristic of the black American struggle. Black militants of the 1960s civil rights struggles—Black Muslims, the Black Panthers, and Black Power—embraced the color line. Black Power advocate Stokely Carmichael based his Pan-African philosophy on racial demarcation. The Black Panthers spearheaded a movement that emphasized racial divisions. This was and remains true of the Nation of Islam. In fact, Nation of

Islam leader Elijah Mohammed and his successor Louis Farrakhan never made secret their advocacy of, and commitment to, the color line, justified largely on pathological and negative characterizations of whites. Mohammed's speeches are replete with calls for constructing and strengthening the color line. His "truth" about the black situation in America is unambiguously racial and racist. As he declared, "We, the Black men are of God. Our oppressors whoever they may be are of the devil. Their nature is evil! They are incapable of doing well."[16] Describing "the nature of the white man," Farrakhan, on the other hand, refers to, "the Caucasian" as "a vessel made for dishonor. He's like a vile olive branch grafted in. He ain't natural, he's not a natural branch, he's grafted in among the peaceful people. This is a graft that is a sucker."[17] The essentialization of race is not isolated to radical fringe elements within the black struggle. Racial essentialism or, more appropriately, the existentialization of color is an integral and critical component of revolutionary black idealism, the best example of which is Afrocentrism.

Molefi Asante, a leading advocate of the Afrocentric genre, articulates and advocates the color line in clearly unambiguous terms in his writings.[18] In one of his books, *Afrocentricity* (1989), Asante emphasizes the need for the development and defense of what he terms the "collective consciousness" of blacks. He stresses the importance of racial unity and harmony, for, in his judgment, blacks remain dogged and threatened by self-abnegating and destructive, hegemonic, Eurocentric values. As he warns, "There can be no effective discussion of a united front, a joint action, and a community of interest until we come to good terms with collective consciousness, the elementary doctrine of economic, political, and social action."[19] Underlining the essence of the collective consciousness, he writes, "Our collective consciousness must question writers who use symbols and objects which do not contribute meaningfully to our victory. *How could a black writer be allowed to use symbols which contradict our existence and we not raise our voice?*" (emphasis added).[20] In this last sentence, Asante clearly establishes the importance of intellectual vigilance on the part of blacks against black writers who betrayed the color line. As constructed by Asante, Afrocentricity represents the intellectual articulation of the color line in all its broader ramifications and implications. But Afrocentricity goes beyond authentication of the color line. Its broader intellectual premise or raison d'être was to challenge and deconstruct Eurocentric denial, and misrepresentations, of black/African history and culture. It advanced a construction of the black/African cultural and historical experiences designed to provide order, rationality, and essence where none had been acknowledged by Eurocentric historiography. It also sought to reverse the negative Eurocentric portraits and renditions of the black and African cultural and historical experiences. In consequence, Afrocentric scholars have made, and continue to make, certain claims about African/black history and culture that often ignore or compromise historical reality, assertions that are socially and therapeutically utilitarian but historically misleading and inaccurate.[21]

Historically, the human drive for essentialist ethos has resulted from, and reflected, the inequality of the human historical encounters. The doctrine of white superiority, affirmation of Eurocentric distinctiveness and distinction, European claims of special and dominant status, assertions of Anglo-Saxon purity and superiority, and advocacy of white solidarity are all part of the historical edifice and repertoire of European hegemony.[22] Over time, this hegemonic disposition reproduced its own contradiction and antithesis. Borrowing from and mirroring the tradition of the hegemonic class, subordinated, oppressed, and exploited groups soon develop "political" and "oppositional" consciousness.[23] In the black American context, this consciousness unleashed countervailing ethos of resistance that crystallized into some forms of essentialism—racial, cultural, or ethnic. Thus, the binary of hegemony-subordination, empowerment-powerlessness, eventually resulted in counterhegemonic essentialist ethos meant to validate and reflect the claims, aspirations, and values of the subordinated and powerless group. Therefore, it could be argued that hegemony is not the exclusive preserve of the dominant powerful class. Subordinated groups have the capacity to develop hegemonic and essentialist ideologies of self-promotion and racial and cultural validation. I focus in this book on the latter type of essentialism, offering an exposition and critique of the cultural, social, historical, and identitarian implications of the essentialist tradition in contemporary black cultural nationalist thought as theorized in Afrocentricity. This work is neither a history of Afrocentricity nor a discussion of the ideology. The focus is not on Afrocentricity per se. The last decade has witnessed outpourings of critical expository, revisionist, and neorevisionist writings on the subject.[24] What I offer is a critique and deconstruction of the social, cultural, historical, and intellectual ramifications and implications of Afrocentric essentialism. The term "Afrocentric essentialism" refers to the use of Africa to advance a monolithic and homogeneous history, culture, and identity for all blacks, regardless of geographical location. Race is a central defining element of Afrocentric essentialism. It is in fact the glue that binds other elements of Afrocentric essentialism such as culture and ethnicity. In Afrocentric essentialist thought, Africa is the embodiment of what are characterized as immutable identitarian elements that unite all blacks: race, ethnicity, and culture. These elements, especially culture and ethnicity, according to Afrocentric essentialist scholars, have not been fundamentally impacted by centuries of separation from Africa and acculturation in America. Put differently, "Afrocentric essentialism" refers to the monolithic construction of the black American and African Diaspora experiences, the location and interpretation of these experiences within a Pan-African historical and experiential paradigm. Though Afrocentric essentialism embodies racial essentialism, it is much broader. Race is just a key defining element, the glue that binds Afrocentric essentialism. Both racial essentialism and Afrocentric essentialism seem synonymous and interchangeable, but the latter is much broader. Algernon Austin provides this apt definition of racial essentialism:

> Racial essentialism means that groups are seen as possessing an essence— a natural, supernatural, or mystical characteristic—that makes them share a fundamental similarity with all members of the group and a fundamental difference from non-members. The essence is understood in racialist thinking as being immune to social forces. It does not change with time or social context. In essentialist thoughts, blacks in the United States share a fundamental similarity with blacks in the African nation of Malawi, for example, and blacks today share a fundamental similarity with blacks in ancient Nubia thousands of years ago.[25]

Austin's definition underscores this use of race to construct a monolithic identity across historical time and space with disregard for historical change. Afrocentric essentialist thought acknowledges the centrality of race. Owing to its problematic character as identitarian construct, however, leading Afrocentric scholars now deemphasize race and highlight ethnicity, broadly and vaguely represented by the concept "Africa." Africa became a much more reliable identitarian construct that embodies something that binds all blacks, something much more substantive than race—*culture*, which, despite centuries of separation, had supposedly survived almost intact among blacks in

Diaspora. Being African (ethnicity) became the essential defining element around which to organize and combat Eurocentric hegemony. Hence, while some Afrocentric scholars acknowledge the social and political construction of race and thus its limited value and diminished status, and elevate Africa as the essential factor, Afrocentrism actually embodies race and nurtures racialist consciousness. Again invoking Austin:

> Afrocentrism is a racial ideology because it ideologically constructs a heritable essential difference among human populations. Within Afrocentric theory, people who are of the African Cultural system are presented as being fundamentally different from people outside this system. These differences are passed on to the descendants of people within this African Cultural System so that centuries later the descendants of Africans are said to be culturally African. Because these cultural differences are not influenced by social forces, they remain present in the same form over millennia.[26]

This continuity is best represented in Afrocentric depiction of continental Africans and all blacks in Diaspora as one people who share identical historical and cultural experiences. Afrocentric scholars consider this monolithic construction of the African and black historical and cultural experiences critical to survival and success in their historical and existential struggles against forces of white/European historical and cultural hegemony. They construct a historical continuum of shared interests, experiences, and challenges unifying Africans and blacks in Diaspora. This is evident in the works of Asante, Marimba Ani, Maulana Karenga, Nai'm Akbar, Amos Wilson, and John Henrik Clarke, among many others.

A defining characteristic of Afrocentric essentialism is the Manichean conception of history. Afrocentric scholars represent history as an arena of irreconcilable conflicts between diametrically opposed cultures—black versus white. They advance a racialized paradigm that delineates boundaries of historical and cultural conflict between blacks and whites.[27] Their affirmation of a uniform and homogeneous Africa and black Diaspora history and culture underscores certain critical cannons of Afrocentric essentialism: the development of a countervailing African epistemology as the modus vivendi for black empowerment and regeneration; the proclamation of a monolithic African identity for all blacks regardless of geographical location; the advancement of the cultural essence and superiority of black and African cosmology; the development and propagation of the "stolen legacy" thesis, a theory that attributes the core values of western civilization to the over-riding influence of ancient civilizations of Africa, particularly Egypt. This theory has become an article of faith among Afrocentric scholars who have used it to advance what some critics depict as a hegemonic universal Afrocentric historiography.[28] Furthermore, Afrocentric essentialist thought underscores the historical depth and authenticity of a positive African consciousness among blacks. Finally, there is also a deemphasizing of New World (metropolitan) influences, consciousness, and acculturation among blacks; that is, the denial of the essence and validity of the New World (American) consciousness and identity among blacks.

To understand Afrocentric essentialism fully, it is imperative that the tradition is appropriately contextualized within the historical discourse of black alienation and resistance. From slavery to the present, blacks have had to struggle against the forces and manifestations of Eurocentric essentialism. Enslavement, racism, and segregation (Jim Crow) were all built on affirmations of white superiority and corresponding claims of black inferiority. As slaves, blacks were deemed subhuman, items to be owned, bought, and sold by whites. As free, they were deemed primitive and inferior, not deserving of close association with the "superior" white race. Historically, Eurocentric essentialism engendered misery, alienation, subordination, depersonalization, dehumanization, and subjugation. Whether in slavery or freedom, it nurtured in blacks alienated consciousness, provoking resistance and ultimately the development and articulation of a combative countervailing essentialist worldview: Afrocentric essentialism. The roots of Afrocentric essentialism can in part be traced to the nineteenth-century black resistant traditions of abolitionism, moral suasion, colonization, and emigration. Modern representations of Afrocentric essentialism are in the "militant" ethos and movements of the black struggle from Pan-Africanism to Black Power and Black Panthers. Modern attempts to revive Pan-Africanism is premised on the conviction that continental Africans and blacks in Diaspora are one people who share identical problems and challenges and are threatened by, and vulnerable to, the hegemonic machinations of the old racial enemy (whites/Europeans). This explains the racial/Afrocentric essentialist construction of the struggle and the location of Africa as the foundation, the edifice of black resistance.

In modern times, early centralization of Africa abounded in Marcus Garvey's philosophy and movement, in the writings and speeches of the "radical" activists of the civil rights struggles such as Stokely Carmichael and Malcolm X, and in the writings and speeches of the late West Indian scholar-activist Walter Rodney. Rodney offered a sound knowledge of African history as a prerequisite for any meaningful and effective confrontation with Eurocentric historiography and world-view and emphasized the imperative of using historical knowledge to rescue blacks from cultural imperialism. African history became a weapon for combating and deconstructing what he termed "European cultural egocentricity."[29] At the roots of Afrocentric essentialism lie African history, African cosmology, African identity, and African epistemology. From the early slave resistance and anti-slavery abolitionism through nineteenth-century emigration movements to the present, the black struggles reflected and entailed efforts, directly or indirectly, aimed at deconstructing ethos of Eurocentric essentialism. This is reflected in the insurrectionary tradition of Nat Turner and Denmark Vesey; the quasi-historical efforts of the pioneers of black intellectual resistance such as William C. Nell, James W. C. Pennington, Robert Benjamin Lewis, James Theodore Holly, William Wells Brown, George Washington Williams, and Martin Delany; the moral suasion ethos of the early nineteenth-century black abolitionist movement spearheaded by the likes of William Whipper and Lewis Woodson; and the nationalist and colonization schemes of the nineteenth century. In different ways, therefore, these efforts constituted attempts to confront and challenge the hegemonic order that had been validated and legitimized by Eurocentric racial and cultural essentialist ethos. The doctrine of white supremacy that justified Europe's claim to cultural and civilizational supremacy also shaped the historical relationships of whites and non-whites and legitimized the subordination and dehumanization of the latter.

Over time, however, the failure of blacks to overcome the experiential impacts of Eurocentric essentialist ethos compelled many to invoke black and African essentialism in response. Thus, racism became a critical element in the development of essentialist ethos. The role of race in the construction of white essentialist ethos laid the foundation for the countervailing development of black and African essentialism. Although there were several occasions in the eighteenth and early nineteenth centuries when race appealed to blacks as a potential framework of constructing resistance and affirming and validating self/identity, the mid-nineteenth-century upsurge of black nationalist and emigrationist consciousness was a major point of maturation, and gradual crystallization, of Afrocentric essentialist consciousness.

Delany's epochal racial essentialist declaration of 1854 noted above was perhaps a critical turning point in the evolution of Afrocentric essentialism. The entire speech amplified the growing disillusionment of blacks with the failure of integration. Delany would go on in his writings and struggles to give greater substance and strength to "Afrocentric essentialist" values that future generations of black nationalists and activists would invoke. He emphasized the imperative of an African-centered epistemology and insisted on a trans-Atlantic nexus of struggle that united Africans and blacks across the Diaspora as people with shared history, culture, identity, challenges, and problems. He used race (that is, the fact of blackness) as the basis of delineating distinct boundaries of historical encounters and struggles and advanced a monolithic interpretation of black history, while also advocating an Africa-black Diaspora unity built on a common platform of struggle.

This book is a critical interrogation of the cultural and intellectual implications and ramifications of Afrocentric essentialism. As defined above, the concept "Afrocentric essentialism" refers to the monolithic construction of the black experience, the location and interpretation of the black experience within a Pan-African historical and experiential paradigm, and perspective, as a countervailing force against the hegemonic influences and impact of Eurocentric essentialism. Afrocentric essentialism is predicated largely on the convictions that "Afrocentric consciousness" is deep-rooted among blacks in Diaspora and that this consciousness of Africa had always been positive and endearing. From this came the Afrocentric call for Pan-African solidarity and for using Africa as the platform of commonality, identity, culture, and struggle. A major defining character of Afrocentric essentialism is the racialization and ethnicization of the black experience; however, the drive toward essentializing the black and African historical and cultural experiences resulted in what many describe as a dehistoricization process.[30] In other words, the need for a homogeneous and monolithic African and black Diaspora worldview led to deemphasizing of the historical process. Afrocentric scholars have found it necessary to deny or deemphasize the processes of historical change and transformation in America. They deem constructing an essentialist tradition of history and culture profoundly critical to group survival and empowerment in the context of what they perceive as the ever-present and potent threat of Eurocentric hegemony. Although in recent years there has been increased scholarly attention to Afrocentric historicism, little attention has been given to examination of the intellectual, social, and cultural ramifications and contradictions of its essentialist projection of black history, especially in relation to issues such as identity, Pan-Africanism, globalization, the historical process, and the historical representations and utility of Africa. For example, as already stated, Afrocentric essentialism projects Africa as a unifying framework for all blacks. The basis of this "African-centeredness" is the belief that blacks in the Diaspora had historically harbored a deep and positive consciousness of Africa and a strong desire to identify with the continent. It is this claim of historical depth and potency of African consciousness among blacks in the Diaspora that inspired a corresponding assertion of historical continuity and confraternity, and advocacy of reconnection with the continent and reactivation of Pan-Africanism. There are pertinent but often neglected paradoxical questions relating to Afrocentric amplification of the "African roots of, and African influence on, western civilization," and the supposed immutability of African culture, while denying or deemphasizing the acculturative influence of the New World: How is it possible that a people whose legacies, according to Afrocentric scholars, so profoundly shaped Western tradition, would remain uninfluenced by Western contacts? How were they able to retain the original African identity and culture intact (that is, remain essentially African)? These questions underscore the central paradoxical and philosophical problematic of Afrocentric essentialism—the claim of cultural originality and exclusivity in a context of historical and cultural contacts, exchanges, and hegemony!

Afrocentric essentialist scholars depict Africans and blacks in the Diaspora as a community of like-minded, historically and culturally congruent people, whose shared history and culture not only transcended space and time but also defied the process of change. The two are considered one, united by commonality of interests, aspirations, and challenges; a people whose shared identity had not been affected by the historical process of change and transformation, despite centuries of geographical and historical separation. Certain key essentialist ideas derive from such narrow racial, cultural, or ethnic construction of the black Diaspora and African experiences. First, the utility of race, blacks and continental Africans defined as one people united by racial identity and shared struggles; a people whose historical experiences were shaped by the fact of race (color), in consequence of the negative and dehumanizing experiences of their encounters with whites and Europeans. Second, the depiction of Africans and Diaspora blacks as

a people of shared "African" culture, the reality of historical separation and transplantation notwithstanding. African cultural retentions
in the New World are projected as historically rooted and, therefore,
evidence of the permanence and indestructibility of the African essence. In Afrocentric essentialism, therefore, all blacks share one African identity regardless of historical experiences and geographical locations. Thus, historical *time* and *space* appear irrelevant and inconsequential. Here, Afrocentric essentialist scholars reject the Du Boisean
duality construct and any suggestion of New World impact on identity. In their judgment, the American experience never significantly
affected the identity and consciousness of the *real* African person.
The Afrocentrist is not tormented or influenced by warring ideals.[31]
The third is the construction of what I characterize as a *gloracialized*
worldview against globalization. Advocates of Afrocentric essentialism reject globalization and the prospect of global cultural citizenship
and affirm instead ethnic and racial identity and consciousness.[32] It
should be noted, however, that Afrocentric suspicion of globalization
is much older than the advent of globalization. It is rooted in what
some of the pioneers of black historiography characterized as the hegemonic character of "universal history." It is rooted in their representation and rejection of universal history as Eurocentric and destructive to blacks, and in their Eurocentric construction of global history.
The advent of globalization has only strengthened Afrocentric suspicion and provoked some of the most virulent anti-globalization ideas.
Even as many applaud globalization as obviating and transcending
the restrictive parameters of the nation state, thus affording greater
opportunity for human interactions and intercultural communication, Afrocentric scholars portray globalization as anti-black. They
perceive globalization as essentially an enlargement of the power of
the hegemonic nation-state and therefore pernicious. This problematizes the conflict between globalization and the nation-state. In other
words, the nation-state remains a problematic entity, the shrinkage
of its traditional boundaries of political influence notwithstanding.
Afrocentric essentialist scholars suggest that it is not possible to embrace globalization without first confronting and resolving the contradictions and limitations of the nation-state. In Afrocentric essentialist
construct, therefore, the global arena is an extended domain of the
problematic nation-state. Thus, in the Afrocentric genre, globalization reflects continuation of Eurocentric hegemony and essentialism,
hence the need for a countervailing Afrocentric essentialist response

and vigilance—which comes in the form of *gloracialization*. I define *gloracialization* as the consciousness of racial distinctiveness, developed and projected on a global scale, unifying all blacks, regardless of geopolitical location, drawn together by perceived threats emanating from European global cultural expansion. This highest and global expression of black racial consciousness is considered the most potent and formidable force with which to negate the cultural hegemonic implications of globalization.[33]

Ironically, Afrocentric scholars erect boundaries of distinct historical experiential performances within the larger context of American national historical performance, and often at odds with it. The hegemonic nature of the larger context of historical performance led blacks to search for, and construct, their own space within which they are able to perform and tell their own story, while highlighting the limitations and hegemonic character of the dominant space. This justified establishment of distinct epistemological and cosmological boundaries outside of the dominant domain. A major problematic is how blacks are able to construct and navigate distinct cosmological and epistemological spaces while living within a Eurocentric space. To understand black history and culture, Afrocentric scholars insist, one must do so within an African-centered epistemology to the exclusion of the acculturative impact of New World geopolitical space. However, Afrocentric essentialism goes beyond just a platform. What makes it distinctive today is not the platform character but the use of the platform as the basis of constructing a homogeneous and monolithic worldview for all blacks and Africans regardless of geographical locations and historical and cultural experiences. As emphasized, Afrocentric essentialism underscores historical and experiential uniformity and conformity for Africans and all blacks across historical time and space, without due acknowledgment of the historicity of *time* and *space*. That is, both *time* and *space* are treated as static and ahistorical entities, and not the conduits of historical and cultural transformations. Africa is at the heart of Afrocentric essentialism; it is the very basis and foundation for a common identity, historical and cultural experiences and affinity, the substructure for constructing uniform and unifying experiential discourses of historical, cultural, and identitarian homogeneity.

This appeal and utilization of Africa as a weapon and the basis of struggle goes back to the early nineteenth century. Enslavement and dehumanization were based on the negative portraits and rendition of the African background and connection. Initially, this elicited rejection of, and alienation from, Africa. The early-nineteenth-century black abolitionist and moral suasion ethos were designed to affect distance from Africa and achieve full integration in America.[34] By the mid-nineteenth century, for many blacks, Africa was becoming an attractive and acceptable basis of constructing a countervailing platform of struggle. For key nineteenth-century black nationalists, Africa became the basis of a counteroffensive against Eurocentric hegemony. Though for them, the underlying objective of constructing a counter-identity and experience based on Africa was to reshape and reform the American condition.[35] Paradoxically, the essentialization of Africa reflected, in some sense, recognition of historical process and transformation. Even as they constructed a monolithic racial platform of struggle, the activism of nineteenth-century black nationalists mirrored ambivalence that itself implied some recognition of the historical process and transformation. In the postmodern context, however, the essentialization of Africa has come to mean deemphasizing and deessentializing of the historical process. Afrocentric essentialism underscores the fragile, porous, and shallow character of New World enculturation. To bridge the divide created by the historical process or transplantation, and New World acculturation, Afrocentric scholars felt it necessary to deemphasize the historical essence of both transplantation and acculturation. That is, transplantation, in Afrocentric genre, represents just a geographical act, not a culturally transforming process. Enslavement simply took Africans from one locale to another without any lasting transformation and impact. Afrocentric essentialism thus exhibits the following attributes: the tendency to impose uniform identity on all blacks, the tendency to advance uniform culture, regardless of geographical locations or historical experiences, and the tendency to locate all blacks within a monolithic epistemological and cosmological tradition. Afrocentric essentialists associate black Americans, cosmologically and epistemologically, with Africa, as opposed to the western epistemological and cosmological traditions. On the basis of the above, Afrocentric scholars advocate reaffirmation of Pan-Africanism as a viable platform and framework of constructing and demonstrating unifying experiential challenges. Thus, Afrocentric essentialism underscores the color line—black separation and alienation—even in the context of a broadening globalization of the human experience.

Although Afrocentric essentialism is deep-rooted in history, the emergence of Afrocentricity in the modern world represents its ideological maturation, the highest point of Afrocentric essentialism. The historical underpinning of contemporary Afrocentric essentialism is the perceived onslaught on blacks in the post-civil rights era, as in attacks on, and reversals of, the gains of the civil rights struggles. This has caused alienation, resulting in calls for strict delineation of the racial and cultural lines, affirmation of black distinctiveness and uniqueness, cultural conflicts, dissonance and divergence, as opposed to convergence and compatibility. The hegemonic character of mainstream historical experience led many blacks inexorably to affirmation of Afrocentric values and distinctiveness. Thus, rejection and negation led to affirmation of, and quest for validation in, Africa.

The hegemony-subordination binary within which the black American experience unfolded problematized the Self-Other identitarian nexus and consciousness. Afrocentric scholars reject the identity problematic that Du Bois represented in dualistic and conflicted terms. While Du Bois emphasized acknowledging the validity of the Self-Other dichotomy, Afrocentric scholars affirm the Self (Negro) while invalidating the Other (American). While Du Bois presented both in historical relational terms as mutually reflective and reinforcing, Afrocentrists present one as the negation of the other, both perpetually at odds. Du Bois described both as engrossed in a conflict of mutuality, with shared historical and cultural experiences. Afrocentrists underscore distinctiveness, conflict, and negating values.

In a recently published provocative study, Debra J. Dickerson attempts further deconstruction of the racial underpinning of the cultural black nationalist worldview. She wrote *The End of Blackness* (2004) in order to prove and promote "the idea that the concept of 'blackness,' as it has come to be understood is rapidly losing its ability to describe, let alone predict or manipulate, the political and social behavior of African Americans. Given its strictures and the limitations it places upon the growth and free will of those to whom it refers, it diminishes their sovereignty as rational and moral actors."[36] She advocates "updating" blackness so that blacks "can free themselves from the past," and stop "defining themselves out of America."[37] Dickerson underscores the depth of racialist consciousness and convictions among blacks and the degree to which such disposition has informed, and continues to shape, black American history and experience. She emphasizes the negative, constricting, and circumscribing influence of race-conscious disposition and how it is both limiting and undermining the possibilities and potentialities of blacks. Dickerson's "gauntlet thrown down to the black powers that be," echoes much of the strictures against the stranglehold of racialist consciousness among blacks. She articulates in profoundly effective and powerful terms the debilitating effect of racial thinking. Unfortunately, as powerful and potentially influential as Dickerson's work is, the fact remains that racialist consciousness has taken such a strong hold among blacks that it has become synonymous with the very survival and success of the race. Especially in the times of "compassionate republicanism," to be race conscious became a defining essence of being "a real black person." In other words, race consciousness and racial solidarity have become countervailing strategies of struggle and survival. There is nothing wrong with being race conscious. It is a manifestation of one's awareness and responsiveness to the realities of daily life. The problem, however, is in using such consciousness as the basis of existential aspirations and struggles; of allowing race to define and determine, and thereby limit, one's choices, aspirations, visions, and goals. It is ironic that a construct that is widely acknowledged for its fragility and artificiality was, and remains, key to defining the character of a people's conception of self and construction of history. It seems equally ironic also that at a time when many are questioning the utility of race, some blacks are heavily dependent on it as a unifying experiential construct and the basis of constructing boundaries and frameworks for existential struggles.[38] Undoubtedly, it is the virulence and potency of racism in America that has provoked and reinforced black people's affinity to race as a viable means of existential validation.

This book illuminates the social, intellectual, and political representations, challenges, and limitations of Afrocentric essentialist consciousness among black Americans. The many complex dimensions of essentialist ethos are identified and analyzed in relation to identity, historical memory, conceptions, and perceptions of Africa; relations between blacks in Diaspora and continental Africans; and the responses of blacks to the challenges and implications of the expanding terrain of human encounters and experiences. I interrogate the prominence of Africa as a construct and frame of historical and cultural reference in black essentialist ethos. I contend that very often the construction of Africa entailed a dehistoricization process that deemphasizes and diminishes the essence of history. Put differently, in order to construct and defend an essentialist construction of the black experience, Afrocentric essentialist scholars often ignore or deemphasize the dynamics of history. I have written this book, first, to develop and analyze Afrocentric essentialism as a comprehensive and dynamic agency in black history and, second, to probe its many-faceted representations in, and impacts on, black American history and consciousness. Most important, this book is meant to illuminate Africa's problematic, conflicted, and ambiguous role, underscoring the contradictions and limitations of Afrocentric essentialist thought. I aim to suggest that while theoretically Afrocentric essentialism seems like a logical response to alienation and the deepening crisis of black impoverishment, it remains historically weak as a means of understanding, or mirroring into, the historical realities of the black experiences in America and the entire Diaspora.

# 1

# Africa and the Challenges of Constructing Identity

In *The Roots of African-American Identity* (1997), Elizabeth Raul Bethel identifies two critical events that shaped black American consciousness and identity in the nineteenth century. The first was the Haitian revolution of 1791–1804, which resulted in the overthrow of French plantocratic hegemony by black slaves. The revolution represented, for blacks in the United States and elsewhere, both a "model of political agency and racial achievement" that was denied to them and the potency and possibilities of nationalism in the context of New World experience. It consequently nurtured optimism on the prospect of transcending enslavement.[1] The second was the 1807–8 federal legislation prohibiting ships flying under the United States flag from engaging in the importation of slaves. Blacks welcomed this as signaling an end to the long sufferings brought upon Africans by enslavement and the transplantation process. This enthusiastic and joyous response betrayed a growing consciousness of affinity with Africans. The legislation thus induced optimistic expectations about the future of Africa and her descendants abroad, and many blacks began to envision eventual reunification with a lost African identity.[2]

The two developments, according to Bethel, "provided fertile psychosocial environments in which memories of the past intersected with realities and opportunities of the moment."[3] This intersection induced ambivalent nationalist consciousness, which in turn nurtured an equally ambivalent conception of identity. Blacks saw the anti-slave-trade legislation as a positive development that they hoped would terminate the nightmarish experience of dislocation and dehumanization that enslavement and transplantation entailed. The Haitian revolution exemplified the ultimate potential of New World nationalism. Celebrating these positive developments, however, entailed coming to grips with an existential problem of self-definition—"Am I an American or am I a Negro? Can I be both?"[4]

Consciousness of African ancestry combined with the exigencies of the American experience to present, in the words of Bethel, "a continuing challenge to identity for African Americans, and it never would be entirely resolved."[5] This challenge mirrored a critical dilemma, that is, double consciousness, which many critics have since identified as the hallmark of black American identity. This dilemma involved critical existential inquiries into the very nature and character of the black American experience designed to ascertain the extent to which the American experience could be deemed positive and satisfying. The critical inquiry is as follows—To what degree has the American experience satisfied the yearnings by blacks for acknowledgment as full-fledged citizens of America, with their interests, aspirations, and values represented, articulated, advanced, and defended within the framework of the larger society? Put differently, has the American experience been positive and satisfying enough to nurture and sustain in blacks a faith in, and a sense of identity with, the larger society? The absence of a correspondence, the reality of divergence, between the aspirations, interests, and values of blacks, and those of the larger society, has been a defining character of black history and has informed conceptions and perceptions of black identity. There is, however, an added factor of equal importance in shaping black American identity—the denial and denigration of the black historical experience, ancestry, and heritage. This perceived lack of correspondence between black values, interests, and aspirations, and those of mainstream white society, has consequently configured and complicated the identity problem.

Blacks manifested double consciousness on identity from the very earliest of times. Many retained memories of Africa, while struggling to be acknowledged as Americans. Rationalizing the identity question, "Who am I?", consumed the attention of blacks, and Bethel is right in suggesting that the question may never be satisfactorily answered. Attempting to answer the question has provoked some of the most contentious debates in the annals of the black experience. The credit for identifying the focus of the modern context of the debate belongs to W. E. B. Du Bois, whose formulation captured the essence of the identity dilemma. His statement that "one ever feels his two-ness,—an American, a Negro: two souls, two thoughts, two unreconciled striving; two warring ideals in one dark body" underscores the status of the black American as a product of complex historical and cultural experiences.[6]

Du Bois, however, portrayed both experiences as vital to the formation of identity and cautioned against sacrificing one for the other, for each possessed intrinsic essence and validity. As he contended, the Negro "wishes neither the older selves to be lost." The Self (Negro) and the Other (America) are intrinsically and inherently essential, each with unique contributions to the world.[7] Du Bois thus conferred both historical reality and permanence to the double consciousness. He soon immersed himself in the struggles to validate both identities: the struggle for the integration of blacks into the United States as full-fledged citizens and the struggle by blacks to contribute to the defense and furtherance of the interests of Africa. The civil rights movement of the 1960s also exemplified this double consciousness as black Americans fought for integration (that is, American citizenship), while culturally and politically embracing and identifying with the struggles and challenges of the African continent.

The historical validation of the notion of double consciousness has not won universal acclaim and acceptance. It remains the subject of intense controversy among scholars, precisely because of its bearings on the identity question. The notion of double consciousness is central to modern discourses on black American identity, and responses to it betray conflicting interpretations of identity. A few years back, Gerald Early, former chair of African American Studies at Washington University in Saint Louis, Missouri, invited a select group of scholars to respond to the Du Boisean duality paradigm. Published as *Lure and Loathing: Essays on Race, Identity, and the Ambivalence of Assimilation* (1994), their responses betray the complexity and conflicting perceptions of identity among black Americans. A few respondents rejected the duality paradigm, denying its historical potency, while strongly counterpoising a monolithic identity construct grounded in African cosmology. Some accepted and validated the notion of double consciousness and thus acknowledged the legitimacy of the Afro and African American construction of identity. Some others embraced a more neutralist formulation and attempted to situate identity within a cosmopolitan and universal construct—humanity, western civilization, and so forth. Advocates of this "universal" construct perceive black identity as neither essentially African nor essentially American but as the product of a broader and complex human experience. Finally, there are those who situate black identity squarely within a Euro-American cultural context.[8]

The above conflicting conceptions suggest fundamental differences on the significance and relevance of Africa. Historically, Africa had constituted a challenge to black Americans, precisely because in order to define themselves, they had to deal with the reality of their African background.[9] The fundamental challenge has been to establish whether blacks are Americans who had completely shed all trappings of their African ancestry, or Africans, residents in an alien and hostile environment, who somehow managed to retain their Africanness, despite centuries of separation from Africa and acculturation in a New World environment. The responses have been diverse and conflicting. Afrocentric scholars such as Molefi Asante, Maulana Karenga, and Marimba Ani (aka Dona Marimba Richards) proclaim the centrality of Africa to the construction of black American identity and insist upon identifying black Americans as quintessentially Africans.[10] These scholars deemphasize the transforming consequences of New World transplantation and acculturation, suggesting a certain shallowness and superficiality to Euro-American cultural impact and, as one critic put it, affirming the "purity, homogeneity and primordiality of African cultural influences among Afro-Americans."[11] The essentialization of Africa in Afrocentric essentialist thought therefore represents a rejection of the Du Boisean duality construct.

The true Afrocentrist is supposedly someone who is rid of double consciousness. Afrocentrism presumes the possibility of expelling or submerging one of the warring ideals—the Euro-American. Marimba Ani has no scintilla of doubt that blacks in the Diaspora are Africans. The retentions of Africanism in music, religion, family structure and norms, and burial practices clearly separate blacks from whites ethnically and culturally. As she put it, "Africa survives in our [i.e., black Americans'] spiritual make-up; that it is the strength and depth of African spirituality and humanism that has allowed for the survival of the African-Americans as a distinctive cultural entity in New Europe; that it is, our spirituality and vitality that defines our response to European culture; and that response is universally African."[12]

In Afrocentric epistemology, however, Africa is much more than an identity construct. Affirming African identity also represents a strong statement of protest. The late Amos Wilson unambiguously proclaimed this protest dimension. To assert the "Afrikan" identity, he argued, is to assume a radical posture against injustice. As he proudly declared, "I love the challenge of being Afrikan in today's world; it's wonderful! I love digging in my heels against the impossible odds of being black in America. What greater challenge could we have in life today than to be Afrikan?"[13] Africa thus acquires a utilitarian function far beyond representing identity. Critics deem the zero-sum stance on the African identity of black Americans that Afrocentrists maintain as grossly reductionistic and absolutist. W. D. Wright, for instance, does not believe that blacks are "hundred percent" African in character. He acknowledges the complex cultural, national, and ethnic factors involved in forging the black American identity.[14]

The Afrocentric absolutist stance on the African identity of black Americans has provoked a countervailing school that totally rejects Africa and posits instead slavery and the American experience as more substantive foundations for constructing the black American identity. Attempts to impose a racial and color line in the social, academic, political, and cultural spheres provoked widespread resentment that compelled interrogation of the complexity of the American and black Diaspora experiences. Many blacks object to being stamped with a racial label or being confined behind a racial boundary line. The monolithic Afrocentric construction of black history, identity, and culture provoked challenges from black politicians, academics, community activists, entrepreneurs, artists, and athletes, who rejected the simplifying and confining character of race and embraced a more complex and mainstream construction of identity. In the universities, and in the field of education in general, there are calls for a nuanced and representative paradigm that captures the complexity of the African and black Diaspora experiences. Many have come to realize the artificiality of race and its social and political character. This slavocentric or Americentric perspective has been articulated and defended more recently by the black American playwright Douglass Turner Ward, and former *Washington Post* Africa bureau chief, Keith Richburg. Among the most recent proponents of the anti-Afrocentric identity paradigm, Turner and Richburg, in different contexts, called for deemphasizing Africa and situating black American identity instead within the context of slavery. In his provocative book, *Out of America: A Black Man Confronts Africa*, Richburg rejects African identity and strongly implores black Americans to turn inward to their American experience to validate their identity.[15] In a keynote address to the Southern Conference on Afro-American Studies in Baton Rouge, Louisiana, in February of 1995, Ward boldly proclaimed himself a slavocentric and urged blacks to locate their identity in the enslavement experience. Between the two extremes of Afrocentrism and slavocentrism lie other perceptions on identity, ranging from the universalistic and humanistic to the existentialist. Essentially, these other perspectives represent attempts to anchor identity to some supposedly neutral ideals and values that are deemed neither essentially African nor essentially American.[16]

The differences and controversies generated by these conflicting perspectives are played out fairly regularly in the media and in scholarly publications and debates. Consequently, this chapter will not delve deeply into the modern debate. Rather, I hope to highlight something glaringly missing in contemporary discourses on black American identity—the historical context. Since Africa is critical to modern configurations of the identity debate among black Americans, it is pertinent to ascertain the depth and strength of the African consciousness of black Americans by examining how they historically responded to, and defined, their African connection. Did Africa occupy a central place as Afrocentric epistemology suggests, or was Africa subordinated to a greater identity? How crucial was Africa to black American conception of identity? What role did blacks assign Africa in their struggles, and how did they define themselves in the contexts of the struggles? Answering these questions would require a critical examination of the historical antecedents of the current controversies on identity.

I have chosen two critical historical epochs during which black Americans grappled with the identity question. The first is the moral suasion epoch (1830–1849), which was essentially integrationist in aspiration, and the second is the emigration phase (1850–1864, 1878–1880s), which has been characterized as essentially a separatist and nationalist phenomenon. The first is associated with the phase of organized black abolitionism, the second with an organized quest for an independent black nationality abroad. Both epochs provide insights into the construction of identity and considerations of the place and relevance of Africa to the process. In the moral suasion phase, the more neglected of the epochs, the focus will be on the debate and controversies generated by the adoption of moral suasion as abolition strategy by leading blacks in the 1830s.

Moral suasion has often been characterized as a conservative movement whose purpose was to reconcile blacks to mainstream American values and, in the process, attain the rights and privileges of American citizenship.[17] Although it is true that the moral suasion crusade envisioned integration, the debate it unleashed entailed spirited arguments on identity. The debate centered around attaining some consensus on the identity of blacks and, most significantly, on how best to affirm and realize that identity. This debate revealed that though advocates of moral suasion shared a consensus on identity, they disagreed sharply on strategies. The African identity did not feature at all in the debate. On the other hand, the emigration phase focuses on the ideologies, policies, and schemes of leading black nationalists. Africa featured prominently in this latter phase. Emigration has been defined and analyzed almost exclusively in the context of nationalism and Pan-Africanism.[18] While this is true to a significant degree, black American nationalist consciousness, especially in the emigration phase, was also about the quest for self-definition and identity. The impulse for emigration developed out of the anguish felt over the intractable problems of identity and self-knowledge. Out of the emigration debate grew and developed a self-definition that shaped, and continues to shape, the identity discourse today. As an ideology of the abolitionist crusade, moral suasion assumed prominence in the 1830s. Since the motivation and underlying impulse for moral suasion developed against the backdrop of the enslavement experience, a brief examination of slavery and its bearings on identity is pertinent at this juncture.

## Slavery and the Challenge of Identity

To understand the fascination of black Americans with Africa, and the ambivalent and contradictory consciousness Africa provoked, and continues to provoke, among them, one needs to examine the very foundation of hegemony that slaveholders constructed. Enslavement and acculturation in the New World entailed a conscious and systematic process of simultaneous deconstruction and construction of identity.[19] Sometime in the early 1700s, a "slave owner Willie Lynch" addressed fellow slave owners on how best to tame and transform blacks into docile and perfect slaves. Widely publicized as "How to Make a Slave," "Lynch's" speech, which supposedly began circulating in 1712, described in great detail how slave owners could break the spirit and obliterate the humanity of their slaves. "Lynch" had no qualms about his barbaric, inhuman admonitions, for in his schema, slaves belonged alongside horses. He offered planters a strategy of stripping slaves of a sense of worth or any quality that might pose a threat to the smooth functioning of the South's "peculiar institution." The speech was indeed a recipe for deconstructing whatever identity slaves had and imposing in its place an identity that was amenable to slavery. Widely circulated today among black scholars, the authenticity of this document is indeed questionable. It is not dated, and there is no information on the publisher. In other words, the document could well be a hoax, and I am convinced it probably is. This notwithstanding, its basic premise of the need to transform blacks into perfect slaves, from human to subhuman identity, is consistent with a practice that, according to modern scholars, was prevalent among antebellum southern planters. As a North Carolina planter once admitted, "It is a pity that agreeable to the nature of things Slavery and Tyranny must go together and that there is no such thing as having an obedient and useful slave, without the painful exercise of undue and tyrannical authority."[20] Frederick Douglass, the famous "graduate of the *peculiar institution*" gave eloquent testimony to the brutalities and inhuman character of slavery in his epic autobiography.[21] On the authority of historian Ira Berlin, we do know that in 1727, some fifteen years after "Lynch's" document supposedly surfaced, one Robert "King" Carter, considered the richest planter in Virginia, purchased a handful of African slaves from a trader who had been trading on the Chesapeake. The transaction was a familiar one to the great planter, Berlin suggests, because "Carter owned hundreds of slaves and had inspected many such human cargoes, choosing the most promising from among the weary, frightened men and women who had survived the transatlantic crossing."[22] Writing to his overseer from his plantation on the Rappahannock River, Carter explained the process by which he initiated Africans into their American captivity; "'I name'd them here & by their names we can always know what sizes theyr are of & I am sure we repeated them so often to them that every one knew their name & and would readily answer to them.' Carter then forwarded his slaves to a satellite plantation or quarter, where his overseer repeated the process, taking 'care that negros both men and women I sent . . . always go by the names we gave them.'"[23]

This process of renaming, according to Berlin, "marked Carter's initial endeavor to master his new slaves by separating them from their African inheritance."[24] Clearly, the deconstruction of the African identity and background was central to the acquisition of mastery over the slaves, and it began with the practice of stripping slaves of their African names and renaming them. This loss of name was only the beginning of "the numerous indignities Africans suffered at the hands of planters."[25] The process of de-Africanization entailed skills and language. According to Berlin, "Since many of the skills Africans carried across the Atlantic had no value to their new owners, planters disparaged them, and since the Africans' 'harsh jargons' rattled discordantly in the planters' ears, they ridiculed them." Thus began "the slow, painful process whereby Africans became African Americans."[26]

The capture and enslavement of Africans and their forcible transplantation to the New World were traumatic experiences that would transform many of these slaves into chattels, items of commerce, property to be bought and sold. Olaudah Equiano gave a vivid and captivating rendition of this trauma and transformation in his epic autobiography.[27] But we also see the essence of his Igbo identity as he takes us into the inner workings of his society—the values, norms, and institutions that defined identity and personhood, and how these were trampled upon and destroyed by slavery. For Equiano, and the thousands, if not millions, of slaves taken from Africa, enslavement struck at the very root of existential consciousness. The auctioning of the slaves and the "scrambling" by planters in Barbados underscored for Equiano and many others a critical stage in the process of deconstructing and reconstructing identity. The deliberate mixing of slaves of different ethnicities during the Middle Passage constituted a telling stage in the deconstruction of the captives' ethnicity. This would continue in the New World. As the likelihood of meeting, and being in the midst of, one's ethnic kin grew slimmer, slaves found themselves among strangers, with no means of effective communication. Suspended in this condition, the slave's gravitation from ethnicity to race began. The only language of communication with other slaves was embedded in the institution of shared misery—the violence and dehumanization of slavery built solely on the color of the skin. Denied the familiarity, comfort, and reassurance of indigenous ethnicity by being kept among strangers with whom there was little verbal communication, slaves inadvertently gravitated toward, and embraced, the familiarity and comfort offered by color. Shared trauma, violence, and dehumanization became the glue that sustained and impressed upon slaves the practicality of color as the basis of identity. But this process was not just mechanical and uncoordinated, neither was it completely a choice that the slaves freely made. In fact, the Europeans themselves coordinated and choreographed the process of singling out color as the new identity for blacks by defining the very nature and qualities of blackness.

When Europeans made the epochal decision to turn to Africa for slave labor, it was a conscious decision that would entail negating the identity and humanity of a people in order to impose a new identity tailor-made for the drudgery of enslavement. Though the slave raids, capture, and enslavement traumatized the captives, these experiences represented the first stage in what would become a complex process of transformation and transmutation from Igbo, Wollof, Mandinka, Fante, Yoruba, Asante, Hausa, and so forth, into something negative and distasteful: a slave, black, nigger, and so on. The dehumanizing experiences of the Middle Passage pushed these slaves further along the path of deconstructing their indigenous identities. Such deconstruction was deemed essential to the success and future of slavery, for the institution could thrive best upon a people completely traumatized and stripped of a sense of worth and identity, of the unity, comfort, and reassurance that indigenous values represented and offered. In the judgment of slave owners, this is the only condition that would enable blacks fully and responsibly to embrace their new roles as slaves. Slavery thus constituted an affront on the personality and identity of slaves—two crucial existential factors. The rupture of capture and transplantation was the first telling blow on the personality. The imposition of slave status completed that depersonalization process as enslavement, in theory and practice, reduced the slave to something less than human.

Thus, the making of a slave society was also the unmaking and remaking of a people's consciousness of self. Slaves came to America not as "Africans" but as Mandingo, Fulani, Yoruba, Fulbe, Asante, Fante, Hausa, Ibo, and so forth. They became "Africans" in the New World. As James Campbell underscores, in the eighteenth century, Africa was the basis of collective identity for blacks. In fact, since colonial times, "African" was an accepted term for referring to blacks in North America.[28] Blacks accepted this collective identity. It was from the onset a problematic identity, however, constructed and conferred for a specific purpose—for a more effective management and control of slaves. The construct "Africa" gave blacks a collective identity, in an environment where one was desperately needed. From the beginning, therefore, it was clear that the only unifying attribute blacks possessed, aside from race, and perhaps because of it, was shared misery and oppression. Becoming "African" exemplified this collective identity of negation and negativism. In a curious way, what masters constructed as a collective identity for effective control eventually became, for slaves, a countervailing construct for affirming a collective identity that would facilitate group solidarity and survival. However, from the master's point of view, the African identity exemplified negative and debilitating qualities such as backwardness, inferiority, and primitivism. For blacks, on the other hand, being African exemplified unity, albeit within a collective identity of negation, shared miseries, failures, objectification, and depersonalization. Thus, even as Africa served as the basis for group solidarity and survival for blacks, it was a troubling and troublesome identity.

From the very beginning, therefore, the experience of slavery underscored the need for collective self-definition and self-affirmation. It also entailed an existential challenge to negotiate and affirm an identity that became a foundation for group survival. In their daily ordeal, blacks continually confronted certain existential questions: Who are we? Why are we treated differently? These questions arose logically out of the dehumanizing experience they were subjected to. They searched for answers to these questions, convinced that such answers would not only explain their ordeal but also point the way to a clearer knowledge of identity. Knowing and affirming identity was considered critical to the success of the struggle for freedom. Enslavement was thus a constant struggle over a contending, complex, and troublesome consciousness of identity. There was a conscious effort on the part of the slave masters to purge blacks of any sense of positive identity, especially one that would negate and compromise the structure and foundation of the institution of slavery.[29] Whether blacks arrived in the New World with their indigenous values and identities intact, or lost them in the process of transplantation and enslavement, the experience that they were subjected to on the plantations raised crucial questions of identity. Slavery was built on a denial and negation of whatever collective existential ethos these slaves brought with them. Blacks were enslaved, according to pro-slavery ideology, because they were primitive and inferior. Slavery thus assumed the character of a civilizing process. The African identity (that is, being black) was considered evil, an identity to be shunned and avoided.[30] The acculturation process that slavery entailed became a medium of being "civilized" in European values. For slaves, therefore, enslavement became the foundation for a new identity. Though overwhelmed and challenged by this experience and consciousness, many blacks stuck to positive memories of Africa, and often invoked "Africa" in crucial moments of their struggles. Thus, Africa became a rallying point, and the basis of self-definition. In the late eighteenth and early nineteenth centuries, free blacks in Ohio, Pennsylvania, New York, and Massachusetts adopted the name "African" for their institutions—churches, schools, and fraternal societies.[31] This is indicative of a consciousness of affinity with Africa. This expression of African consciousness served as the framework for the advancement of the black struggle for freedom and equality.

Slavery nurtured in blacks what Samuel Dubois Cook termed "a tragic conception of history," contrived to destroy any desire for self-fulfillment.[32] The de-tribalization or de-Africanization process began on the slave ships of the Middle Passage. Through a deliberate process of intermingling slaves of different ethnic and linguistic origins, slavers hoped to prevent the emergence of any corporate sense of identity that would threaten the stability of slavery. As Eric Lincoln describes it, "History was suspended, and that part out of which all status and all relationships derive, and which constitutes the only sure reality in African cosmology, was summarily denied or leached away. American slavery offered 'no place to be somebody.'"[33]

The process of discrediting and nullifying the African heritage and inducing self-abnegating consciousness in blacks intensified on the plantations. Pro-slavery ideologists unleashed a barrage of negative propaganda aimed at controlling the slave's consciousness. As Leonard Curry surmised, "White superiority—and, hence, the 'innate' inferiority of Negroes—was . . . a concept requiring neither scientific nor theological justification, nor documentation by evidence. It was a given, a timeless verity applicable to all societies in all ages."[34] To solidify the institution of slavery, slaves must first be made both to acknowledge the poverty and nullity of their backgrounds and to internalize consciousness of helplessness and vulnerability that would render them totally dependent on the masters for almost anything, including self-definition and identity.[35]

Slavery thrived on what Charles Mills aptly terms a "racial contract"; one that "establishes a racial polity, a racial state, and a racial juridical system, where the status of whites and nonwhites is clearly demarcated, whether by law or custom. And the purpose of this state . . . is, *inter alia*, specifically to maintain and reproduce this racial order, securing the privileges and advantages of the full white citizens and maintaining the subordination of nonwhites."[36] Fortunately, or unfortunately (depending on your status), this "partitioned social ontology," this "universe divided between persons and racial subpersons"[37] (to borrow Charles Mills' descriptions) did not function as expected. Masters never achieved the total domination they sought over slaves. Despite the efforts of the slave owners to attain total control and regulation of slave lives, slaves were able to develop their own world that "was influenced but by no means totally controlled by the Slaveholders' regime."[38] Though some blacks internalized self-abnegating values and became "good slaves," many others rebelled, becoming what Kenneth Stampp termed "troublesome property."[39] For the latter, the challenge of self-definition, of asserting and affirming one's identity, became a daily preoccupation.

In their struggles to transcend the boundaries of enslavement and counteract imposed and debilitating conceptions of identity, many blacks espoused emancipatory, counterestablishment ideas and developed positive self-conceptions. Examples of such counterestablishment and positive conceptions of the self abound in the numerous Nat Turners, Denmark Veseys, Gabriel Prossers, David Walkers, Paul Cuffees, and Lott Carys that the institution of slavery nurtured.[40] By 1830, however, the year blacks inaugurated the convention movement and the beginning of organized black abolitionism, it had become clear to perceptive blacks that violence, or any radical confrontational approach to slavery and racism, was at best suicidal. The brutal and savage responses of southern whites to slave insurrections, both real and imagined—the surge of anti-black violence and pogroms, beginning in Cincinnati in 1829, and spreading to other northern cities—clearly demonstrated the depth and virulence of racism. They also underscored the relative powerlessness of blacks.[41] Leading blacks confronted a dilemma. On the one hand, they perceived the specter of a nation rife with racism and bigotry, and seemingly determined to keep blacks permanently degraded. On the other hand, the surge of reform movements in the North compelled attention and inspired hope and optimism in many blacks. In the Second Great Awakening, from 1825 through 1835, liberal and reform-minded whites in New York and New England unleashed religious evangelical crusades aimed at radically transforming society into a better place for all, with slavery coming under close scrutiny and criticism.[42]

Utilizing the weapon of moral suasion, these reformers, the rank of which included Charles G. Finney of New York, Benjamin Lundy of Baltimore, James Birney of Alabama, and Lyman Beecher of New England, endeavored to change society for the benefit of all, regardless of race or ethnic backgrounds, convinced that societal evils resulted not from any innate deficiencies or inabilities but from moral failures—failures that, in their judgment, individuals possessed the moral capacity to undo.[43] As one authority put it, they "believed in a new, more immediate relation between man and God and man and his fellow creatures—one that emphasized perfectibility rather than inability, activity rather than passivity, benevolence rather than piety."[44] The reformers had strong faith in the individual's capacity both to attain perfection and actively and positively to transform society. They consequently conferred on the individual a moral responsibility to partake in actually changing and redressing societal wrongs.[45] Rejecting orthodox Calvinism, they "minimized original sin and preached instead the doctrine of free will. Sin was voluntary, and thus every individual could do good and become good."[46]

The surge of religious evangelism inspired hope and optimism in blacks. Instead of folding their arms in resignation, or succumbing to fatalistic ethos, or even escaping to Canada or some safe haven abroad, blacks portrayed themselves as a people with the capacity to assist in transforming America. As white abolitionists including William Lloyd Garrison, the Tappan brothers, Arthur and Lewis, Simeon S. Joycelin, Benjamin Lundy, and John Greenleaf Whittier armed themselves with the weapon of moral suasion and nonviolence, and mounted frontal attacks against slavery, blacks felt encouraged to invoke the long-tried tradition of self-help, cooperative activities, and economy that had shaped the reform efforts of eighteenth-century free blacks in New York and Pennsylvania. They officially launched the convention movement and proclaimed moral suasion as their guiding principle. Since the prevailing ideology exalted the individual, blacks, individually and collectively, became actively energized and projected themselves as active agents of change. They hoped to accomplish this, however, by first changing themselves and their communities with the weapon of moral suasion. Moral suasion thus became the underlying ideology of the black convention movement, and the convention itself provided the forum for further enunciation of, and debate on, moral suasion. In moral suasion, blacks found an ideology that, they hoped, could reform their communities, while peacefully and nonconfrontationally convincing whites to accept them as full-fledged citizens of the United States. The moral suasion debate was thus inspired by the need to affirm and secure a cherished identity—becoming full-fledged American citizens. Blacks, according to James Oliver Horton, saw themselves as "special Americans, dedicated to the spirit of American liberty as few others were. They were not alienated Americans even though for them American society was alienating. They were not discouraged Americans, even though the racial restrictions were discouraging. They were committed Americans, determined to improve the country's treatment of its people."[47]

## Moral Suasion

The moral suasion phase witnessed the origin and development of organized black abolitionism. For the first time, free blacks took the momentous step to organize and deliberate on how to change their condition. The need for organized efforts by blacks could in fact be traced to John Ruuswurm's clarion call to blacks in the founding edition of his *Freedom's Journal* in 1827. Ruuswurm was Jamaican-born and the first black to graduate from an American college (Bowdoin College). *Freedom's Journal* became the first black newspaper published in the United States. Its first editorial stressed the importance of blacks assuming more active roles in articulating and projecting their cause. As the editorial put it, "We wish to plead our own cause. Too long have others spoken for us."[48]

Although Ruuswurm and his coeditor Samuel Cornish talked in terms of journalistic representation, by the late 1820s, the rising tide of anti-black sentiments and pogroms would induce other black leaders to recognize the urgency of organized movement. The immediate factor was the outbreak of anti-black violence in Cincinnati, Ohio, in 1829. Alarmed by the sudden increase in the free black population of the city, whites decided to enforce the provisions of the Ohio Black Code, which required free blacks to post a bond of five hundred dollars as guarantee of good behavior and providence. Violence erupted, compelling many free blacks to flee the city.[49] The resurgence of violence, not only in Cincinnati but in other cities such as New York, Philadelphia, Boston, Charleston, Pittsburgh, Washington, Baltimore, and Providence, impressed on blacks the need for organized response, thus inaugurating the convention movement in 1830.[50] Between 1830 and 1835, blacks met in five different conventions to deliberate on how best to bring about positive changes in their experiences of racism, marginalization, and rejection.[51] Not being acknowledged as full-fledged members of the American polity was a major motivation. The denial of the American identity was, therefore, a key factor in the rise of organized black abolitionism.

Several studies underscore the centrality of identity to the convention movement. Bethel describes it as "the first mass civil rights movement in the United States."[52] By the 1800s, the vast majority of the black American population was American-born, with little recollection of Africa. Whatever knowledge or consciousness of Africa that existed was colored by pro-slavery propaganda and values, which served to alienate many blacks from, rather than endear them to, the continent. Africa was not a place to cherish or with which to desire identification. Many blacks perceived themselves as "negative Americans" or "aliened Americans," people denied any positive self-definition and knowledge.[53] The need to define and assert an identity, therefore, became a central focus of the black abolitionist crusade.

Though brought together by the desire to organize and fight back in the face of overwhelming adversity, the platform that black abolitionists produced betrayed a deep sense of wanting to be acknowledged as Americans. These early conventions clearly revealed a strong integrationist consciousness.[54] Though some blacks embraced emigration and colonization as avenues of escaping the ugly and harsh realities of their lives, the vast majority refused to give up. Delegates overwhelmingly rejected and condemned colonization and invoked passages of the Constitution and Declaration of Independence in justification of their claims to American citizenship. For most blacks, colonization or permanent relocation to another country was anathema. It was tantamount to a voluntary relinquishing of identity.

The rising tide of anti-black violence notwithstanding, many blacks retained strong faith in the potency of moral suasion to bring about meaningful change. The ambition of every black person was to transcend the boundaries and limitations created by slavery and racism and be identified as an American citizen with all the accompanying rights and privileges. For example, in Philadelphia, the city with the largest concentration of free blacks in the country, blacks remained "convinced that although the path to acceptance and accomplishment in America was strewn with obstacles, it was the road to be taken."[55] To achieve this end, however, blacks had to subscribe to, and inculcate, values and goals that the mainstream society had identified as constituting the distinguishing characteristics or essence of being American—industry, thrift, economy, education, and moral uprightness. These values became the constituent elements of moral suasion. As they enthusiastically declared at the second convention in 1832, "We yet anticipate in the moral strength of this nation, a final redemption from those evils that have been illegitimately entailed on us as a people. We yet expect by due exertions on our part . . . to acquire a moral and intellectual strength, that will inshaft the calumnious darts of our adversaries and present to the world a general character, that they will feel bound to respect and admire."[56]

The first five Negro national conventions, therefore, embraced these moral suasion values, convinced that the cultivation of these values would open wide the gate to full America citizenship. Moral suasion was a crusade for identity. Blacks were denied American identity in Constitution and in practice. They were either slaves or free blacks, but not citizens, not Americans. Being a slave, or not being one, defined their identity. The establishment in effect imposed a slavocentric construction of identity on blacks. Blacks were good only as slaves, or in subordinate positions. In fact, many pro-slavery preachers affirmed that blacks had been chosen and set aside by providence to be slaves.[57] Getting out of this restrictive slavocentric mold became the preoccupation of the early black conventionists. Black abolitionism, therefore, was a search not just for freedom but also for a sense of identity. Even if free, the life experience of blacks was still very much shaped by the fact of belonging to a race for whom enslavement was deemed appropriate. Moral suasion was aimed at breaking out of this slavocentric identity and establishing the basis for the affirmation of American identity. What is unique about this period was the consensus among blacks on the desirability of the American identity. There was hardly any black person who did not envision or desire to become an American citizen in the practical sense of it. Moral suasion was essentially the strategy devised for attaining this goal. It set the guidelines or framework for the realization of a cherished identity.

Prominent leaders such as William Whipper and the Reverend Lewis Woodson spearheaded the moral suasion crusade. They strongly asserted their claim to American identity. In consonance with the dictates of moral suasion, they acknowledged that the primary reason for the denial of the American identity to blacks was largely shortcomings in the black condition, that is, situational deficiency, and declared a commitment to addressing those deficiencies. Race was not considered a significant factor. In defining themselves, therefore, black leaders espoused an ideology that emphasized the possibility of attaining

American identity. They projected themselves as Americans held back and down by deficiencies in their condition, deficiencies that could be remedied through moral suasion.

Although oppressed, alienated, and marginalized, blacks felt they shared a lot in common with whites and, therefore, worked hard to bridge the gap. In defining themselves as Americans, these leaders invoked certain universalistic ideals that they claimed united them with whites. The crusade for moral suasion symbolized an affirmation of American identity, a determination to be fully American, a demonstration of compatibility with classic American traditions and values. Moral suasion was consequently as much an explanation for black subordination as an affirmation of identity. It was an integrative and optimistic ideology, influenced by faith in the potency of universal values, values that supposedly impacted humanity regardless of race. Advocates therefore defined progress as the result of the triumph of those values. The proliferation of those universal values would eventually acquire for blacks the long-denied American identity.

The first three conventions were held in Philadelphia, Pennsylvania. The proceedings and declarations emphasized the primacy and efficacy of moral suasion. Blacks pledged to be industrious, economical, thrifty, and morally upright.[58] Controversy surfaced at the fourth convention in 1834 in New York. According to one source, disagreement developed between the New York and Pennsylvania leadership over moral suasion. The more radical and race-conscious New York leadership began to question the efficacy of moral suasion. To prevent a radical change in the focus of the convention, the venue was quickly moved back to Pennsylvania the following year. The 1835 convention, the last of the early national conventions, established the American Moral Reform Society, the framework for propagating moral suasion.[59] The founding of this society underscored the determination of blacks to become fully American through peaceful character reform, and William Whipper became the prime mover and spiritual leader of the moral suasion crusade.

Information on Whipper's early life is sparse. Born in 1804 in Little Britain, Lancaster County, Pennsylvania, by 1828 he had settled comfortably in Philadelphia, Pennsylvania, and become one of the most successful black businessmen in the state. Though victimized by the prevailing climate of racism, Whipper, undoubtedly influenced by his economic success, developed strong faith in the potency of industry to break through racial barriers. Imbued with a strong sense of identity as an American, Whipper believed that the denial to blacks of American citizenship was only temporary and that with the success of moral suasion they would become fully integrated. He assumed the responsibility of providing blacks with the ideological guidance, and he believed that character reform would satisfactorily resolve the problem of black identity.

For Whipper, the resolution of the question of whether blacks were Americans or not lay in certain divinely given universal ideals. Though human destiny and the relationships between individuals and among groups are shaped by the functioning of those ideals, one's identity also has a lot to do with behavioral inclinations. In essence, blacks had a choice in determining how they defined themselves and how others responded to and perceived that self-definition. Underlining his universalistic inclination, Whipper fully embraced the Garrisonian precept, "My country is the world, my countrymen are all mankind."[60] He presented himself as color-blind, one who saw every human being as brethren. With this outlook, Whipper defined black subordination as the failure of blacks to live up to the dictates of moral suasion and, in consequence, the failure by the entire society to fully embrace and live according to those universal ideals.[61] Once these deficiencies were remedied, the problem of black identity would become resolved, as the barriers separating the races would disappear and whites would recognize and acknowledge blacks as fellow citizens. Whipper proclaimed, "God's moral ethics" as the foundation on which to build the black struggle, the legitimizing factor against which to measure demands by blacks for citizenship and equality.[62]

The notion of "God's moral ethics" underlined his belief in a universal standard, based upon the idea of one God, one humanity. Black leaders accepted the notion of the existence of an overriding divine moral order, one that mandated a uniform standard of morality for humanity, regardless of race or geographical location. As a strong believer in universalism, Whipper maintained that "virtues" and morality, rather than the color of the skin, or some other primordial factor, should differentiate people.[63] These moral and virtuous qualities resulted from adherence to those divinely established universal moral standards. One concept dominated his thought: *reason*. He described reason as "the noblest of all goals that brings man closer to God." *Reason* allows human beings to rise above, and transcend "physical inflictions that are offspring of passion"—for example, pains and grief resulting from racism and slavery. *Reason* was, in effect, a weapon for neutralizing the painful and crippling effects of slavery. It generates stoical quality in human beings, enabling them to transcend, and consequently ignore, earthly pains and suffering. It also motivates people to seek solutions in "something higher than human power"—God's moral power.[64]

Whipper challenged humanity to perfect its reasoning capacity, and move closer to God, a situation that instantaneously neutralizes all physical pains and suffering associated with slavery, racism, societal inequities, and other forms of man's inhumanity to man. Once *reason* predominates, government actions and policies are transformed as they bear the imprints of divinity, resulting in universal peace and love.[65] Consequently, though Whipper acknowledged the existence of discrimination, his explanation of its causes pointed not to race, or policies of particular individuals, but to humanity's deviation from the path of *reason*. To be guided by reason, he opined, is to be propelled by love, eventuating in universal peace and harmony.[66]

Color became irrelevant as a factor in the denial to blacks of American citizenship. Since the key problem emanated from moral failures, the proffered solution tended to deemphasize race. Racial distinction and prejudices originated, according to Whipper, "in the spirit of selfishness, cultivated and sustained by a religious and moral delinquency in principle, in utter disregard of the divine will . . . and every element that is calculated to cement the interest of society in one universal brotherhood."[67] He consequently rejected the notion of a racially exclusive movement. Once *reason* prevailed, blacks would attain American citizenship. The doctrine of universal brotherhood would prevail in the aftermath of the reign of *reason*. Society would become colorblind, and black identity as Americans would be an acknowledged fact.

Whipper's ideas and convictions provoked angry response from blacks who felt that race and racism occupied prominent places in the struggle for identity. Since blacks and whites shared separate paths and experiences, the black struggle ought to reflect this separation. Those who espoused this view urged blacks to adopt clearly a conception of the self that reflected divergence from whites. Blacks were not Americans and could never become fully American until universalism was abandoned and the distinct experience and identity of both races were acknowledged. In order to become fully American, blacks must first begin by acknowledging racial and cultural distinctiveness. In essence, the struggle for universalism and the American identity

must first be waged on a racially distinct platform. Those who advocated this separatist perspective belonged to the more "radical" New
York leadership group, including the likes of Samuel Cornish, William
Hamilton, and Samuel Hardenberger. Despite their desire for reform,
these leaders rejected Whipper's universalism.

Cornish called upon the Moral Reform Society to evolve a clear
and definite plan, identify concrete goals, and develop a definite strategy for attaining them, rather than engaging in what he perceived as
a spurious and deceptive universalism that was "destined to influence
nobody."[68] The problems of "the poor, proscribed, down-trodden and
helpless people" deserved more time and efforts. Societal reality revealed, Cornish observed, that some people occupied comfortable
positions, sustained by the exploitation and subordination of others.
Universalism blurred both this reality and its fundamentally racial
character.[69] Cornish's paper, *The Colored American*, therefore pushed
for a racially exclusive strategy and ideology. Whipper objected, and
denounced separatism as a measure destined to erode the moral legitimacy of the reform movement. He implored blacks, as members
of the human family, who are also susceptible to universal values, to
join forces with, rather than oppose, whites in the quest for a better
society.[70]

Cornish disagreed, and accused the Moral Reform Society of assuming national responsibilities instead of zeroing in on critical black
problems. Putting it bluntly, he charged Whipper with endeavoring to
"elevate whites to the neglect of blacks" and also make blacks "beasts of
burden" by placing the entire nation on their shoulders. He proposed
a redefinition of the society's mission to emphasize issues pertaining
solely to "the proscribed colored people."[71] It should be emphasized
that Cornish was not opposed to the American identity. He equally
cherished this identity and believed that blacks were as entitled to it
as whites. He disagreed, however, with Whipper on strategy, that is,
the means for attaining that identity. Given what he perceived as the
depth and pervasiveness of racism, Cornish considered universalism
unrealistic. In order to attain the citizenship status of whites, blacks,
in Cornish's view, had to adopt, and proceed on, a separatist platform.
In other words, Cornish urged blacks to situate their quest for the
American identity on a solid foundation of racial distinctiveness.

Thomas Sidney, another respondent to the moral suasion debate,
quickly declared his opposition to universalism. "In an effort for freedom," he argued, "there are several important and indisputable quali-

fications, which the oppressed alone possess." He identified two inter-related qualifications as the most critical. First, a sense of actual suffering and, second, a determination to end suffering. Sidney insisted upon a convergence of both the feeling (that is, consciousness) and the purpose (that is, reaction) of those who suffer in order to effect any meaningful and effective strike for freedom. Put differently, to struggle effectively and legitimately against oppression, one had to have experienced oppression. Consequently, in the estimation of Sidney, blacks alone possessed the moral legitimacy to organize against slavery. Underlining the necessity for a racially exclusive movement, Sidney linked the elevation of a people to "the inward rational sentiments which enable the soul to change circumstances to its own temper and disposition." It "is not measured by dependent upon external relations" (or forces). In his view, "the relative position and the relative duties and responsibilities of the oppressed and the oppressors" constituted the only ground upon which to predicate any argument for or against "complexionally distinctive organization." Whenever a people are oppressed peculiarly, he noted, "distinctive organization or action is required on their part to destroy oppression." Creating a distinct identity was crucial to Sidney, and he implored blacks to adopt the name "Colored American," a term Whipper had vehemently opposed on the ground that it undermined universalism, favoring instead the appellation "Oppressed American." Sidney, like Cornish, advocated a racially distinctive platform.[72]

Whipper was not the only focus of the moral suasion controversy. Another contributor, whose views perhaps generated even more heat, was the Reverend Lewis Woodson. A fugitive from Virginia, Woodson rose rapidly through the ranks of Philadelphia black leaders. His was equally a success story. He owned several barber shops and assisted in establishing and running the only colored school in Philadelphia. As a member of both the religious community and the elite black intelligentsia, Woodson would have had difficulty isolating himself from the controversies surrounding moral suasion. Furthermore, his deep commitment to the black struggle rendered such an isolationist posture unlikely. His approach seemed, in the estimation of contemporaries, critical of Whipper. On closer examination, however, his ideas tended to complement Whipper's. In a seven-part series titled, "Moral Work For Colored Men," he underlined the peculiarity of blacks and the need for special attention and strategies: "The relation in which we have for generations been held in this land, constitutes us a distinct class. We have been held as slaves, while those around us have been free. They have been our holders, and we the held. Every power and privilege have been invested with them, while we have been divested of every right. The distinction of our classification is as wide as freedom and slavery."[73] He too approved of the moral reform efforts, strongly believing that blacks were miserably deficient in education, morality, and industry and, therefore, needed to be elevated in order to justify any claims of American citizenship. Writing under the pseudonym "Augustine," Woodson acknowledged black deficiencies but stopped short of endorsing a racially exclusive movement. Like Sydney, he too welcomed the sympathy and support of whites, while emphasizing the prime responsibility of blacks.[74]

In its totality, Woodson's strategy paradoxically seemed to steer blacks in the direction of Whipper's universalism. He praised whites and expressed faith and optimism in the inevitability of change. He perceived a flexible and malleable society, one that was susceptible to moral arguments. Colored persons of healthy state of morals, he observed, attracted the respect and admiration of whites and were encouraged, rather than discriminated against, thus underscoring the situational imperative of prejudice. In his words, "I have noticed that the intelligent Colored man of polished manners, and pleasing address, is always well received and well treated, while some others, who are even wealthy, but who had paid no attention to the cultivation of the manners and habits of polished society, were rejected." He too, like Whipper and many others, placed greater burden on blacks. To benefit from the reform impulse of American society, and attain the much sought after American citizenship, blacks had to demonstrate both the will to improve, and also take the first tentative steps in that direction.[75]

Woodson's most contentious views resulted from his notion of the dual character of humanity—that it was possible for blacks to succeed, even in the most prejudiced environment. The oppressive legal system was not the problem, he intimated, but the demeanor and condition of human beings, especially blacks. The most direct path to an inclusive society, therefore, remained the cultivation of pleasing manners and unquestionable integrity. However violent or virulent racism was, it would crumble once confronted by a colored man of a healthy state of morality. The immortal side of man, that is, his inherent divine nature, allowed him to live and escape the evil effects of cruel laws. Though every individual possessed this divine quality, it is, however, functional and effective only in those who invoke it, and invoking it entailed a conscious effort to live according to the tenets of moral suasion. Prejudice, consequently, was most pronounced, he believed, whenever blacks were immoral, corrupt, and illiterate. Such negative qualities induced mistreatment from whites and a disposition on their part against integration. He referred to his personal experience in justification of the notion that "condition and not color" was the major cause of prejudice. He outlined the following as the "qualifications" for the admission of blacks into "polished society": hard work, polished manners, and physical and material condition. When these qualifications are achieved, he suggested, "a man slides into his proper circle with ease."[76]

The subject of emigration featured prominently in Woodson's discourse on moral suasion. Since one of the goals of moral suasion was economic elevation, Woodson believed that the acquisition of land would best facilitate this objective. He thus urged blacks to emigrate from densely populated and racially tense environments to the "West," identified as comprising Indiana, Illinois, and Ohio, where, according to him, land and other avenues of economic advancement abounded. The West was the new frontier for blacks, with promises of a more comfortable and desirable life. Such economic development would facilitate integration.[77]

He envisioned America as a liberal and open society, compelled to engage in discriminatory practices by the deficiencies and failures of blacks. His strong objection to "political action," or actions aimed specifically at the repeal of repressive laws, underscored an unflinching faith in moral suasion. He deemed such actions misdirected efforts. Bad laws did not originate slavery and racism. The twin evils were, he argued, products of an unrighteous and corrupt mind, or, as he put it, of "the corrupt moral sentiment of the country."[78] Once the moral sentiment was purified, slavery and all accompanying evils would disappear. He thus elevated man's moral quality to a height of prominence—the key determinant of human action and societal condition. The condition of this moral impulse influenced societal values and institutions. This led him to yet another conclusion; "that a morally good man cannot do a physically bad deed," suggesting a correlation between morality and virtue. There is undoubtedly a strong element of Whipperian universalism in Woodson's moral interpretation of human actions. His ultimate goal, it seems, was to reform the "corrupting element" in the moral fiber of society, and slavery would cease as "the great source from whence it springs would be dried up."[79] Both he and Whipper saw blacks as the major source of the corrupting element. Overall, Woodson advanced a very optimistic philosophy. He saw American identity as very much within the grasp of blacks. He did not perceive any conspiracy or concerted efforts by whites to deny blacks access to citizenship. The problem, in his judgment, was that blacks had yet fully to explore and exploit all available possibilities.

The debate and controversies over the implications of moral suasion notwithstanding, blacks remained faithful to the basic premise that moral improvement would result in the realization of American citizenship. It is no exaggeration to suggest that in this early phase of the black abolitionist crusade, most blacks sought American nationality and identity and were optimistic that a gradualist, reform-oriented platform would lead eventually to the desired goal. Though blacks disagreed on the exact character of the platform, they shared a consensus on the goal—American citizenship. Moral suasion thus remained entrenched, even as blacks began to organize politically vocal state conventions in the 1840s. They hinged everything on the potency of reason, on man's presumed desire and inclination for progress, on the reality, and compelling force of universal values, and perhaps most significantly, on a strong faith in humanity, guided by universal, divine values. Given this faith in the inevitability of change, blacks jettisoned confrontation in favor of cooperation. Even when they acknowledged extraneous circumstances, they often emphasized their own failures. Moral suasion was supposed to serve as a dynamic, intertwining ideology that would ultimately bridge what was deemed an ephemeral racial schism.

Paradoxically, it would take the success of moral suasion to reveal its deficiency as a reform strategy. By the late 1840s, the number of morally upright and economically elevated blacks in Philadelphia and other parts of Pennsylvania had more than doubled. Evidence from other parts of the country—Boston, New York, Cincinnati—clearly revealed determined efforts on the parts of blacks to cultivate habits of thrift, industry, economy, and temperance, and they achieved success measured by the wealth and economic successes of individuals and organizations.[80] Their rewards, however, came in the form of opposition, resentment, and increased anti-black violence. In his study of Philadelphia, Bruce Laurie underscores the economic efforts and accomplishments of the city's black population and the corresponding negative and violent reactions of whites.[81] Other studies reveal that this trend was not isolated to Philadelphia. In several northern cities, wherever blacks manifested the desire and determination to conquer economic poverty as a step toward political elevation, they encountered violent responses from whites. Perpetrators of violence targeted wealthy blacks and symbols of black economic power.[82] One study describes the Moyamensing riots of 1842 in Philadelphia as "one of the prime examples of whites denouncing blacks for their degradation while simultaneously destroying those institutions which sought to eradicate that degradation."[83] It dawned on many that the key factor was not *condition* but *race*, and, consequently, some blacks concluded that no matter how hard they worked to cultivate moral suasion, the chances of integration remained bleak. At a gathering in Harrisburg, Pennsylvania, these blacks voiced their frustration over the failure of moral suasion. According to them, "The barrier that deprives us of the rights which you enjoy finds no palliative in merit—no consolation in piety—no hope in intellectual and moral pursuit—no reward in industry and enterprise." They underlined the fact that they were denied opportunities of elevation "because we are not 'white.'"[84] Moral suasion then gave way to immediatist and political strategies.

The failure of moral suasion clearly impressed on blacks the problematic of identity. The upsurge of anti-black movements, violence, and policies suggested a stronger racial dimension to identity. This affected a shift in black consciousness. Many became fully aware of the place of race in the denial to them of the American identity. This did not, however, lead to a total abandonment of moral suasion. Moral suasion became part of a broader platform of protest. The conventions of the 1840s, both state and national, emphasized both moral and political agenda. Though moral suasion failed, blacks did not relinquish their claim to American identity. By all available criteria that whites had used to claim that identity, blacks continued to press their own claim.

A strong declaration of affinity with America and a desire to be acknowledged in theory and practice as Americans characterized the proceedings of the 1840s conventions.[85] Henry H. Garnet perfectly captured the feelings of other blacks in a speech delivered at the Seventh Anniversary of the American Anti-Slavery Society in 1840. After affirming that blacks had satisfied all criteria for American citizenship, he declared, "With every fiber of our hearts entwined around our country, and with an indefeasible determination to obtain the possession of the natural and inalienable rights of American citizen, we demand redress for the wrongs we have suffered, and ask for the restoration of our birthright privileges." He repeated the same theme in his epochal speech at the Buffalo convention three years later in which he told the slaves, "forget not that you are native-born American citizens, and as such, you are justly entitled to all the rights that are granted to the freest."[86] In an address to the people of the state of New York, black delegates to the state "Free Suffrage Convention" of 1845 declared, "We love our native country, much as it has wronged us . . . *We are citizens*; this we believe would never have been denied, had it not been for the subserviency of the people of the free states to slavery" (emphasis added).[87]

Blacks were hopeful and optimistic that a combination of reform, petition, and peaceful protest would eventually convince whites to concede their citizenship rights and privileges. In the conventions of the 1840s, black leaders implored their respective communities and constituencies to continue to cultivate those same moral suasion ideals as keys to American citizenship. The underlying objective was to demonstrate to whites that there was nothing inherently wrong with blacks and that, given the right conditions, blacks were fully capable of self-improvement. This, they believed, would facilitate integration.

By the late 1840s, however, it became clear that the combination of moral suasion and political activism had not changed white perceptions and dispositions and that the quest for citizenship and American identity remained as elusive as it had ever been. But the failure of moral suasion alone would not induce blacks to turn completely away from their aspiration of attaining American citizenship. Subsequent developments, however, underlined the centrality of race and impressed on many the futility of integrationist aspiration and the elusive character of the American identity. The Fugitive Slave Law of 1850 was one of such developments. Under the provisions of the law, the federal government pledged its resources and assistance to the apprehension and return of fugitive slaves. This law convinced many that racism was pervasive and perhaps even permanent, and that blacks had no safe haven from slavery. The hope of becoming American became even dimmer. The law sharpened the debate on identity and convinced many of the need for a new identity external to the American context. Emigration became an attractive option for some, and Africa became the obvious choice. It should be emphasized, at this juncture, that the moral suasion debate, this very critical discourse on black American quest for, and affirmation of, identity, did not feature Africa. The disputants disagreed on strategies, but there was never a dispute on their objective—American citizenship.

### Emigration and Nationalism

Martin Delay, the acclaimed black nationalist and advocate of an independent black nationality and identity, was initially a staunch advocate of moral suasion. He had in fact been among the most forceful advocates of the ideology and had spent the years 1847–49 propagating the doctrine to free black communities in the North.[88] Delany strongly believed that blacks were as qualified as, if not more qualified than, whites for American citizenship. This optimism sustained the integrationist and moral suasion phase of his career. The passage of the Fugitive Slave Law in 1850, however, destroyed this optimism. The law revealed a radically different America than he had hoped for. It established America, in his judgment, as a land "for whites only" and stripped blacks not only of considerations for citizenship but, most critically, of any protection, thus rendering them vulnerable to perpetual subordination. He described the law as a violation of the constitution, saying it debased blacks "beneath the level of the recognized basis of American citizenship."[89] Blacks were now clearly an alien people. There was consequently an urgent need for a new identity. Delany assumed the responsibility of helping blacks map out strategies and modalities for realizing this new identity. In several publications, he defined this new identity as African and Pan-African.[90] The depth and pervasiveness of racism convinced him that blacks had no hope of attaining American identity. This conviction led him to a racial essentialist construction of the black struggle. For Delany, "a question of Black and White" became "the great issue, sooner or later," that would determine "the world's destiny."[91]

Delany exhorted blacks to reclaim their African heritage as the basis of a new identity. They were not only black but also Africans, and as Africans, they shared historical and cultural experiences with Africans on the continent. Since America was irredeemably racist, blacks could never be accorded their cherished American identity. Delany soon began to spearhead and galvanize the emigration movement. Between 1850 to the outbreak of the Civil War, he urged blacks to relinquish the never-ending search for the American identity. The creation of a new black nationality in Africa would serve as the solid foundation for a new black identity. His travels in Africa from 1859 to 1861 bolstered his faith in the possibilities and future of a black nationality and identity based on Africa. He returned in early 1861 and began to campaign vigorously for emigration. He proclaimed his resolve to relocate to Africa and urged wealthy and enterprising blacks to consider relocating and assuming the African identity.[92]

Opponents of emigration such as Frederick Douglass objected strongly to externalizing the struggle. Douglass portrayed emigration as a dangerous distraction. In fact, the struggle between Douglass and Henry H. Garnet on African nationality and emigration was, in essence, a debate on conflicting consciousness of identity.[93] Garnet, like Delany, advocated a new nationality in Africa based on the development of a cotton economy. Douglass strongly opposed emigration, which he viewed as tantamount to voluntarily relinquishing all claims to American citizenship. He reminded blacks of the role and sacrifices of their forebears in helping to develop the American wilderness. Consequently, Douglass insisted, blacks had as much right to nativity as any white person.[94] He emphasized the possibility of a cultural pluralistic America in which blacks could remain, and still maintain their distinct identity, values, and institutions. Few emigrationists shared Douglass's optimism. In fact, Delany maintained that it was impossible to have an America in which blacks would be integrated with their racial/cultural distinctiveness intact. By the late 1850s, he had come to the conclusion that the quest for full integration and American identity jeopardized the racial and cultural essence of blacks.[95]

Emigration, a movement that developed in response to rejection and the failure to realize one identity, was soon redirected at the reaffirmation of another identity—the racial and cultural essence of being African. Preserving the racial and cultural distinctiveness of blacks became a matter of life and death for Delany. In his judgment, coexistence with whites threatened the racial and cultural heritage of blacks. In essence, the price of integration, if it was possible to become fully American, would be a sacrifice of one's African identity. In Delany's estimation, blacks would have to commit cultural suicide, cease being black and African, in order to be fully accepted as Americans. This was too high a price to pay for American citizenship.[96] Nothing, he insisted, was worth sacrificing his blackness and African identity for. He offered emigration to blacks as the key to remaining black and African. In his strong defense of, and articulation of the imperative of, the African identity, Delany set the tone for future Afrocentric discourse. Despite his sense of alienation and depth of nationalism, Delany soon abandoned his quest for, and advocacy of, the African identity. By 1863, with the progress of the Civil War, he saw prospects for the American identity and nationality in the war, and joined Frederick Douglass, Henry H. Garnet, and other black leaders in supporting the Union cause. He exhorted blacks to focus inward and strengthen their faith in American nationality and identity.[97]

The ease with which Delany abandoned emigration and the quest for the African identity underscored the strength of his American consciousness and desire for American identity. But his expectations and those of blacks in general would be disappointed. The revolution of rising expectations that the Civil War engendered soon collapsed. Though the war destroyed slavery, and the reforms of the subsequent Radical Reconstruction era (1866–1876), particularly the Fourteenth and Fifteenth Amendments, conferred citizenship and the franchise on blacks respectively, including the promise of legal equality, implementation of these constitutional reforms and guarantees proved difficult. The vast political landscape that Reconstruction opened up for blacks soon shrank as conservatives and defenders of the antebellum status quo gradually and viciously fought their way back to positions of authority in the South. By the end of Reconstruction in 1877, blacks were citizens in name only. The rights and privileges they had won were compromised and revoked. In other words, the Civil War and Reconstruction failed to resolve the problem of black identity. By the late 1870s, it was obvious that blacks remained alien to the American nation and would be accommodated only in subservient and subordinate roles. The return to power in the South of members of the *ancient regime* in consequence of the Compromise of 1877 sealed the fate of blacks. The "redeemers," as they fondly referred to themselves, assumed power with a vengeance, determined to undo every vestige of radical Reconstruction and return blacks to the status they had occupied, and roles they played, before the war. This development brought to the fore, once again, the age-old question of black identity.

Blacks, many of them among the most optimistic of the civil war and Reconstruction era, turned outward in a desperate search for a separate and external identity. Again, many turned to Africa, including Martin Delany. But the activist phase of Delany's African identity search was over. It would be left to two other black nationalists to propagate and vigorously pursue the realization of the African/black nationality and identity in the post–Civil War epoch: Alexander

Crummell and Henry McNeal Turner. Both men emphasized the urgency of developing a strong African identity.

After he and other blacks were forced out of the Georgia legislature by whites, Turner denounced his American identity and enjoined blacks to embrace Africa as a viable alternative identity.[98] He was very critical of integration-minded blacks such as Booker T. Washington, whose brand of nationalism suggested enduring faith and hope in the possibility of realizing the American dream and identity. Turner expressed the same degree of concern over the possibility of blacks losing their identity. He stressed the urgency of an independent black nationality, and a new African identity.[99] Like Delany, Turner envisioned a dark and gloomy future for blacks in America. Africa provided the basis for regeneration and for the construction and consolidation of a new nationality and identity. He made several trips to Africa in the 1890s in pursuit of his black nationality scheme.[100] In his own response, Crummell proposed a Pan-African Christian community of Africans and blacks in the Diaspora. He expressed pride in his African ancestry and declared a commitment to the development and redemption of Africa. His writings and public lectures underscored experiential and identity linkages between Africa and black Diaspora. He implored black Americans to become more actively involved in the elevation and development of Africans. He soon moved to Liberia, West Africa, and immersed himself in the spread of literacy, Christianity, and "civilization" among the indigenous people.[101] All three men (Delany, Crummell, and Turner), at different times, went to Liberia and traveled extensively in other parts of the west coast of Africa.

Thus, leading nationalists of the nineteenth century strongly affirmed their African identity. Being black and of African heritage mattered the most to them. They considered the African heritage and identity worth affirming and defending in the context of rejection and alienation in the United States. They all espoused a Pan-African construction of identity, which they believed unified all blacks, regardless of geographical location. This Pan-African identity became the means of combating the ever-threatening Eurocentric cultural hegemony. Prompted by the elusive character of the American nationality and identity, these black nationalists mobilized Pan-African consciousness and sought the realization of a new nationality and identity through cooperative endeavors between Africans and black Americans. In different ways, Delany, Crummell, and Turner, attempted to make Pan-

Africanism the basis of responding to the challenges of blacks in Africa and the Diaspora.

A critical examination of the history of Pan-Africanism, particularly of the strategies devised by nineteenth-century black nationalists for actualizing the Pan-African ideal and solidifying African identity, reveals a deep cultural distance and alienation from Africa, a consequence, no doubt, of the acculturation process in the New World. While these nationalists declared interest in assuming African identity, once in Africa, their utterances and activities betrayed ambiguities with respect to the projected African identity. It became clear that the Pan-African construction of identity was not as deep-rooted and strong as the expressions and rhetoric suggest. In other words, there was a certain superficiality to the Africa identity construct. These nationalists manifested a much stronger attachment to their elusive and cherished American identity.

From the birth of organized abolitionism in the early nineteenth century to the present, Africa had always served black Americans as the basis of articulating identity and an inspiration in the struggle for freedom and survival. The tendency by modern Afrocentric scholars to inject some mutuality or consensual ethos into the historical relationship of Africans and blacks in Diaspora misrepresents the reality. Such tendency ignores the complexity of the relationship. A critical look at the crucial nineteenth century would illuminate the contradictions and disharmony within black American nationalist and Pan-African thought. While blacks in Diaspora espoused Pan-African ideals and expressed a desire to identify with Africans, their activities betrayed cultural alienation from Africa. Though they acknowledged being black and of African ancestry, culturally, Delany, Crummell, and Turner distanced themselves from Africa. Their expression of cultural identity was unambiguously Eurocentric. They opted for shaping Africa according to the Eurocentric images that had shaped their own acculturation.

Delany, Crummell, and Turner were in Africa in the crucial period from 1850 to the 1890s, when European relationships with Africa began to change from "cooperation" to confrontation and occupation, a change that led inevitably to formal colonialism. During this momentous epoch, Europeans debated what to do with Africa and how to go about implementing this new aggressive policy. Whether by design or not, these black nationalists embraced this new aggressive policy. During a visit to Britain in 1861, Delany advocated the use of force against Africans to stem the tide of what he presented as an endemic crisis among indigenous African states, a crisis that he insisted inhibited the orderly and peaceful flow of civilization. He urged European missionaries to resocialize Africans away from what he perceived as barbaric indigenous traditions and modes of living.[102] Similarly, Turner also characterized Africans as barbaric and backward people in need of the civilizing touch of external forces.[103] Crummell referred to Africans as barbaric, restless, violent, and crude people against whom the use of indiscriminate force was legitimate. Crummell advocated violence as a potent weapon for controlling what he characterized as the wild barbarism of indigenous Africa, and he implored the British not to be restrained by democratic considerations. In his view, no price was too high for Africans to pay in return for the benefits of European civilization. He advocated systematic reeducation of Africans in Anglo-Saxon values.[104] There was, therefore, a discrepancy between the rhetoric of African and black confraternity, nationality, and identity that these nationalists popularized, and their distant, condescending, and hegemonic attitudes toward Africans.

The implications of their contradictions and ambivalence for the notion of identity are clear. Visiting and living in Africa exposed all three to realities that challenged the romanticized images and expectations that undergirded their quest for African identity. Most significantly, as I argued elsewhere, exposure to African realities revealed their unAfricannesss. They saw and realized their own cultural difference and distinctiveness.[105] They realized that, though of African ancestry, they had become culturally different and that the acquisition of African identity was more complex and problematic. In other words, exposure to Africa confirmed their American and Anglo-Saxon essence. Though driven by rejection and alienation to seek the African identity, these nationalists soon realized that culturally they shared more in common with Americans and Europeans than with Africans. They realized how difficult it was to presume that simply relocating to Africa made one an African. Though they initially proclaimed African and black identity, as they became conversant with Africa, they soon realized that the basis of their identity and affinity with Africa was purely *racial*, not *cultural*. The realization of cultural distance from Africa and the feeling of alienation from African tradition and customs necessitated strengthening and reaffirming the cherished but elusive Euro-American identity. With renewed vigor, all three embarked upon the difficult task of reasserting cultural affinity with Euro-America.

Without really saying it, their denunciations and negative characterizations of Africans revealed that they did not see themselves as wholly African. They envisioned themselves as blacks with strong American, European, and Anglo-Saxon cultural connections. But then, there was a problem. What was the benefit of being black and Anglo-American in an epoch when European imperialist ideology defined all blacks (that is, peoples of African ancestry) as primitive and inferior? Delany, Crummell, and Turner felt challenged to legitimize and justify their claim to Anglo-American identity. To do this, it was necessary both to emphasize distance from Africa and to close the cultural gap with Europe, a gap established by the ideology of white supremacy. They found the answer in the very institution that had brutalized and dehumanized them—*slavery*. Invoking religious historicism, they theorized that the enslavement of Africans was divinely inspired and sanctioned as a foundation for the fulfillment of God's purpose for Africans. Enslavement brought many out of "dark" Africa into close proximity with Europeans. Socialized and acculturated in superior European values, these blacks would now return to Africa as bearers of light and civilization to those still languishing in barbarism. Furthermore, enslavement closed the cultural gaps with Europe. Consequently, black Americans could no longer be classed in the same cultural category with indigenous Africans. As Delany emphasized, though involuntary and evil, slavery bred an educated, enlightened, and civilized black American population destined for greater responsibility and greatness in Africa.[106] All three nationalists shared Delany's interpretation of slavery. For Crummell, slavery was the "Fortunate fall," an embodiment of positive experience.[107] In Turner's view, slavery was "the most rapid transition to civilization for the Negro."[108] He predicted that in the future the world would become more appreciative of slavery.[109] I have done a more exhaustive analysis of the religious historicist contents of nineteenth-century black nationalism elsewhere.[110]

Edward Wilmot Blyden was another nationalist who used Africa to propagate the myth of African inferiority and backwardness and also rendered a positive construction of slavery. In an address titled "The African Problem and the Method of Its Solution," which he delivered at the seventy-third anniversary of the Colonization Society in Washington, D.C., January 19, 1890, Blyden acknowledged the civilizational and historical accomplishments of Egypt, in contrast to the darkness and backwardness of the interior of Africa. He characterized indigenous Africans as backward and primitive people who have resisted the touch of superior European civilization. Blyden, who was then the principal of Liberia College, a post he assumed in 1880, urged black Americans to come to Africa and heed her cry for help. He then provided a providential rationalization of slavery. God sanctioned slavery largely for the preservation and civilization of a portion of Africa so that the preserved would return to uplift those left behind. According to him,

> The Negro race was to be preserved for a special and important work in the future. Of the precise nature of that work no one can form any definite conception. It is probable that if foreign races had been allowed to enter their country they would have been destroyed. So they brought them over to be helpers in this country and at the same time to be preserved. It was not the first time in the history of the world that a people have been preserved by subjugation to another. . . . Slavery would seem to be a strange school in which to preserve a people; but God has a way of salting as well as purifying by fire.

Blyden's positive rendition of slavery was popular among black nationalists. Africa, Blyden continued, was enveloped in darkness and primitivism, while the Americas were opened and developed. The solution to Africa's problem lay in colonization. In fact, Africans desperately called for it in their cry, "Come over and help us." Further emphasizing the need for colonization, Blyden declared, "It is a significant fact that Africa was completely shut up until the time arrived for the emancipation of her children in the western world." He presented himself as a messenger sent by Africans to convince black Americans to come to Africa and help rescue them from barbarism.[111]

Enslavement, therefore, was a necessary price to pay for the benefits of western civilization. Though this redefinition of slavery was done partly to bridge the cultural gap between Europeans and black American nationalists, it was in essence an exercise in identity construction. Being part of the enslavement experience amounted to a nullification of the African identity they initially proclaimed affinity with. What was most significant for Delany, Crummell, Turner, and Blyden was that slavery had brought them closer to the American identity. What this reveals is that despite their criticism of Euro-American values and influences, and a determined search for a new identity, these nationalists failed to project any consistency on the crucial question of identity. Their nationalist values and schemes betrayed cultural ambiguities. They were driven by alienation in America to seek African identity, only to be driven by revulsion and cultural alienation from Africa to assert and reaffirm their Euro-American identity. They perceived themselves no longer as Africans but as products of a historical experience mandated by slavery, an experience that had transformed them culturally into something different from Africa. Delany, Crummell, and Turner exhibited a complex and troubling consciousness of identity, exemplifying Du Bois's duality construct.

The search for a rational answer to the existential question "Who are we?" preoccupied blacks. Their response was unambiguous: Americans. Failure to achieve this identity, however, led many to embrace Africa. But their profession of affinity with Africa and Africans betrayed ambivalence and evoked conflicting passions of love, dislike, confraternity, and distance.

# 2

# Conceptual and Paradigmatic Utilizations and Representations of Africa

Africa has been a crucial component of black Diaspora struggles from the very beginning. How blacks in Diaspora perceived, conceived, and utilized Africa is a reflection of both the prevailing and dominant images and constructions of Africa, and the dynamics of the ever-changing experiences of blacks over historical time and space. Five paradigms/perspectives defined and shaped black Diaspora perceptions of, reactions to, and utilization of Africa. These paradigms reflect the functions Africa served and continues to serve (negatively and positively) in the black Diaspora struggle through historical times. They provide insights into how blacks conceptualized, utilized, and responded to Africa. They are civilization, cultural-nationalism, black nationalism and Pan-Africanism, instrumentalism, and Afrocentricity. These paradigms are not necessarily mutually exclusive, neither are they spatially and temporally confined. In fact, as this chapter will demonstrate, there is a very thin line between them, suggesting a mutually reinforcing relationship.

## Civilization

The first encounter between Europe and Africa brought two fundamentally different civilizations together, neither of which really understood the other. This lack of mutual understanding and appreciation bore the seeds that would germinate in estrangement and eventual hegemony of one over the other. Europe eventually became the dominant and domineering power. In a bid to strengthen their hegemony, Europeans felt compelled to deny the historicity of civilization in Africa and to denigrate and demonize Africans. This was accomplished largely through the intellectually fraudulent practice of denying the reality of civilization in Africa and through deliberate misrepresentation of the historical realities of the continent and its peoples. Initially, this misrepresentation of African history and civilization grew out of a genuine sense of awe, mystification, and ignorance the Europeans felt at encountering a civilization about which they knew absolutely nothing and one that was particularly striking for its exoticism. Encountering these strange, exotic, and enigmatic African civilizations and cultural realities undoubtedly mystified the Europeans. Later, such misrepresentation and denigration of Africa became deliberate and conscious. The strangeness and exoticism of Africa became, for the Europeans, a reflection of its essential inferiority and lack of substance. This set the stage for future flowering of racist and aristocratic ideological thoughts that legitimized exploitative and hegemonic institutions and experiences such as slavery and colonialism. The civilizational paradigm thus became the earliest structure within which the Europe-Africa encounter was defined and analyzed. For Europeans, the alleged absence of civilization in Africa justified the subordination of Africans and blacks in Diaspora. Over time, however, blacks used the civilizational paradigm as a medium of resistance and constructing identity.

The supposed absence of civilization in pre-European Africa, and the alleged primitive, backward, and heathenish nature of its indigenous societies, coupled with the negative connotations of blackness in European thought, provided justifications for the enslavement of Africans. From the mid-eighteenth century on, pro-slavery advocates developed powerful ideological justifications of slavery based on alleged cultural and historical poverty of Africa. James Walvin contends:

> in the eighteenth century, it was important for slave owners to deny the claims of black humanity and to resist demands that they convert and Christianize their slaves. To admit slaves to the brotherhood of the church was to accord them an equality that might conflict with the claims that they were people destined by origins and race to a humbler, less-than-human role in life. Of course plantocratic ideology is best seen in its starkest form in the daily, brutal operation of their properties, and took its most clearly defined form in the legal system they erected around them. There was, however, a more public and metropolitan aspect of that ideology, in the form of pro-slavery tracts and pamphlets, growing in volume as the eighteenth century advanced . . . Time and time again, these plantocratic tracts turned to the issue of colour and race. The African connection, the reality of blackness (race) became the sustaining pillar of slavery. Several derogatory terms manifest the disdain with which Europeans regarded peoples of African ancestry. Terms such as "moors", "blackamoors" and "Ethiopians" evolved and over time gave way to the generic "Negroes", or "blacks."[1]

In Walvin's view, "the transmutation of the African from a subject of cultural curiosity, viewed as inferior and beyond the pale, to being regarded as an object, a non-person, was the story of plantation slavery and its consequences for African enslavement and transportation."[2] The denial of African civilization thus pushed people of African descent into the abyss of depersonalization and objectification. They became objects, chattels, to be owned, bought and sold, and people with whom the "superior" Europeans should have the minimal of contacts, except in the relationship of superior-subordinate. Walvin provides ample evidence of this relationship in his study, *Questioning Slavery* (1996). In one example, in 1772 one Samuel Estwick proposed a law to preserve the British from the stain and contamination of blacks. He was a strong believer in the hierarchical ordering of races into groups and subgroups, with Africans and their descendants at its lowest level of creation.[3] European scholars theorized and pamphleteered in defense of slavery, often supporting their contentions with bogus theories and scientific postulations. Again, in Walvin's view, "their theories justify enslavement, and helped to create an intellectual and social climate that gave a veneer of respectability to long held prejudices about black humanity—here are people so far beyond the pale of civilized behavior that it was folly to think of conferring full citizenship rights on them . . . slavery was presented as a civilized force; shaping uncivilized beings into useful and productive workers."[4] Corroborating the above, George Frederickson contends, "prior to the 1850s, black subordination was the practice of white Americans, and the inferiority of the Negro was undoubtedly a common assumption, but open assertions of permanent inferiority were exceedingly rare. It took the assault of the abolitionists to unmask the cant about a theoretical human equality that coexisted with Negro slavery and racial discrimination and force the practitioners of racial oppression to develop a theory that accorded with their behavior."[5]

The presumed and alleged inferior and backward condition of Africa served as the building block for developing this racist and hegemonic theory. As Frederickson further argues, in order to justify slavery "as a necessary system of race relations, the proslavery theorists of the 1830s and 1840s developed an arsenal of argument for Negro inferiority which they repeated *ad nauseam*. Heavily emphasized was the historical case against the black man based on his supposed failure to develop a civilized way of life in Africa. As portrayed in pro-slavery writings, Africa was, and always had been, the scene of unmitigated savagery, cannibalism, devil worship, and licentiousness." In pro-slavery ideology, therefore, blacks "were much better off in slavery than they had been in Africa."[6]

This early denigration and objectification of Africans challenged the "African consciousness and disposition" of eighteenth-century free blacks in Pennsylvania, New York, and other northern states, who, still conscious of their African background and heritage, utilized Africa in identifying institutional structures of survival and struggle. The word "Africa" appeared in several of their institutions; strongly projecting Africa as their pillar of support and identity. By the late eighteenth and early nineteenth centuries, however, under the onslaught of anti-slavery and abolitionist criticisms, a strong pro-slavery ideology emerged, sustained by deliberate and forceful attacks on Africa and her descendants in the Diaspora. This denial and denigration of African historical heritage became the legitimizing basis of white superiority and black inferiority. Blacks were denied citizenship, equality, and access to social, economic, and political resources. Thus the civilizational deficiency of Africa served to tighten the knot of bondage and subordination on all blacks. Pro-slavery ideology depicted Africa as a primitive and problematic continent and African descendants in Diaspora as inferior, and thus inheritors and reflectors of Africa's cultural decadence. Racists and paternalistic solutions were proposed ostensibly to uplift Africans and their descendants through the introduction to both civilizational values and conditions from Europe. Of particular significance was the portrayal of the institution of slavery as a civilizing process for the enslaved African descendants. Removing blacks from "primitive" Africa and enslaving them in Christian white societies elevated them on a higher pedestal of civilization.[7]

The experience of enslavement and the indoctrinating effect of pro-slavery ideology would, over time, induce in blacks an alienated and paternalistic disposition toward Africa. Many of them began to espouse a variant of Eurocentric diffusionist thought—the civilizational export thesis—that is, the conception of Europe as the source from where civilization came to Africa, a theory that tied Africa's development and civilization to the infusion of ideas and values from "civilized" Europe. Europe was the center of civilization and progress, while the rest of the world, particularly Africa, represented zones of inertia and cultural sterility, and therefore in need of the infusion of civilized values and institutions from the European center.[8] This export thesis acquired its earliest manifestation in the colonization movement of the early 1800s. The American Colonization Society was founded in 1816 to facilitate the relocation of free blacks to Liberia in West Africa. The society was inspired, some suggest, by altruistic considerations. The founders hoped to secure a place where free blacks would have opportunities to realize their potentialities to the fullest, while also serving as bearers of civilization and progress to the rest of Africa.[9] In this latter goal, the society reflected the dominant perception of Africa as backward and primitive. From the 1820s through the 1840s, the society tried to persuade free blacks to relocate to Liberia. It did not achieve much success since the majority of blacks saw colonization as essentially a pro-slavery institution designed to rid society of the disturbing presence of free blacks.[10] However, some blacks soon embraced the scheme, and became convinced of its underlying premise of Africa as a primitive and backward place, of Africans as a people in need of civilization, and of black Americans as ideal agents for the transfer of civilization to Africa. This denigration of Africa provided black Americans with a sense of self-exaltation and emancipatory consciousness.

Although still considered backward in relation to Europeans, sharing a geopolitical and cultural space with Europeans situated blacks on a civilization pedestal above indigenous Africans. Many blacks therefore gladly and enthusiastically accepted designations as agents and bearers of civilization and culture to primitive Africa. But there was another troubling dimension. According to advocates of colonization, Africa offered the ideal and authentic basis of identity for identity-hungry and deprived black Americans who, because of inherent deficiencies, were deemed incapable of coexisting with whites on the basis of equality. The American identity, and all its accompanying rights and privileges, were reserved for whites only. The colonization society, and the African alternative it dangled, offered blacks two fundamental imperatives: identity and self-exaltation. The entire colonization doctrine convinced blacks that they were going back to Africa no longer as they had come, primitive and savage, but as changed and civilized beings who were now culturally superior to Africans. It also assured them that colonization was a step toward rediscovering their lost African identity. This dual consciousness explains many of the conflicts that would later develop between black Americans and indigenous Africans in Liberia. Colonization thus offered solutions to Africa's civilizational challenges in the early eighteenth century. If immersion in Euro-American values was the route to civilization, then the only conceivable means by which Africa would become civilized was through colonization, which would transfer those elements of Euro-American civilization to the continent. Colonization, therefore, represented the earliest representation of the modernization theory. Colonization thus encouraged and nurtured paternalistic and racist assumptions about, and postures toward, Africa. Africa and Africans were perceived more like objects to be shaped and reshaped into configurations determined and defined by others. Black Americans who equally imbibed this perception of Africa assumed paternalistic postures towards the continent. Many blacks embraced colonization, which they then draped in quasi Pan-African robes, imploring blacks in Diaspora and Africans, by virtue of shared heritage and identity, to cooperate in pursuance of mutual interests. They conceived this cooperation within the racialist and paternalistic ethos of the era and advanced a linear trajectory of influences from black Diaspora to Africa. In other words, black American subscription to colonization implied acceptance of Eurocentric conceptions of Africa's problems and the suggested solutions.

Paul Cuffee (1759–1811) and Lott Cary (1780–1828) are two of the earliest black American promoters of colonization and the Pan-African genre. A Quaker of mixed Negro and Indian heritage, Paul Cuffee supposedly developed interest in Africa early in life and became concerned with alleviating Africa from degradation. As he once declared, "The travail of my soul is that Africa's inhabitants may be favored with reformation."[11] Convinced that indigenous Africans lacked civilizational attributes and habits, Cuffee sought to encourage blacks to colonize Africa and assist in promoting habits of industry, sobriety, and frugality among the natives. He was undoubtedly a product of his time, for his vision of Africa was shaped by the larger and prevailing Eurocentric conceptions and depictions of Africa. Consistent with prevailing disdain for African traditions, Cuffee advocated the eradication of facets of African traditions that he deemed primitive. He found the African practice of carrying loads on the heads particularly distasteful. As he averred, "Instead of carrying loads on their heads, how much better would it be if the colonists had a wagon on which to haul the loads." Removing this and other primitive practices would facilitate "mercantile relations . . . between Africa and America." The eventual outcome would, he hoped, supplant the obnoxious slave trade with other economic activities, such as "whale fishery on the western coast of Africa." Living at a time when British abolitionists were involved in the establishment of the colony of Sierra Leone, Cuffee turned to the British for permission to take a few black Americans to Sierra Leone. His colonization plan would, he reasoned, rid Africans of the slave trade and replace it with badly needed "civilization and Christianity."[12]

Lott Cary was licensed to preach by the First Baptist Church of Richmond, and almost immediately he began to speak in favor of missionary activities in Africa. His efforts led to the formation of the Richmond African Baptist Missionary Society in 1815. Blacks in Richmond conceived their missionary scheme within providential dynamics, according to which God sanctioned the enslavement of Africans so that those brought to the New World would become converted to Christianity and civilized. Transformed from savages to civilized beings, these blacks would then return to evangelize to the rest of Africa. This mission spirit energized blacks in other states, resulting in the creation of African mission societies in Philadelphia, Virginia, New York, and Georgia. These facts clearly suggest a developing consciousness of affinity with Africa and concern for resolving Africa's problems, albeit derived from a negative Eurocentric construction of Africa. Embracing the prevailing negative depictions of Africa, these blacks saw themselves as destined by providence to be the saviors and redeemers of Africa. It is within this context that Cary's mission was later endorsed by the American Colonization Society. Like Cuffee, he became a convenient conduit for the transmission of superior European civilizational values to Africa. Cary was endorsed by the Baptist Board of Missions in 1819 and also by the Colonization society. Before his departure for Africa, Cary delivered a farewell speech in the meetinghouse of the First Baptist Church in Richmond. His speech reflected the prevailing paternalistic and racist conception of Africa and disdain for the continent. According to him, "I am about to leave you and expect to see your faces no more. I long to preach to the poor Africans the way of life and salvation. I don't know what may befall me, whether I may find a grave in the ocean, or among the savage men, or more savage wild beasts on the coast of Africa."[13]

Although Cary, Cuffee, and other black colonizationists betrayed in their utterances and writings genuine concern for Africa and the slave trade, and declared a commitment to alleviating Africa's problems and ridding the continent of "barbarism," they framed their solutions within the paternalistic and racist ethos of the age, by endorsing a scheme (colonization) that the majority of blacks rejected for precisely the reasons that Cuffee and Cary embraced and advocated it—that Africa was primitive and backward and that blacks are not Africans but Americans who were denied their rights and privileges. Thus, sharing the same perceptions of Africa, one group used that perception to advance missionary and colonization scheme while the vast majority, skeptical of colonization, used the same perception to insist upon American citizenship. This missionary and paternalistic conception of Africa induced a dualistic interpretation of the relationship of blacks to Africans: the former, elevated and civilized; the latter, still trapped in decadence and primitivism. In a speech endorsing colonization as a solution to Africa's problems, delivered in Philadelphia in October of 1877, in the aftermath of the collapse of Reconstruction, renowned journalist John Edward Bruce made this remark: "one hundred and fifty millions of our people are on the other side of the broad Atlantic, groveling in darkness and superstition; five millions are on this side surrounded by all the advantages that could be desired in the march toward civilization. It is our duty to carry to those benighted, darkened minds a light to guide them in the march toward civilization."[14]

Although colonization was not popular among blacks, the conception of Africa as a primitive place was widespread. But there were other blacks who equally embraced Eurocentric perceptions of Africa while rejecting colonization. Though they acknowledged Africa's "primitive," nature, these blacks vehemently opposed any scheme that entailed removal from the United States. The ambiguity represented by the acceptance of a racist portrayal of Africa while rejecting colonization surfaced in a speech by the Reverend Peter Williams Jr. at St. Philips Episcopal Church. In his judgment, "Africa could certainly be brought into a state of civil and religious improvement without sending all the free people of color in the United States there. A few well-qualified missionaries, properly fitted out and supported, would do more for the instruction and improvement of the natives of that country than a host of colonists." He ridiculed the contention that colonization would help improve the character and condition of black Americans. It was illogical, he argued, to envisage improving a people by sending them "far from civilized society." "What is there in the burning sun, the arid plains, and barbarous customs of Africa, that is so peculiarly favorable to our improvement?" he asked sardonically. Emphasizing the American identity of blacks, Williams declared, "We are natives of this country, we ask only to be treated as well as foreigners. Not a few of our fathers suffered and bled to purchase its independence. We ask only to be treated as well as those who fought against it. We have toiled to cultivate it to its present prosperous condition; we ask only to have equal privileges with those who came from distant lands; to enjoy the fruits of our labor."[15]

In their reactions to the condition of black alienation and marginalization, future advocates of emigration would reflect the same racist, paternalistic, and Eurocentric constructions of Africa. They would not only embrace the Eurocentric worldview but also concede Europe's preeminent claim to civilization. Consequently, many exhibited disdain for, and alienation from, Africa. Like the Europeans, they too proposed paternalistic and racist solutions for Africa's alleged civilizational deficiencies.[16] As described later in this study, these blacks turned the civilization-export thesis, to which they had subscribed, on its head, counterpoising the civilizational preeminence of Africa over Europe. At a convention in Michigan in 1843, blacks laid down in detail evidence not only of the antiquity of civilization in Africa but also of the preeminence of African civilization over European. This evidence not only enhanced their self-worth but also provided strong grounds for demanding radical change in their condition—demands for citizenship and equality.[17]

### Cultural-Nationalism

Culture constituted a central component of the civilizational paradigm. To be civilized meant that one possessed a vibrant culture and cultural heritage. Africa, and by extension, her descendants in Diaspora, were denied a viable cultural heritage. Since Africa presumably did not produce a civilization, it seemed logical to conclude that Africans lacked a vibrant culture. Plantocratic ideology denied the existence of African culture. Africa was depicted as a place without a culture and Africans as a people without a cultural heritage. This nullification of African culture held sway for decades. When it became implausible for pro-slavery advocates to continue to deny blacks and Africans a cultural tradition and heritage, they switched to characterizing African culture as intrinsically barbaric and primitive. They represented African culture and lifestyles as the lowest in the scheme of human development. Spokespersons resorted to ethnophaulisms to describe African peoples and their cultures. This denial of African culture became the legitimizing weapon of domination. Such a culture was not endearing to black Americans, and many of them became alienated from Africa and searched desperately for identity in Euro-American culture. Just as with the concept of civilization, "culture" evoked both endearing and alienated responses in black Americans toward both Africa and Europe. Both consciousnesses developed for the same end—affirmation and defense of an identity, the definition of which changed and often vacillated between Europe and Africa. At times, some black leaders found conceding that Africa was indeed primitive necessary in order to affirm their own cosmopolitan New World identity. This pattern of denial and denigration of African culture occurred even as many blacks invoked and utilized their African heritage to fashion values and institutions of survival under slavery. At other times, they found that contesting Africa's alleged primitivism and demonstrating Africa's cultural worth and authenticity eroded the legitimacy of European hegemony in the New World. Affirming African cultural worth thus became for some a weapon of pride, of enhanced self-conception, and of psychological, if not cultural, emancipation from the domineering and alienating Euro-American geopolitical and cultural contexts. African culture thus served as a weapon of struggle, of self-definition, and of counterhegemonic identity construction. Authenticating African culture enabled blacks to reject and contest both Euro-American cultural influence and essence and its claim to universality and superiority. In the beginning, therefore, the denigration and denial of African culture and the alienation slavery induced only further forced blacks to embrace Africa as the basis of their cultural and institutional apparatus of survival and identity. Soon, however, the ideology would have the negative effect of alienating blacks from Africa. Many blacks became publicly disdainful of African culture and sought cultural meaning and identity in Euro-America.

A strong sense of alienation and distance from Africa and an equally strong determination to demonstrate cultural affinity with Euro-America propelled the struggle for integration, especially from the rise of organized black abolitionism in the 1830s to the mid-1850s and beyond. A consciousness of distance from African culture informed the integrationist and cultural-pluralistic genres. While the former sought integration in the United States, in preference over emigration to Africa, the latter envisioned a cultural pluralistic America where all races would coexist, while each maintained its cultural identity and values. Neither sought identification with Africa; however, the hardening of racism and the alienated consciousness it engendered compelled many blacks to fall back upon and exalt African culture, extolling the virtues of her traditions, as a counterweapon of struggle and a means of affirming a counterhegemonic protest identity. These cultural nationalists now found African culture a potent weapon of struggle and began to espouse some degree of economic, political, and cultural independence for blacks.

At various times in the black Diaspora experience, individuals and groups invoked cultural-nationalist strategies. Rejection and marginalization induced negative and alienated consciousness in blacks, and, as integration proved elusive, they developed positive attitudes toward Africa. This was reflected in declarations of pride in African culture, affirmation of the uniqueness, wealth, and even superiority, of African culture; and pride in a positive rendition of African historical heritage. Although such glorification of Africa was most pronounced in the late nineteenth century, it existed much earlier, as in William Whipper's eulogy to the British abolitionist, William Wilberforce. In this eulogy, delivered in Philadelphia on December 6, 1833, Whipper unambiguously proclaimed the antiquity of civilization in Africa. According to him,

to have established the fact that Africa was once the cradle of science—the seat of civilization—and her sons as its early votaries and boasted cultivators, who in their search after wisdom and scanned the "azure pathway of the heavens" and laid the foundation of some of the most abstruse sciences, they might only have referred to the Ptolemaic age or to that mammoth receptacle of their collected wisdom, the Alexandrian library, that by the decree of Omar was consumed by fire. . . . the light of its conflagration was followed by an age of darkness; and its incensed smoke appears in its fall to have brought down barbarism and superstition. Let history mourn the event.[18]

In 1833, Whipper was just condemning slavery, and there is no indication that he meant his exaltation of Africa for anything other than to negate and debunk prevailing racist contentions that had been used to legitimize slavery. Whipper was more interested in using this adulation of Africa to advance the cause of freedom and equality in America. Robert Benjamin Lewis, a black Bostonian, wrote *Light and Truth* (1844,) in which he identified Ethiopia as the fountain of many civilizations in antiquity and highlighted the accomplishments of prominent blacks in antiquity. Then there was James W. C. Pennington's *A Text Book of the Origin and History of the Colored People* (1841). An ex-slave who became a minister and abolitionist, Pennington attacked and contested many of the false ideas that have been used to justify enslaving the Negro. Through such exposition, Pennington hoped to facilitate integration. In his own writings, George Washington Williams, a graduate of Howard University, focused on the African background of black America. He discussed the ancient kingdoms and states in Africa, including the Yoruba, Asante, Benin, Liberia, and Sierra Leone, underscoring their civilizational and cultural worth. This particular tradition of exalting African culture as a protest culture became more and more pronounced in the second half of the nineteenth century.[19]

As indicated in the previous chapter, Martin Delany spearheaded the emigration crusade of the 1850s. He rejected Europe's claim to civilizational preeminence and provided evidence of the antiquity of civilization in Africa. Contesting the hamitic theory, Delany described ancient Egyptian civilization as authentically Negroid. As he asked rhetorically, "Who were the builders of the everlasting pyramids, catacombs, and sculptors of the sphinxes? Were they Europeans or Caucasians, Asiatic or Mongolians? . . . Among what races of men, and what country of the globe, do we find traces of these singular productions, but the African and Africa? None whatever. It is in Africa the pyramids, sphinxes and catacombs are found; here the hieroglyphics still remain." And, he continued, "Is it not known to history that Egypt was the cradle of the earliest civilization, propagating the arts and sciences, when the Grecians were an uncivilized people, covering their persons with skins and clothing, anterior to the existence of the she-wolf." Further, he opined, "It is also the glory of the black race to know that they have had these qualities in sufficient measure to build a great political fabric long before the whites, imparting to them the first germs of civilization and enlightening the world by their wisdom." Delany extolled the virtues of indigenous Africa in several of his writings and pronouncements; yet nothing compares to that of his lecture titled, "The Moral and Social Aspect of Africa." Here Delany rejected claims of African inferiority. He invoked his three thousand miles of travels in Africa and acquaintance with all facets of African social and moral life. In the lecture, he showered praises on indigenous Africans, all in a bid to convince black Americans of the potentialities and prospects of emigration to Africa. Referring to Africans, he wrote, "The language of the people is a good sign of its civility, and the African language is derived from fixed roots, it is not a jargon . . . the people speak clearly and well . . . The people are very polite." He described Africans as a people of high moral standard and praised their institutions, cultures, industry, values, and mode of living.[20]

Other blacks also wrote forcefully in defense of African civilization, underscoring both the antiquity of civilization in Africa, and Africa's immense contributions to world civilization. Instead of Europe, therefore, these blacks projected Africa as the quintessence of civilization. This positive rendition also entailed the exaltation of African culture as the basis of self-affirmation and definition and the foundation for staging a counterstruggle against Eurocentrism. In other words, African history and culture became the substructure for constructing a strong nationalist consciousness. Juxtaposing Africans and Europeans as equal contributors to building the New World, and invoking Providentialism, Blyden wrote, "To take their place as accessories in the work to be done God suffered the African to be brought hither, who could work and would work, and should endure the climatic conditions of a new southern country, which Europeans could not." In his judgment, since both Africans and Europeans contributed equally to the development of the New World, they both deserved the glory and celebration. As he emphasized, "Englishman, Hollander, and Huguenot, Nigritian and Congo came together. If Europe brought the head, Africa furnished the hands for a great portion of the work which has been achieved here."[21]

The ambivalent responses of blacks to African culture predominated in the nineteenth century. This ambivalence reflected the influence of European thought. For much of the eighteenth and nineteenth centuries, the values of Euro-American socialization and acculturation shaped black American conception of Africa. This conception manifested ambiguity, often changing with the vagaries of racism. These blacks had become reflections of the acculturation process in European thought. Perhaps without realizing it, they became deeply enmeshed in European thought and unable to develop and sustain a clear-cut independent policy; however, the exaltation of African culture was more rhetorical than substantive in the nineteenth century and earlier. By the mid-twentieth century, blacks became more forceful in embracing Africa and began to move beyond rhetoric to practical manifestations of African culture in their lifestyles. Regardless of how good they felt about Africa, however, they were not willing to live independently of America. Hence, their ideology reflected a crisis of identity that confirmed their essentially American character. By the twentieth century, there was a move toward reviving African culture, giving it the respectability it deserved. Thus, African culture acquired attraction in the wake of the civil rights movement. The rise of the countercultural movement led blacks to embrace African culture and lifestyles in an unprecedented manner. African culture became weapon of protest, affirmation of a counteridentity, and rejection of Euro-American culture. The Afro hairstyle, *dashiki* outfit, name change, celebration of Kwanza—all became African cultural artifacts of protest and identity. African cultural identity is today very strong among black cultural nationalists who assume a posture of cultural defiance and rejection of Euro-American culture.

In order effectively to debunk European claims to civilizational pre-eminence, black leaders confronted the issue squarely and promptly. Delany, Crummell, and Turner countered Europe's conception of civilization with a more culturally constructed version, one that exalted African cultural attributes. For example, Crummell viewed civilization as encompassing "not only the elements of technology and materialism" but also "personal responsibility . . . the honor and freedom of womanhood, allied with the duty of family development . . . an elevated use of material things."[22] Turner, on the other hand, constructed civilization as the contemplation of "the fraternity, civil and political equality between man and man . . . regardless of his color or nationality."[23] Both definitions were meant to highlight attributes lacking or deficient in western societies—what was wrong with, and missing in, Western civilization—an acknowledgment of its imperfections. Despite western economic and technological advancement, nineteenth century black nationalists advanced a conception of civilization that seemed to privilege attributes that they associated with Africa. They underlined other culturally constructed values that are conspicuously missing in, and perhaps even alien to, western civilization: political equality, social equality, respect for rights and privileges of fellow beings, civility, justice, courtesy, and so forth. They invoked aspects of civilization that the Europeans neglected or overlooked in order to counter Europe's claim to a monopoly of civilization.

At different times, these nationalists attempted to illuminate positive aspects of Africa, primarily to debunk the myth of the "dark continent" and enhance black American chances of becoming accepted as the equals of whites. They aimed their constructions of a progressive African culture primarily at qualifying, not necessarily invalidating, the universalistic and absolutist claims of western civilization, qualification that many hoped would erode the cultural chauvinism and ethnocentrism that characterized European thought. The moral, ethical, and cultural authority of Africa became a positive force against Eurocentric claims and pretensions of both civilizational and cultural superiority. Aside from the positive reaction that Eurocentric propaganda generated among blacks, compelling many to seek integration into the Euro-American world, these blacks also evinced a negative attitude and response toward Africa. Many blacks became disdainful of African values, believing that these could be replaced entirely with Euro-American culture and values. Many of them actively advocated the obliteration of indigenous African cultural norms and values that were deemed primitive by Euro-American standards. Paul Cuffee, for instance, was averse to the African practice of carrying loads on the head.[24] Decades later, in an effort to justify Europe's civilizing mission, Delany identified several African practices that he deemed abhorrent and advised their displacement with European habits; among them was the African practice of sitting and eating on the floor. He deemed this a mark of inferiority and primitivism. Crummell equally loathed African languages and dialects, which he depicted as symbols of primitivism.[25] Succumbing to Eurocentric socialization, many blacks became disdainful of African culture and norms and adopted distant and standoffish postures vis-à-vis the continent. In the judgment of these black Americans, Africans practiced customs and traditions that were indeed barbaric and primitive and had to be civilized. The primitive and decadent character of Africa compelled many black Americans to seek their identity, both cultural and national, within a Eurocentric mold.

### Black Nationalism and Pan-Africanism

In proslavery thought, the denigration of African culture and concomitant denial of African civilization justified the denial to blacks of Americans citizenship. The alleged absence of civilizational heritage and cultural worth in consequence of the African ancestry provided grounds for black subordination, depersonalization, and denial of American citizenship, with all its accompanying rights and privileges. Blacks became, in the words of Delany, "a nation within a nation," an alienated minority whose only option, in the judgment of many, was the creation of an alternative black nationality abroad.[26] The first challenge therefore that blacks confronted immediately on arrival in the New World, derived from their suspension in what one may characterize as a nationality void. By the mid-nineteenth century, after struggling unsuccessfully for integration as full-fledged members of the American nationality, many black leaders embarked upon an earnest search for this alternative nationality, spurred on by a strong conviction in the benefits and potentialities of shared African ancestry and heritage. It should not be forgotten, however, that this search for a black nationality external to the United States, this manifestation of national consciousness, derived from the conception of Africans and blacks in Diaspora as one people united by shared cultural and historical heritage, was the product of rejection and alienation.

Consciousness of African civilization and of the utilitarian worth of African ancestry and nationality surfaced very early in the black American struggle. The use of Africa for identification of churches, fraternal societies, and self-help organizations exemplified one of the earliest invocations of Africa for the construction of a countervailing corporate national identity. This was particularly noticeable among free blacks in New York, Pennsylvania, and New England in the late eighteenth and early nineteenth centuries. They began with using Africa as identity construct, and over time the prospect of using Africa as the basis of constructing a national identity gained popularity. The invocation of African ancestry and shared historical experience as the basis of rallying all blacks and Africans behind a consensual perspective of the struggle surfaced very early in the black experience. An early representation and articulation of Africa as the rallying point of "nationalism" can be found in the writings of Henry H. Garnet, Martin Delany, James W. C. Pennington, and William Wells Brown.

During a trip to Jamaica, Henry Garnet came to the realization that the conditions of West Indian blacks were in some ways similar to those of blacks in the United States. This led him to the conviction that emphasis on the struggle in America was too narrowly focused. He advocated a broadly based international movement to promote unity within the entire black world, from Africa to the Caribbean. Thus, Garnet saw Africa as the rallying point of a trans-Atlantic struggle for blacks. In furtherance of this, in the summer of 1858, Garnet and several other blacks and interested whites founded the African Civilization Society, and Garnet was elected its first president.[27]

Garnet was not just advocating unity between blacks in Diaspora and Africa, he was also interested in a program of economic relationship that would help strengthen the two and create the foundation for mutual development. He proposed the development of a cotton economy in Africa, the success of which, he hoped, would undermine cotton and slavery in America. By 1859, he was convinced that the founding of a powerful nation in Africa "would do more to overthrow slavery, in creating respect for blacks. The African Civilization Society which he helped found, became the vehicle for the advance of commerce and civilization in Africa." In a speech delivered in 1860 at the Cooper's Institute, New York, Garnet outlined the objectives of the African Civilization Society to include Christianizing and civilizing Africa through the medium of black emigrants, overthrowing idolatry and superstition, destroying the slave trade, and establishing civil government.[28]

Delany was perhaps the most vocal and articulate advocate and defender of African nationality in the second half of the nineteenth century. He was very conscious and proud of his African ancestry from youth, and a major part of his life was spent in the pursuit of integration. As suggested earlier, when it became obvious to him in the 1850s that blacks would never be granted full citizenship and equality, Delany fell back upon his African ancestry for succor. In several of his publications, he offered the resources of Africa as the foundation for an independent black nationality, especially in the 1850s when meaningful equality and integration seemed far-fetched in the aftermath of the Fugitive Slave Law and the Dred Scott decision (1857). Africa offered the only hope; by relocating to Africa, blacks would be among their own kind. Delany saw other potentialities the African landmass, natural resources, and population offered: abundant land for agricultural projects, cheap labor for cultivating the land, the ideal climate and soil for producing a strong cotton economy that would challenge and undermine that of the American South.[29] Thus, Africa offered the edifice for a grand black nationality that would serve as the rallying point for all blacks. This perspective became more pronounced from the 1850s through the 1880s, with the rise of emigration and back-to-Africa movement. I have already mentioned Henry McNeal Turner and Alexander Crummell, who were both instrumental in advocating emigration, and the moral, economic, and cultural transformation of indigenous Africa into the black man's "city on a hill."[30] This scheme assumed greater urgency after the collapse of Reconstruction and the gradual erosion of the rights that blacks had won in the aftermath of the Civil War. Disillusioned by the dramatic turnaround in the 1880s and 1890s as returning "Bourbon" politicians frantically sought to return blacks to the antebellum status quo, blacks again embraced Africa, as the foundation for a future independent and affluent black nationality. While Delany was active in the 1850s and 1860s, Turner and Crummell dominated the late nineteenth and early twentieth centuries. Although riddled with contradictions, their nationalism reflected their complex historical and cultural experiences, and although they did not succeed in sponsoring emigration of any magnitude, by articulating a nexus between blacks in Diaspora, the Caribbean, and Africa, these nationalists are credited with laying the foundation for Pan-Africanism.

Thus, just as Africa served as the rallying cry of nationalism in the early nineteenth century, so did it become the substructure of Pan-Africanism in the twentieth century. In advocating the emigration of blacks to Africa, John Edward Bruce, a powerful advocate of Pan-Africanism in the early twentieth century, outlined the benefits that Africa offered to blacks—ancestral heritage, meaningful freedom, and the opportunity fully to realize potentialities and the economic resources for economic development. As he declared,

> I shall endeavor to show tonight why the colored American should emigrate to Africa—first, because Africa is his fatherland; second, because, before the war, in the south He was a slave, and in the north a victim of prejudice and ostracism; and third, because since the close of the war, although He has been freed by emancipation and invested with enfranchisement, He is only nominally free, and lastly, because He is still a victim of prejudice, and practically proscribed socially, religiously, politically, educationally, and in the various industrial pursuits.[31]

Bruce went on to outline the necessity for emigration. According to him, "First, then he should emigrate to Africa because it is his fatherland. Africa is a country rich in its productions, offering untold treasures to the adventurer who may go there. It has a peculiar claim upon the colored American in this country, and that claim is just and as equitable as any could be."[32] The Pan-African philosophy and movement of Marcus Garvey, the Jamaican-born advocate of black independence and emigration, preceded the emergence of the Pan-African Congress tradition. Enraged by what he perceived as a worldwide European conspiracy to degrade and exploit blacks, Garvey arrived in the United States in 1916, armed with an organization that he had founded in Jamaica—the Universal Negro Improvement Association (UNIA).[33] He also came armed with a strong conviction of the imperative of unity among blacks in Africa and the Diaspora in order to effectively combat and survive the onslaught of European economic, political, and cultural hegemony. Almost immediately, Garvey's appeal and message struck a responsive cord among the masses of black Americans. As one writer suggests, "Garveyism represented the subterranean counter-point of the elite Pan-African Congress tradition that was controlled and organized by black intellectuals." Garvey appealed to the masses. As one authority contends, he "brought the notion of the links between the black world and Africa to a mass audience, creating a new working-class Diaspora consciousness. By linking the entire black world to Africa . . . Garvey made the American Negro conscious of his African origins and created for the first time a feeling of international solidarity between Africans and peoples of African descent."[34] Garveyism, the Pan-African Congress tradition and movement of the late nineteenth and early twentieth centuries marked the highest expression of black nationalism.

Apprehensive of the rising tide of Europe's global imperialism, and the tenacity of racism, blacks in Diaspora, led by Henry Sylvester Williams of Trinidad, inaugurated the Pan-African Congress movement, which brought Africans and Diaspora black representatives together to deliberate on crucial matters arising from their common African heritage.[35] The unifying factors were the negative experiences that characterized their relations with Europeans, out of which developed ethos of mutuality that further strengthened the Pan-African bond. It was the black American W. E. B. Du Bois who captured the defining character of the epoch in his often-quoted identification of the problem of the twentieth century as "the problem of the color-line, the question as to how far differences of race—which shows themselves chiefly in the color of the skin and the texture of the hair—will hereafter be made the basis of denying to over half the world the right of sharing to their utmost ability the opportunities and privileges of modern civilization."[36]

Essentializing the color line constituted a strong clarion call for unity among peoples of African descent against those on the other side of the racial divide. Du Bois's publications highlighted the positive accomplishments of blacks and the contributions of Africa to civilization. A scholar par excellence, the massive force of his scholarship provided compelling evidence of African civilization and culture. His

*The World and Africa* (1947) was written "to remind readers of the crisis of civilization, and how critical a part Africa had played in human history, past and present."[37] Du Bois used his scholarship to fight both the internal war against black subordination, and the external force of European imperialism in Africa. By demonstrating the historical and civilizational worth of African history, Du Bois simultaneously weakened the ideological edifice of imperialism. Underscoring the importance and imperative of African independence, he urged the nations of the world to "respect the integrity and independence of the free Negro states of Abyssinia, Liberia, Haiti and the rest, and let the inhabitants of these states, the independent tribes of Africa, the Negroes of the West Indies and America, and the black subjects of all nations take courage, strive ceaselessly, and fight bravely, that they may prove to the world their incontestable right to be counted among the great brotherhood of mankind."[38]

Essentially, both Garveyism and the Pan-African Congress tradition were built on shared African ancestry and historical experiences; that is, Africa was the rallying point, the very nexus and nerve of Pan-Africanism. The Pan-African Congress movement met five times between 1900 and 1945. The combined efforts of Diaspora blacks and Africans brought pressure to bear on European powers, resulting in accelerating the process of decolonization in Africa.[39] The Pan-African tradition did not end with Africa's independence. Africa and her descendants abroad continued the tradition, albeit with reduced vigor and a lack of consensus on goals, focus, and strategies. The last Pan-African congress was held in Kampala, Uganda, in 1993; however, a Pan-African Movement summit took place in January 2007 organized by the World Africa Diaspora Union. This was preparatory for a 2008 Pan-African celebration of the 108th anniversary of the launching of the Pan-African Movement. Africa continues to serve blacks in Diaspora as the basis of constructing a solid platform of struggle against the forces of domination and exploitation.

Consciousness of shared African ancestry was the basis, the underlying force, of the Pan-African tradition. Shared negative experiences of racism and colonialism became the precipitating force. Both racism and colonialism were justified, again, as with slavery, on negative characterizations and vilification of Africa and Africans. According to this reasoning, blacks were subordinated because of the facts of African primitivism and cultural and civilizational sterility. Advocates of black nationalism and Pan-Africanism built their ideology

and movement, that is, their appeal for black unity across Atlantic
space, largely on African considerations: shared culture, history, and
experience. Like their nineteenth-century predecessors, twentieth-
century Pan-Africanists based their cause on realities of Africa; what
Africa meant, represented, and offered. Pan-Africanism represented
a corporate construction of identity and struggle based upon shared
experiences—historical and cultural. Blacks in Diaspora invoked this
corporate Africa-centered identity, in order to present a united front
against domination and exploitation. Many scholars have characterized this corporate consciousness as historically deep-rooted and
pervasive, best represented in the thoughts and schemes of Du Bois,
Henry Sylvester Williams, Edward Wilmot Blyden, Martin Delany, Alexander Crummell, Henry McNeal Turner, Marcus Garvey, Stokely
Carmichael (aka, Kwame Toure), and Malcolm X. Pan-Africanism became instrumental in the decolonization of Africa and in the nationalist upsurge in black Diaspora—for example, the civil rights movement
of the 1960s. Many black Americans, like Malcolm X, and Stokely Carmichael, believed in invoking Pan-Africanism and internationalizing
the civil rights movement by tying it to the plight of Africans, since
both supposedly shared identical problems and challenges.[40] Thus,
Africa occupied a central and elevated platform in the nationalist and
Pan-Africanist paradigm. Africa was the center of and the very foundation upon which rested the superstructure of historical and cultural
experiential unity that nurtured the corporate ethos that the militants
of the 1960s advocated. "Of all our studies," Malcolm X once observed,
"History is best qualified to reward our research." Here, Malcolm emphasized the importance that historical knowledge of Africa offered
to the struggles of black Americans. He urged black Americans to attain strong grounding in African history as the means and vehicle of
reclaiming themselves and of expunging seeds of self-denigrating consciousness implanted in them by Europeans. He was very emphatic on
broadening the parameters of the civil rights movement to include the
struggles of Africans, for success in one was inconceivable without the
other. He presented a positive rendition of ancient African civilization
and history, one of a glorious accomplishment before the advent of
Europeans. The European misrepresentation of African history and
culture implanted inferiority and self-hate in blacks. To reverse this,
blacks must turn to Africa and reclaim their legacy and heritage. As
he reasoned, "Why should the black man in America concern himself since he's been taken away from the continent for. Three or four

hundred years?—Having complete control over Africa, the colonial powers of Europe projected the image of Africa negatively . . . it was negative to you and me, and you and I began to hate it . . . in hating Africa and in hating the Africans, we ended up hating ourselves."[41]

Stokely Carmichael, a leading advocate of Black Power militant ideology and Pan-Africanism in the 1960s, also offered knowledge of Africa to blacks as the most potent weapon of freeing themselves from subordination. He implored blacks and Africans to unite and strengthen Pan-African ties. Success was inconceivable without a strong Pan-African framework. He defined Pan-Africanism as "the highest political expression of black Power." Black Power and Pan-Africanism seemed inextricably tied. As he argued, "Black Power means that all people who are black should come together, organize themselves and form a power base to fight for their liberation. That's black power." Furthermore, he insisted, "We're an African people and Africa belongs to all African people. It is our homeland! . . . We must ask ourselves what relationship Africa has to us while we are here in the western hemisphere. We must ask what our relationship to Africa is and how do we survive here at the same time." Pan-Africanism enabled Carmichael to tie Africans and black Americans as a people with a "Common enemy, common problems . . . Victims of imperialism, racism." The Pan-Africanism that he espoused and propagated as a medium of struggle and freedom for all blacks had "Mother Africa as its *sine qua non*."[42]

It is, therefore, clear that Africa served dual functions for blacks in Diaspora in both domestic nationalism and external Pan-Africanism. For the former, it was a weapon of struggle and survival, of blunting the edges of the negative and debilitating impact of the ideology of subordination and depersonalization, of proffering a counterhegemonic identity and culture in the face of denial and objectification. For the latter, Africa functioned as the foundation for trans-Atlantic unity, for generating the unity needed to combat perceived common threats, problems, and challenges confronting all blacks. A more detailed analysis of the Pan-African paradigm is provided in the next chapter.

Instrumentalism

Instrumentalism is essentially a historiographical genre that grew out of the fight to combat Eurocentric historiography and its misconceptions about, and misrepresentation of, the African historical heritage. From the 1830s on, history assumed a position of potency as a weapon in the ideological arsenal against anti-slavery thoughts and movement. Historians were active in contributing their "scholarship" to proving the lack of historical heritage in Africa; the inherent inferiority of all blacks, and the marginality of the black presence to American and New World history and development. The denial of African history provided legitimacy to slavery and racism. Denied a historical tradition and heritage in Africa, blacks were logically regarded as a people without culture and civilization. Just as historical and other scholarships were marshaled to objectify, depersonalize, and dominate blacks, a few blacks began to mobilize the limited and modest historical knowledge at their disposal to dispel several of the historical fallacies of Eurocentric scholarship. The use of evidence of African historical wealth and civilization to counter Eurocentric claims became forceful among free blacks in the second half of the nineteenth century. According to Earl Ofari, "A few blacks examined the positive dimensions of black history. To them it was a source of pride and a means of combating the racist myths about blacks in Africa and America perpetuated by whites. Henry Garnet must be included among this group of pioneer black historians."[43]

In an address before the Female Benevolent Society in Troy, New York, in February of 1848, Garnet dealt at length with the history of ancient Africa. He placed the blame for the destruction of African institutions on western society and went on to describe the Ethiopians and Egyptians as blacks who had originated science and learning. Africa had produced an enlightened and orderly society while the Europeans were still groping in ignorance and superstition. "At this time when these representatives of our race were filling the world with amazement," he argued, "the ancestors of the now proud and boasting Anglo Saxons were among the most degraded of the human family. They abode in caves under ground, either naked or covered with the skins of wild beasts." Garnet was very insistent upon the Negroid nature and origins of ancient Egypt. As he contended, "Ham was the first African. Egypt was settled by an immediate descendant of Ham, who in sacred history is called mesraim—menes. He rejected the claim of ancient Egyptians as Caucasians. He credits the Egyptians with civilization, arts sciences."[44]

Several nineteenth-century black intellectuals wrote and published to underscore the antiquity of civilization in Africa and rehabilitate

African history from obscurity, among them Delany, Pennington, William Wells Brown, and George Washington Williams. Collectively, they used evidence of African history and African cultural wealth to assert their humanity, worth, and claim to citizenship and win recognition as contributors to world history and progress.[45] In several of their writings, we find seeds of a future Afrocentric genre. Delany had no doubt about the African origin of ancient Egyptian civilization. As he quizzed rhetorically, "Who were the builders of the everlasting pyramids, catacombs, and sculptors of the sphinxes? Were they Europeans or Caucasians, Asiatic or Mongolians? . . . Among what race of men, and what country of the globe, do we find traces of these singular productions, but the African and Africa?" His answer was unequivocal and emphatic, "None whatever. It is in Africa the pyramids, sphinxes, and catacombs are found; here the hieroglyphics still remain. Among the living Africans traces of their beautiful philosophy and symbolic mythology still exists." He also emphasized the antiquity of civilization in Africa, declaring, "And is it not known to history that Egypt was the 'cradle of the earliest civilization,' propagating the arts and sciences, when the Grecians were an uncivilized people, covering their persons with skins and clothing, anterior to the existence of the she-wolf." He published comparative studies of African and European civilization and found Africa preeminent and superior.[46]

It was not until the early twentieth century that a sustained movement to use African history as the basis and weapon of struggle began. Two individuals helped lay the foundation of and advanced this movement: Du Bois and Carter G. Woodson. They were both preceded by G. N. Grisham, professor and principal of a high school in Kansas City, Missouri, described as "one of the ablest educators and most practical philosophers in the country." In a speech he delivered during a reception to the graduate club at the residence of Professor Kelly Miller in Kansas City, on December 28, 1897, Grisham emphasized the importance of historical scholarship as a weapon of resistance, and urged black scholars to rise up to the challenge of developing a revolutionary epistemological weapon. "In the social organism," Grisham argued,

> every kind of human power has its special place, and every grade of intelligence has its function. Men of will trace with their swords the bounds of empire, or as statesmen enter the affairs of nations; men of feeling fashion the cults of picture with pen or brush half-uttered yearnings of races; men of scholarship have likewise their functions of scholarship in the higher

sense of the word. The scholar is the interpreter of civilization, as well as its guide. In him is renewed the spirit of the past, in him are the aspirations of the future, which color the best deeds of the present.

Furthermore, he continued,

The Negro scholar must do something for his race. He can and should offer defense against unjust criticism and wrong. He should in his exalted personality, furnish a standard for building aspiration, and his superior intelligence and keen foresight should offer guidance over the thousands of moral, social and political difficulties that throng the dark and devious pathway of the people. The race has a right to look to him for helpful suggestions, for kindly, sympathetic criticism, for a clear outline of policy and for the inspiration which can come alone from those lofty reaches of thought enable them to contemplate the depths from the standpoint of the heights.

Grisham believed firmly that "the Negro scholar must form the connection between his race and civilization," for "in him they breathe its spirit, think its thought, grapple with its difficulties, and aid in the solution to its problems. The Negro scholar must not confine himself to Negro questions. He must, in action, manifest the breadth of Terence. ... mankind, humanity." Thus, Grisham placed immense responsibility on the Negro intellectual. His call was essentially for an instrumentalist history, one specifically designed for enhancing the self-esteem and elevation of blacks. To generate this type of scholarship, blacks had to turn to their own history and heritage in Africa. The tradition of rehabilitating African history that Delany and other nineteenth-century free blacks inaugurated flowered in the early twentieth century.[47]

Long before Grisham's admonition, black lecturers routinely referred to the glory and achievements of Africa. In an address in 1832, David Nickens declared that "all the now civilized world is indebted to Africa for the arts of civilization."[48] In numerous publications, free blacks underlined the historical accomplishments and worth of Africa. Examples include Pennington's *Text Book of the Origin and History of the Colored People* (1841) and William G. Allen's *The Origin and History of the Africans* (1850). For blacks, demonstrating the historical and cultural worth of Africa became a potent weapon of waging an intellectual battle against the forces of oppression and alienation. This became more structured, organized, and historically more credible from the late nineteenth century on. Carter G. Woodson, Du Bois, and members of the New Negro History movement researched African history to demonstrate the wealth of that history and in the process reversed the debilitating impact of Eurocentric historiography on black consciousness. In his *African Heroes and Heroines* (1939), Woodson underscored the accomplishments of African leaders, portraying them as positive historical actors. His more enduring legacy was in the organizational efforts to encourage scholarship in African history in order to counteract and uproot entrenched fallacious ideas about the African and black historical past. In 1915, Woodson founded the Association for the Study of Negro Life and History (now Association for the Study of African American Life and History—ASAALH), followed closely by the *Journal of Negro History*. The purposes of this journal were "the collection of sociological and historical data on the Negro, the study of peoples of African blood, the publishing of books in this field, and the promotion of harmony between the races by acquainting the one with the other."[49] The last of the objectives clearly underscores the essentially integrative dynamics of Woodson's scholarship. The prime objective of encouraging scholarship in African history was to facilitate mutual understanding between the races as a prelude to the integration of blacks. Woodson's organizational efforts had African historical reconstruction as its underlying dynamics. Scholars were encouraged to research African history and expose and debunk the myths of Eurocentric scholarship and historiography. Their combined efforts led to the flowering of studies and interests in African history and the publication of books and articles that developed an enhanced sense of historical worth and positive self-image among black Americans. Today, Woodson's ASAALH and his journal remain among the leading organizations and media of disseminating knowledge and scholarship about the African historical experience.[50]

Marcus Garvey used African history to develop and sustain a positive self-image in his followers. As he asked rhetorically,

> But, when we come to consider the history of man, was not the Negro a power, was he not great once? Yes, honest students of history can recall the day when Egypt, Ethiopia and Timbuktu towered in their civilizations, towered above Europe, towered above Asia. When Europe was inhabited by a race of cannibals, a race of savages, naked men, heathens and pagans, Africa was peopled with a race of cultured black men, who were masters in art, science, and literature; men who were cultured and refined. . . . Black men, you were once great; you shall be great again. Lose not courage, lose

not faith, go forward. The thing to do is get organized; keep separated and you will be exploited, you will be robbed, you will be killed. Get organized and you will compel the world to respect you.[51]

Garvey offered his followers knowledge of African history as the basis and foundation for Pan-African unity, for uplifting blacks worldwide. He built his Universal Negro Improvement Association on the principle of pride in African race, culture and heritage. His slogan was "Africa for Africans," meaning that "Negro peoples of the world should concentrate upon the object of building up for themselves a great nation in Africa." Garvey here trumpets the African nationality idea and scheme that nineteenth-century nationalists like Delany, Turner, and Garnet had earlier espoused. Exploited, alienated, and dejected, Garvey offered blacks in Diaspora hope in a return to, and reconstruction of, Africa for all Africans at home and abroad. Africa provided Negroes the basis of a "Country and government of their own" and the opportunity to "make our own impression upon a world of injustice and convince men by the same means or methods of reasoning as others by their strength do." Diaspora blacks had no alternative route to elevation, respectability, recognition, than through a return to Africa. As Garvey insisted, "if you must be heard and respected you must have to accumulate, nationally, in Africa, those resources that will compel unjust man to think twice before he acts."[52] This tradition of using African historical scholarship as a weapon of struggle and response to domination and objectification blossomed in the 1960s. As part of the civil rights movement, some black historians began advocating a new combative historiography, one that would mobilize African history in the service of the black revolution. This instrumentalist history would scathingly indict, and totally reject, Eurocentric historiography, while enhancing the self-esteem of blacks. Knowledge of African history, instrumentally constructed, became crucial to the social agenda of the instrumentalists. Among the leading advocates of this historiography were Vincent Harding and Sterling Stuckey, both of whom were skeptical of mainstream historiography and advocated a distinct black American history, one that is critical and condemnatory of mainstream ideas and values and is designed specifically for advancing the black struggle.[53] Understanding and reconstructing Africa's historical and cultural foundations became the nerve center of the new instrumentalist historiography. Here we see the microscopic beginning of the construction of African history and cosmology as the substructure for black Diaspora epistemology and cognitive development. African history became an arm of the black liberation movement in the 1960s. Knowledge of African history became sine qua non for self-liberation for blacks. It thus became a central component of black epistemological struggle that later flowered into the Afrocentric genre. Informed knowledge of Africa became a crucial weapon of liberation scholarship against colonialism and neocolonialism. Many scholars, particularly those of Marxist persuasion, sought to use African history to construct a liberation ideology against foreign domination. A leading example was the late Walter Rodney, whose scholarship remains among the most combative of black liberation epistemology. As he once declared, "One of the major dilemmas inherent in the attempt by black people to break through the cultural aspects of white imperialism is that posed by the use of historical knowledge as a weapon in our struggle. We are virtually forced into the invidious position of proving our humanity by citing historical antecedents; . . . the white man has already implanted numerous historical myths in the minds of the black peoples; and those have to be uprooted, since they can act as a drag on revolutionary action in the present epoch."[54]

Rodney urged the study of African history directed at "freeing and mobilizing black minds."[55] He went on to a successful career as one of the most prolific African historians and scholars of his generation who researched African history and used their findings to debunk and derail long-entrenched myths and misconceptions that had served to legitimize European domination and exploitation of blacks and Africans. Rodney's study of the Upper Guinea Coast enabled him to challenge and debunk prevailing Eurocentric notions about slavery in traditional African societies.[56] His study of imperialism in Africa resulted in his iconoclastic work, *How Europe Underdeveloped Africa* (1972). Written from a Marxist perspective, the book traces the historical, social, economic, political, and cultural development of Africa before the denuding and devastating encounter with Europe and the inauguration of a systematic underdevelopment of the continent. Rodney found in African history ample solid evidence to negate the misrepresentations of Eurocentric scholarship. Underscoring the functional use of African history, Rodney declared, "an overall view of ancient African civilizations and ancient African culture is required to expunge the myths about the African past, which linger in the minds of black people everywhere. This is the main revolutionary function of African history in our hemisphere."[57]

The instrumentalist tradition of using African history as the medium of developing and sustaining a revolutionary liberation pedagogy intensified and by the mid-1980s had developed into the Afrocentric paradigm, characterized by bold and combative scholarship, predicated on the color line.

## Afrocentricity

The Afrocentric perspective, perhaps the most forceful today and premised on centering Africa as the foundation of black Diaspora epistemology, developed logically from the instrumentalist tradition. Its roots can be traced to the efforts of such nineteenth-century "intellectuals" as Pennington, Delany, and Williams, down to the tradition of Du Bois and Woodson. Although the terminology is twentieth-century, its fundamental tenets surfaced much earlier. By the second half of the twentieth century, however, it had become more structured and ideological. This ideological character reflected a conviction that America was irredeemably racist. Afrocentric scholars urged blacks to turn to Africa and recapture their lost identity. Afrocentricity became even more combative and ideological in the 1980s under the Reagan counter-civil rights policies. Among its leading scholars today who have published extensively in the field and endeavored to popularize a rehabilitationist and redemptionist African historical and cultural studies as a means of black development and mental and psychological emancipation are Molefi Asante, Maulana Karenga, Na'im Akbar, Marimba Ani, the late John Henrik Clarke, and Chancellor Williams. These scholars reject Eurocentric construction of knowledge and what many perceived as the universalistic thrust of western epistemology. Afrocentricity portrays Africans as historical actors and Africa as the basis of self-definition and identity for blacks in Diaspora. Afrocentricity uses African history and values, indeed the entire African cosmology, as the foundation of black Diaspora identity and the basis of self-affirmation.[58] This paradigm has become a weapon of defense against what is perceived as an ever-threatening and debilitating cancer of Eurocentrism. Premised on a Manichean conception of reality as a theatre of unending cultural wars between the races, Afrocentricity offers re-Africanization to all blacks as the only viable weapon of resistance, survival, and eventual triumph. As "Africans who have lived amidst Europeans on the land of the ancestors of the Native Americans," and have in consequence been exploited materially and

psychologically, and whose historical heritage has been misrepresented and maligned, Asante offered black Americans strong grounding
or centering in African history as the foundation for liberation from
Euro-American cultural and political domination and exploitation.
Reestablishing connections with Africa became for blacks an essential
step toward empowerment.[59] The attempt to claim universality for the
African worldview is a critical dimension of this paradigm. This is a
curious contention given the vehement rejection of the universalistic
claims of Eurocentric cosmology. For example, Na'im Akbar, a psychologist and leading Afrocentric scholar, advocates making the African worldview the foundation for a liberation social science pedagogy.
Such attributes of African cosmology as emotionalism, esoterism,
irrationality, and the unity of body and spirit are, according to him,
capable of infusing education with a humane and moral imperative.
When applied as the foundation of scholarship, the African worldview
becomes an instrument for eradicating the evil consequences of the
materialist and objectivist inclinations of positivist cosmology—such
evil consequences as slavery and racism.[60]

Afrocentric scholarship is heavily reliant on Africa as its foundation for reversing the debilitating impact of Eurocentric education on
blacks. Africa provided blacks with a rich antiquity of history, culture, and civilizations, the very basis of identity, and a rallying point
for group/corporate initiatives against Eurocentric emasculation.
Afrocentricity attracted scholarly interest and has acquired quite a
following within black communities because it spoke directly to the
frustrations and alienation of blacks. It mirrors the feeling that blacks
have of alienation from, and rejection by, mainstream America. It underscores a deeply felt conviction that the interests and aspirations of
blacks are not central to or represented by the dominant white society
and government. The conservative slant in contemporary American
politics, coupled with attacks on and erosion of the gains of the civil
rights movement and affirmative action reinforced black alienation.
Neither does the international global context offer any solace.

Since the negation of African civilization and culture had served to
justify the subordination and alienation of blacks, it was deemed imperative to contest vigorously those negative portraits and images in
order to affirm, albeit philosophically and psychologically, an African
identity and homeland. Reversing the centuries-old "tragic conception
of their history" was critical to blacks' sense of worth and self-esteem.
Afrocentric scholars are convinced that blacks could never benefit

from American identity. In Afrocentric epistemology, to be both black and American seem contradictory and antagonistic. Afrocentrists portray America as an arena of conflict between two irreconcilable worldviews, each propelled by distinct values, products of the age-old contest over history, civilization, and culture. Afrocentric historiography, therefore, emerged primarily to challenge claims of European preeminence in history, civilization, morality, and culture. Afrocentric scholars are determined to bring this battle over history and civilization to its resolution in the affirmation of Africa's superiority. They advanced what some critics perceive as an Afrocentric universal history that situates Africa at the apex of global historical development. They then coupled this history with a mythic construction of identity for blacks that completely ignored the historical transformation of almost four centuries of New World enculturation.[61]

Asante believes that to undo the psychological damage of Eurocentric miseducation, black education must be grounded in a philosophy that affirms blacks as "active historical agents." This is the underlying rationale of Afrocentrism—a paradigm that offers blacks an empowering and regenerative consciousness of history. To do this effectively, the Afrocentric scholar must contest claim of European superiority and offer blacks an ennobling version of history. Like nineteenth-century black leaders, modern Afrocentrists reject the contention that Africa had no history and civilization. They focus on two key challenges. First, reconstructing and validating a homeland and history. Second, affirming a countervailing African protest identity. The African identity, as black psychologist Amos Wilson acknowledged, is essentially and functionally a protest identity. To be African is to embody and reflect anti-European ethos.

The late Senegalese scholar Cheikh Anta Diop is the philosophical godfather of Afrocentrism. His writings serve as reference points for the genre. He focused his research on solidifying the utility of ancient Egypt to Afrocentric historiography. He advanced not only Negroid origin of ancient Egyptian civilization but also its influence on classical Greece. Blacks needed Egypt to provide the same foundation and reference point that the classical Greco-Roman world provided for Europe. According to Diop, "For us the return to Egypt in all fields is a necessary condition to reconcile African civilization with history, to be able to build a body of human sciences and to renew African culture . . . a look toward ancient Egypt is the best way of conceiving and building our cultural future."[62] Agreeing with Diop's contention, Asante writes, "Afrocentrism reestablishes the centrality of the ancient Kemetic (Egyptian) civilization and the Nile Valley cultural complex as points of reference for an African perspective in much the same way as Greece and Rome serve as reference points for the Western world."[63] Asante presents ancient Egyptian civilization as the foundation of Africa's classical civilization and the progenitor of European civilization. By focusing on ancient Egypt, blacks, Amos Wilson argued, "are trying to take back what European historiography has stolen, completely falsified, to erase the new false identities it placed on the Afrikan Egyptian people."[64]

Afrocentric scholars such as Molefi Asante, Marimba Ani, Na'im Akbar, Maulana Karenga, and the late John Henrik Clarke focus on proving three key facts: the antiquity of history and civilization in Africa, the superiority and influence of African civilization over European, and the universality of the African worldview. In this respect, they turned historiography on its head, replacing Eurocentric diffusionist theory with an Afrocentric one. Africa, instead of Europe, became the epic center of world civilization. Africa's pride, ancient Egypt, influenced European civilization, through its nurturing of Greek science and philosophy. Hence, the Greeks, considered progenitors of western civilization, were supposed to have studied in and borrowed copiously from ancient Egypt.[65] The exaltation of Greek science and philosophy without due acknowledgment of Egyptian influence led many Afrocentrists to invoke the theory of the "stolen legacy." This theory is discussed in detail in George G. M. James's *Stolen Legacy* (1954), a book that has become a standard text of the Afrocentric genre. The underlying purpose of the *Stolen Legacy*, as the author contends, is "an attempt to show that the true authors of Greek philosophy were not the Greeks; but the people of North Africa, commonly called the Egyptians; and the praise and honor falsely given to the Greeks for centuries belong to the people of North Africa, and therefore to the African continent. Consequently, this theft of the African legacy by the Greeks led to the erroneous world opinion that the African continent has made no contribution to civilization, and that its people are naturally backward."[66] The denial, or deemphasizing, of Egyptian influence on Greece, the proclamation of European superiority, and the corresponding devaluation of African history and civilization have compelled Afrocentrists to advance the "stolen legacy" thesis, depicting Western civilization as the product of "stolen" ancient Egyptian and African legacies. The Alexandrian conquest of Egypt is identified as a key point in this theft and pillage. Leading Greek philosophers allegedly accompanied Alexander on his rampage of Egypt and pillaged the ancient libraries of the Egyptian temples.[67]

The instrumentalist and utilitarian underpinnings of history mandated Afrocentric mythologizing. To strengthen their case, many Afrocentrists found it necessary to mythologize and deny historical facts. For example, some Afrocentric scholars claim complete immunity from the acculturation process, especially as it impacts identity. Du Bois had proclaimed the black American as a product of dual cultural and identity experiences.[68] Du Bois's contention is applauded by many as a perceptive and more accurate reflection of the historical reality. Afrocentrists, however, disagree. Anxious to deny any lasting metropolitan influence on blacks, they contest Du Bois's duality paradigm, proclaiming instead the permanence and immutability of the African identity. Asante, for example, insists he was never afflicted by any consciousness of double identity. Contesting the Du Boisean duality, Asante affirms, "I was never affected by the Du Boisean double-consciousness. I never felt 'two warring souls in one dark body' nor did I experience a conflict over my identity."[69] The true Afrocentrist, therefore, according to him, retains his/her Africanness intact. Afrocentricity thus constructs an ahistorical identity as a weapon of empowerment, to fill a void created by the denial of American identity. According to Yaacov Shavit, a major problem of Afrocentric universal history is the attempt to split the duality of the black American, to magnify one dimension of identity (African) and deny the other (American).[70] By mythologizing identity, Afrocentrists were able to impose a unified identity on all black people, ignoring the multiple, complex historical and cultural experiences. A detailed and exhaustive analysis of the problematic of Afrocentric identity is provided in the next chapter.

By exalting ancient Egypt, Afrocentrists continue a tradition that nineteenth-century blacks had inaugurated. The novelty of Afrocentricity, however, lies in its ethnocentric and cultural jingoistic overtone, a trait that has provoked the most criticisms. To enhance black self-esteem, Afrocentrists advanced a monolithic construction of black Diaspora identity, a romanticized view of the African past (pre-European), a past of harmony, of advanced cultural and civilizational achievements. They depict Africa as a continent inhabited by people who are morally and ethically superior to all others. In his scathing criticism of Afrocentrism, Shavit rightly observes that Afrocentrists use "strategies of cultural self-affirmation to offset a sense of collective inferiority by boosting national self-esteem or express a sense of collective superiority."[71] But the Afrocentric ideology was not directed solely at enhancing black self-esteem but also at eroding the cultural arrogance of whites. Thus, Afrocentric historiography advances black superiority and produces some of the most ridiculous theories in history. A case is point is Leonard Jeffries's dichotomy between the superior Sun (Africans) people and the inferior Ice (whites) people![72] Thankfully, this theory has crawled quietly into obscurity. At the root of Afrocentric mythology, Shavit contends, is the desire for antiquity to establish originality and distinctiveness, a desire undoubtedly driven by the denial of African antiquity. A claim to antiquity, Shavit concludes, is "an important tool in a vanquished nation's struggle for pride, dignity and status."[73]

Egypt provided Afrocentrists with the basis for affirming antiquity. But Egypt became the basis not only of proclaiming the genesis and evolution of culture in Africa but also of constructing what Shavit terms a grand scale universal history. Afrocentrists use Egypt to affirm the diffusion of African culture both "among black and non-black people around the globe."[74] "Ancient Egyptian history was thus searched," he suggests, "in the hope of finding within it the origins of a black centered philosophy, a foundation for group unity and identity, a source of resistance to alien domination, and a basis for independence and creativity." This resulted in the postulation of what Shavit called "a Greek dependency theory," the logic of which reads thus: If Greece is the alma mater of western culture, and if it could be proven that Greek culture was heavily influenced by Egypt, then, it could be argued that western civilization was a direct and legitimate descendant of non-whites. In Afrocentric historiography, Egypt is represented as the cradle of science, philosophy, and mathematics, the place to which Greek scholars trooped to study, before returning to shape western civilization.[75]

Historian Clarence Walker attributes Afrocentric celebration of ancient Egypt as the primal site of world civilization to a problematic conflation of two concepts—*life* and *civilization*. The claim that *life* began in Africa is often mistaken for another—that *civilization* began in Africa. The truth of the former, Walker suggests, did not necessarily establish the latter. He offers the possibility that civilization could have had multiple origins. Furthermore, Walker seriously questions the Negroid construction of ancient Egyptian civilization. Afrocentrists, he argues, tend to read too much of racial essentialism into ancient Egypt. Walker proffers a much more complex origin of ancient Egyptian civilization, one that includes Mediterranean and Asia Minor influences. He accuses Afrocentrists of "a selective reading of Egyptian cultural production as biological," and applying modern racial categories to a context (ancient Egypt) that did not recognize those categories. These five paradigms and perspectives exemplify, reflect, and nurtured the seeds of racial/cultural essentialism. Africa and elements of African realities enabled blacks to construct a countervailing essentialist worldview as a platform of struggle.[76]

# 3

# Essentialist Construction of Identity and Pan-Africanism

In July 1992, at a symposium organized by the African Students Union of Tulane University, a black American male asked the panelists, all of them Africans, to suggest how black Americans and Africans could best develop and sustain a viable Pan-African relationship as a strategy against threats posed by the political and cultural dominance of white Americans and Europeans. In April 1993, the Pan-African Movement U.S.A. (PAMUSA) held its annual convention in Atlanta, Georgia. The conference focused attention on the necessity and strategies for re-vamping Pan-Africanism. In December 1993, the epochal Seventh Pan-African Congress took place in Kampala, Uganda. Delegates from the United States, Latin America, and the Caribbean met with Africans to deliberate on how to develop and sustain a strong Pan-African con-nection. In the last two decades, delegations of black Americans have met on several occasions with African leaders to discuss modalities for mutual cooperation and struggle. The most recent took place in December 2006 in Lagos, Nigeria. What was tagged "The Black Heri-tage Summit" "brought together intellectuals and academics as well as creative and cultural entrepreneurs, in a three-day meeting designed to build bridges of understanding and create a sustainable platform for cooperation and collaboration between Africans on the continent and in the Diaspora."[1] A Pan-African Movement Pre-Summit meeting took place on May 5, 2007, at Howard University, Washington, D.C. This pre-summit was in preparation for the subsequent Pan-African Movement (PAM) Summit in Kingston, Jamaica, July 11–18, 2007. The goal of the Jamaica summit was to forge a strong Diaspora union and create an "all African government in Africa as a mandate of Pan-Af-ricanism." Representatives of various Pan-African organizations and communities, including the UNIA, the Rastafari Movement, Repub-lic of New Africa (RNA), and the All African Peoples Revolutionary Party (AAPRP), met at Howard University to support the creation of an Afrikan Diaspora Union (ADU) as "historic and sacred mission to re-integrate former enslaved Africans as part of a continental union of Africans." Warning against what he termed "a new scramble for Africa," in his opening address, Elombe Brath urged creation of a strong Diaspora union to protect mutual interests of Africans and blacks in Diaspora and prevent recolonization.[2]

Radical cultural-nationalists bemoan what they perceive as the lack of unity among black Americans and Africans, owing in large part, they suggest, to the lack of sufficient awareness and appreciation of shared historical experiences, cultural values, and interests. Most critically, they lament the failure of black Americans and Africans to acknowledge the commonality of their problems and challenges. Not only do Africans and black Americans share historical ties, common interests, and identity, but also, according to the cultural-nationalists, they confront common problems emanating largely from a common foe—Euro-Americans.[3] This is referred to generally as the Eurocentric threat, a threat of cultural alienation, annihilation, and perpetual domination. This threat supposedly embraces every facet of black American and African lives—cultural, social, economic, and political. Eurocentrism is depicted as an ideology designed to create a world order of white supremacy, sustained by the pains, miseries, and subordination of blacks, and Pan-Africanism is proposed as the tool for dealing with this threat. As Dona Marimba Richards implores, "We must retrieve and create our own myths. We must turn our spirituality, our ethos, our Africanness into a political tool. We must harness the energies that lie dormant and diffused throughout Pan-Africa, and forge them into a powerful political force for liberation and self-determination."[4] Perhaps the most distinguishing characteristics of Eurocentrism are its glamorization of its own historical heritage and experiences and its negation of the historicity of blacks, inducing in many blacks the loss of a sense of history, cultural heritage, and identity, rendering them vulnerable to Euro-American cultural manipulation and domination.[5] Pan-Africanism emphasizes the unity of Africans and blacks in Diaspora in a joint struggle, a struggle ordained by the pains of the deep historical wounds inflicted by slavery, racism, colonialism, and neocolonialism. Memories and knowledge of the success of an earlier cooperation between Africans and Diaspora blacks, a cooperation that was instrumental to the dismantling of colonialism have reinforced faith in Pan-Africanism. Many black Americans today associate progress with reactivation of the old Pan-African cooperation. According to this conviction, in combination, Africans and black

Americans would more effectively withstand the hegemonic threat of Euro-Americans in the United States and vestiges of neocolonialism and neoimperialism in Africa.

The Pan-African and identity paradigms are most forcefully expounded and defended in Afrocentricity—the intellectual arm of the cultural-nationalist and politico-nationalist struggles within the American university system. According to Molefi Asante, a leading Afrocentric scholar, Africans and blacks in Diaspora share a "collective consciousness," one that has not been impacted by history of separation. Furthermore, he insists, "We have one African Cultural System manifested in diversities . . . We respond to the same rhythms of the universe, the same cosmological sensibilities, the same general historical reality as the African descended people . . . All African people participate in the African Cultural System." Invoking Maulana Karenga, Asante contends, "Our Africanity is our ultimate reality." Furthermore, he constructs a strong "Pan-African" world based on the essential Africanness of blacks in America. He rejects any notion of difference between continental Africans and blacks in America. As he reasoned, "There are some people around who argue that Africans and African-Americans have nothing in common but the color of their skin. This is not merely an error, it is nonsense. There exists an emotional, cultural, psychological connection between this people that spans the ocean and the separate existence . . . we are not African-Americans without Africanity; we are an African people, a new ethnic to be sure, a composite of many ancient people, Asante, Efik, Serere, Touculur, Mande, Wolof, Angola, Hausa, Ibo, Yoruba, Dahomean, etc."[6] W. D. Wright's description of the "Pan-African" sweep of Afrocentric essentialism is worth quoting at length:

> Africa, for Asante and the Africancentrists, is not simply the African continent. It is wherever there are what they describe as black African people, which would apply to the aborigines of Australia, the black people of the Fiji Islands, New Guinea, and Hawaii and it would apply to the black people in India, the Middle East, Africa, and any place in the Western Hemisphere. Thus, for Asante and other Africancentrists "place", "location", "context", "African centrality" of "African cultural centrality"—terms of the philosophy/methodology—have no boundaries, except what is called the "African world", which is global.[7]

As highlighted in the previous chapter, there are several problems with the identity and Pan-African paradigms. The depiction of black

Americans and Africans as one people united by cultural attributes and historical experience is seriously flawed at the levels of both theory and practice. Can black Americans truly claim African identity? Do black Americans and Africans really share common interests and challenges? Have both been drawn together historically by shared experiences? In other words, has there always been a "Pan-African" tradition? If yes, how old? These are pertinent questions whose answers compel a reconceptualization and reassessment of the historical or traditional representation of the relationship and experiences of Africans and black Americans, as well as a critical interrogation of the Pan-African and identity contentions of Afrocentricity.

Afrocentricity emphasizes similarities in the historical and cultural experiences of black Americans and Africans and implores both to unite in the spirit of Pan-Africanism. Advocates of this Pan-African strategy maintain that black Americans and Africans confront similar problems and challenges—economic marginalization, political domination, and cultural alienation in the United States; political instability, poverty, and neocolonialism in Africa—problems directly or indirectly linked to Eurocentrism. Afrocentric scholars presume a certain antiquity to Pan-Africanism and trace its roots to the nineteenth century and beyond. They depict Pan-Africanism as a movement informed by a deep consciousness of mutuality—that black Americans and Africans had always been drawn together by common interests and that they had always stood together in furtherance of those interests. The identity claim is a critical underpinning of the Pan-African construct—the contention that Africans and blacks in Diaspora are one people who share cultural (and, some even suggest, ethnic) attributes, centuries of separation notwithstanding. Undoubtedly, Asante is a leading advocate of Afrocentric Pan-Africanism. His numerous publications, especially the earlier ones written in the 1980s, testify to the depth and strength of his faith in Pan-Africanism.[8] Asante identifies Eurocentrism as a major threat to blacks in America. According to him, this problem has been with blacks since the dawn of history and has remained intractable in spite of emancipation and the gains blacks accomplished through the decades. Eurocentrism remains a potent threat to the cultural, social, economic, and political survival of blacks.[9] Eurocentrism has destroyed African culture, de-Africanized the consciousness of blacks, retarded their economic and cultural development, and remains a potent threat to the cultural, social, economic, and political existence of blacks. To combat this, Asante and his ideological cohorts propose Afrocentricity, which he defines

as "a frame of reference wherein phenomena are viewed from the perspective of the African person . . . (and which) seeks in every situation the appropriate centrality of the African person." This solution
entails strengthening black American knowledge and awareness of
African historical and cultural heritage by making Africa the foundation of black American epistemology. The objective is to instill in
blacks an awareness of their African identity and culture as a defensive
weapon against a pervasive and domineering Eurocentric worldview.
Afrocentricity involves resocialization designed to rid black American
consciousness of the "tragic conception" of their history, culture, and
heritage. It is supposed to bring blacks closer to Africa as they develop
in knowledge of Africa.[10]

There are three critical implications of Afrocentric epistemology.
First, the depiction of blacks in Diaspora as essentially African in identity, culture, and ethnicity de-emphasizes the transformative nature
of the New World experience. Second, deep-seated alienation from,
and suspicion of, mainstream American society and its values justifies
rejection of the mainstream as essentially and inherently hegemonic, and consequently culturally antagonistic to the existential needs
of blacks. The third is the representation of Africa as the source and
foundation for a countervailing black epistemological and pedagogical
paradigm, perennially at odds with the mainstream. The Afrocentric
critique has thus far been built on two critical forces: race and culture.
The two represent the trajectory of the Afrocentric response, from
a Pan-African construction of race to a Pan-African construction of
culture. For long, race served as the defining and unifying construct.
Africans and people of African descent in the Diaspora supposedly
share racial identity. Blackness, the basis of oppression, became the
underpinning of identity and the framework for unity in a struggle
against a racially defined and equally monolithic Euro-American establishment and world order. The color line became the defining and
distinguishing character of the black struggle in all its dimensions—
politics, economics, education, and culture. Race was also the medium
not only for understanding the nature of the challenges and struggles
of blacks but also for constructing an effective counteroffensive. The
racial line allowed for no consideration of neutrality. To be neutral in
this struggle was tantamount to identifying with the enemy and op-
pressor.

Asante is not the sole proponent of the cultural-nationalist perspective. Others, including Maulana Karenga, Na'im Akbar, Amos

Wilson, Dona Marimba, and the late Bobby Wright and John Henrik Clarke, have all contributed to explicating and defending the Afrocentric perspective. In numerous articles and books, Karenga established and defended the historicity of the African and black Diaspora experience, and continues to contribute to scholarly discourse on issues critical to the experience. His most enduring contribution, however, lies in the area of culture. He is credited with founding *Kwanza*, which has become a popular event among black Americans.[11] Amos Wilson's scholarship strikes at the very heart of Eurocentric historiography, exposing its misinterpretations of, and damages to, the historical consciousness and heritage of blacks.[12] Dona Marimba has equally been critical of the influence of Eurocentric civilization. Her seminal work *Yurugu* (1994) is a massive exposition of the hegemonic character of the European worldview. She is also among the most ardent defenders of the identity paradigm.[13] Psychologists Na'im Akbar and Bobby Wright emphasize the denigrating and hegemonic effects of Eurocentric values on the mental and psychological balance of blacks.[14] Some Afrocentrists portray the late Vivian Gordon as perhaps the best representative of the Black Womanist perspective, a critique of feminism. Though aware of the contributions of other black feminists such as bell hooks, Alice Walker, and Patricia Hill Collins, who have also been critical of the Afrocentric tendency to essentialize race to the neglect of sex and class, Afrocentrists applaud the perspective advanced by such Afrocentric critics of feminism as Vivian Gordon, Kariamu Welsh Asante, and Dona Marimba.[15] In fact, Gordon's book *Black Women, Feminism, and Black Liberation: Which Way?* (1991) remains the reference source on the black womanist perspective for many Afrocentric scholars and students. Gordon argues that black women and white women had nothing in common besides gender, and that gender oppression, however real, did not constitute a sufficient basis for black women to cooperate with white women. In terms of interests and culture, the two are incompatible, she insists. She denies that black women had any business participating in feminism. Gordon characterizes the location of gender at the core of the struggle as a ploy to hoodwink black women into an engagement that would eventually result in cultural suicide. Regardless of how vocal white women are against gender discrimination, they constitute part of the white power structure that has exploited, and continues to exploit, blacks. In other words, white women constitute an arm of the white cultural war against all blacks. As wives, sisters, and mothers, white women perform crucial functions in the inculcation and perpetuation of racist values and thus perpetuate white cultural hegemony. Gordon consequently deems co-operation with white women dangerous for black women. Instead, she advises black women to forge greater ties with their male counterparts in the United States, and with African and Third World women with whom they share common interests and challenges. Gordon's Pan-African paradigm, like that of Asante and other Afrocentric scholars, advances a conspiratorial theory that discerns threat to blacks in con-spiracies allegedly concocted by "Others"—white Americans and Europeans.[16]

All the scholars cited above subscribe to, and defend, the Pan-African and identity paradigms. They are intellectual Pan-Africanists whose writings underline conflict, divergences, and discord between two opposing worldviews, African and European. Asante, however, remains the most vocal and accomplished defender of both para-digms. His spirited defense is encapsulated in the ideology of Afro-centricity. As indicated, Afrocentricity developed as a response to the intellectual challenges and perceived threat of a mainstream histori-ography that was deemed Eurocentric. It is premised on a reconstruc-tion of African history and the experience of peoples of African de-scent abroad with a view to debunking prevailing historical fallacies and misrepresentations. Its ultimate objective is to build and enhance black self-esteem and induce positive self-conception. Confronting, combating, and debunking entrenched Eurocentric assertions and values that have served to denigrate, objectify, and negate the black historical experience is central to Afrocentric epistemology. Asante has written articles, books, and pamphlets on virtually every aspects of the black experience. His writings, along with those of other Afro-centric scholars, are critical and revisionist, reconstructing the Afri-can and black Diaspora experience from an "African perspective," a context that identifies Africans and blacks as historical actors, high-lighting the positive accomplishments and realities of their history.[17] The entire Afrocentric paradigm is shaped by a strong faith in the po-tency of Pan-Africanism. Afrocentricity seeks to strengthen cultural awareness and unity among blacks in the United States and also to infuse in them knowledge and appreciation of their historical identity and heritage as a distinct group. It proposes Africa as the source of self-definition, self-affirmation, and identity for blacks in the United States and throughout the Diaspora. In essence, Afrocentricity iden-tifies African culture and values as the solid foundation upon which to build a strong resistance against the onslaught of Euro-American cultural and political hegemony.[18] Asante emphasizes "confraternity and continuum" as the defining character of the relationship between Africans and black Americans, a relationship he portrays as essentially and historically Pan-African. He conceives of Pan-Africanism as "a political perspective and a political ideology as well as a social theory. The one does not negate the other. Actually, when we speak of the political dimension of the concept, we are also talking about how Africans see themselves as social units." Afrocentricity represents the social expression of the Pan-African ideology. Its primary function is to bring to fruition the "collective consciousness" that is the essence of Pan-Africanism. The attainment of this Afrocentric consciousness by blacks constitutes the foundation for the flowing of Pan-Africanism. Asante stresses the importance of this collective consciousness. It is the level at which Africans and blacks in Diaspora manifest "shared commitment, fraternal reactions to assault on (their) humanity, collective awareness of (their) destiny." This "Afrocentric state" combines awareness with action. As he contends, "there can be no effective discussion of a united front, joint action, a community of interests until we come to good terms with collective consciousness, the elementary doctrine of economic, political, and social action."[19]

Thus, Pan-Africanism is a central component of the Afrocentric paradigm. Afrocentrists are proud of their supposed state of mental decolonization, a consciousness born of a radical revision and reinterpretation of African and black history. The entire Afrocentric paradigm is geared toward the development and defense of a new historiography focused on Africa, one that articulates a history more in sync with the African and black experience. As discussed in the last chapter, in Afrocentric historiography, Kemetic Egypt serves as the cornerstone of African and indeed, via Greece, world history. This history is definitely positive and capable of enhancing black self-esteem. The glorious and accomplished character of the African historical past is a dominant theme in Asante's writings. Asante is not just defending the historicity of the African and black experience, but, in terms of heritage, accomplishments, and contributions to humanity's growth, he situates that experience at par with, if not above, Western/European civilization. Most significantly, his works underscore the depth and ubiquitous nature of the Pan-African ethos; however, as many critiques have pointed out, though psychologically therapeutic, such history is essentially bad history, steeped in myth-making and dubious claims of originality.[20] Asante's "African perspective" sustains a romanticized, abstract, and idealized Africa and emphasizes a nonexistent harmony and consensus. There is emphasis on glorious accomplishments while neglecting to deal critically with the contradictions and ambivalence. Many scholars have criticized the Afrocentric rendition of African and black history, particularly its tendency to romanticize and misrepresent the African and black American past, and to elevate ideology over scholarship.[21] As Sidney Lemelle contends, "Anyone who has seriously studied African history . . . realizes that a multitude of attitudes and cosmologies produced many African cultures—none of which were 'universal.' Africa is made up of people from different ethnic, religious, and linguistic groupings."[22] In correcting historical fallacies, therefore, Afrocentric historicism tends to assert pseudohistorical claims, create myths, and engage in a reductionism that oversimplifies the complexity of the African and black Diaspora experiences. The Pan-African and identity constructs represent two critical areas of such oversimplification and reductionism. Afrocentric writers and scholars have a tendency to view Pan-Africanism, rather uncritically, as a movement that reflected the inherent unity and harmony of Africa and black Diaspora relationship. Afrocentric Pan-Africanism rests on the presumption of a harmonious historical relationship unifying Africans and Diaspora blacks. Both supposedly share an unbroken chain of history, culture, and identity. A survey of the historical development of that relationship is pertinent in order to ascertain the profundity and authenticity of the Pan-African and identity paradigms as defined and defended in Afrocentric historiography.

There is no consensus on the definition of Pan-Africanism. Some scholars portray it as essentially a politico-nationalist phenomenon contrived to affect the unity of Africans and blacks in Diaspora in a common struggle for mutual advancement and redemption. Others emphasize its cultural dimension, portraying it as the expression of a trans-Atlantic black cultural unity. There is agreement, however, on several of its essential elements. P. Olisanwuche Esedebe identifies the following essential attributes: the notion of Africa as a homeland for persons of African descent, solidarity among Africans and peoples of the African Diaspora, belief in a distinct African personality, rehabilitation of Africa's past, pride in African culture, and the hope of a united and glorious African future. He defines Pan-Africanism as "a political and cultural phenomenon that regards Africa, Africans, and African descendants abroad as a unit. It seeks to regenerate and unify Africa and promote a feeling of oneness among the people of the African world. It glorifies the African past and inculcates pride in African values."[23] The notion of shared identity between blacks in Diaspora and Africans and efforts toward mutual upliftment, development, and defense of mutual interest are at the heart of Pan-Africanism. The contention that blacks in Diaspora and Africans share historical experiences and ought to unite in the face of compelling and overwhelming adversity is historically rooted. As this study has shown, from the very dawn of the black American experience, blacks had nursed and nurtured this feeling, frequently invoking African values and institutions in defense of their struggles. In the nineteenth century, free blacks in cities such as New York, Boston, and Philadelphia frequently invoked African values in their struggle for survival. Many were propelled by the feeling of affinity with Africans to advocate programs for mutual elevation. Pioneers of this "Pan-African" tradition included Paul Cuffee, and Lott Cary, whose contributions are discussed in chapter 2. Both men expressed interests in helping to redeem Africa from poverty and moral degradation. As demonstrated in chapter 2, Cuffee was one of the earliest to draw a linkage between the experience of black Americans and Africans. In his estimation, blacks, regardless of geographical location, could not hope for meaningful advancement unless and until Africa was developed. He urged black Americans to engage in partnership with philanthropists and governments in the United States and Britain for the development of Africa.[24] Cary also took up the cause of Africa, insisting that black Americans had a responsibility to contribute to the development of the continent.[25] Both men saw promise for the future of Africans and black Americans in the encouragement of colonization and commerce in Africa. They invoked the African linkage as a means of nurturing a sense of responsibility toward Africa among black Americans and inspiring a commitment to the development of the continent.

Other blacks emphasized the African connection as a means of generating a collective consciousness among blacks; a consciousness considered crucial to group survival in a hostile environment. One such was David Walker, who is acclaimed by some as the father of black nationalist theory. His *Appeal to the Colored Citizens of the World* (1829) has been described as one of the earliest articulations of Pan-African consciousness among black Americans.[26] Walker wrote the book not only as a critique of slavery and racism but also to inspire a collective sense of obligation and responsibility among blacks for

mutual salvation. Other blacks, among the more enlightened and educated, manifested their African consciousness by engaging the intellectual biases of their times—the denial and denigration of the black
and African historical past and heritage and the negation of the black
Diaspora historical contributions. This group included James W. C.
Pennington, William Wells Brown, William C. Nell, George Washington Williams, and Martin Delany.

The second half of the nineteenth century was perhaps the most
critical phase in the development of the Pan-African consciousness.
Prompted by the elusive character of the American Dream, leading
blacks mobilized Pan-African consciousness and sought the realization of a new nationality and identity through cooperative endeavors
between Africans and black Americans. As discussed earlier, the height
of this Pan-African tradition came in the mid-nineteenth century with
the emigrationist tradition spearheaded by Martin Delany. Frustrated
by the persistence of racism, Delany began to advocate a return to
Africa and the development of a black and African nationality. From
1852 to the outbreak of the Civil War, he persistently advocated a new
nationality for blacks built on cooperation between blacks in Diaspora
and Africa, who supposedly confronted debilitating Eurocentric challenges to their existence.[27] Delany drew the racial boundary line, delineating the struggle as one between blacks and whites. Race was in
fact the basis of his Pan-African ideology. This is evidenced in his 1854
address before the emigration convention cited in the introduction
to this study. The "great issue . . . upon which must be disputed the
world's destiny," he opined, "will be a question of black and white."[28]
As established, for much of the 1850s and early 1860s, Delany steered
the emigrationist and black nationality movement, along with such
other black nationalists as Henry H. Garnet, James Theodore Holly,
William H. Day, and M. H. Freeman. Their plan was to resettle a few
wealthy and enterprising free blacks in Africa who would develop a
strong economy patterned on the cotton-rich South. The success of
this economy, they hoped, would eventually undersell American cotton on the international market, rendering slavery uneconomical and
superfluous. Most critically, this nationality would serve as the rallying point for blacks throughout the world in their struggle against
domination and exploitation. Delany traveled to Africa in 1859 and
spent a little over a year visiting communities in Liberia, Sierra Leone,
and other parts of the west coast.[29]

But as argued earlier, the outbreak of the Civil War unsettled Delany's plans as he became seduced by the liberal and democratic promises of the War. The next phase of Pan-Africanism occurred in the 1880s and 1890s, led by Henry Turner and Alexander Crummell. These nationalists advanced Pan-Africanism as the framework for constructing a powerful and successful African-Black Diaspora struggle. They were all driven by the failure of the promises of the American Dream, to which they had subscribed, and concern over the global advance of racism and imperialism. Their contributions to black nationalism and Pan-Africanism are discussed at length in previous chapters and exhaustively elsewhere.[30]

A next major phase in the growth of Pan-Africanism coincided with the emergence to prominence of Marcus Garvey in the early twentieth century. Garvey espoused a strong cultural-nationalist brand of Pan-Africanism. He appealed to race and envisioned a glorious future for blacks in Africa. The appeal to return to Africa generated a massive response. Garvey offered a strong organizational base within his UNIA. The promise of a future in an independent Africa was alluring to a black American populace entrapped in a vicious circle of poverty, violence, and despair. Like Delany and Turner, Garvey emphasized the racial boundary line and expressed disdain and hatred for imperialism and for European values and influences.[31] Garveyism flowered within the same historical epoch as other Pan-African traditions, most notably the Pan-African Congress Movement. As mentioned earlier, Du Bois was part of the intellectual movement among blacks in the early twentieth century with a strong Pan-African overtone—the New Negro History Movement, a movement spearheaded by a "New Negro," an intellectual and dynamic personality, emboldened by the resilience and entrenchment of racism to resist with the weapon of history. There were determined efforts to rediscover the African heritage, to reaffirm its historicity and authenticity, and, more critically, to define an identity.[32] Du Bois emphasized the roles and contributions of blacks in American society and challenged the hegemonic thrust of American historical scholarship. Along with Carter G. Woodson and members of the New Negro History Movement, Du Bois launched a strong intellectual defense of the historical wealth, resources, and heritage of blacks in Africa and abroad. Du Bois would later move from his intellectual defense of African and black American history to become a force in the evolution of Pan-Africanism as a movement.

The Pan-African Congress tradition that began in 1900 (some trace its origin to the late 1890s and beyond) achieved tremendous success in harmonizing Diaspora blacks with Africans in a joint struggle for mutual advancement against colonialism, racism, and imperialism. Five Pan-African Congresses resulted from this tradition, spanning the period from 1900 to 1945. These congresses were organized by representatives of Africans and Diaspora blacks including Du Bois, Henry Sylvester Williams, Edward Wilmot Blyden, George Padmore, Kwame Nkrumah, and J. E. Casely-Hayford. They were all drawn together by the consolidation of colonialism and the global trajectories of imperialism and racism. Shared experiences and the conviction that all blacks confronted similar problems shaped the deliberations of the congresses.[33] After the Fifth Congress in 1945, no congress was held until the Sixth in 1974 in Tanzania.

This postcolonial congress revealed the growing complexity of the Pan-African movement. Though the common enemy (and rallying point), colonialism, was politically dead, it was clear to some that a new foe had emerged. A controversy ensued between two perspectives, one defended by an American delegate, the other, a Marxist perspective advocated by Walter Rodney. The black American delegation came to defend a race agenda and platform, insisting that Africans and Diaspora blacks confronted similar challenges emanating from racism. According to a spokesman, "There is nothing metaphysical about defining the white race as the traditional enemy of the black race."[34] Walter Rodney, a West Indian who had studied African history at the University of London, and was then lecturing at the University of Dar es Salaam, in Tanzania, had profound knowledge of, and familiarity with, the crises of African political economy and leadership. Rodney was a Pan-Africanist of a completely different ilk. He envisioned Pan-Africanism "not as a utopian blueprint of *a priori* racial unity, but rather as the means of forging empirical criteria for assessing the social bases of contemporary African and Caribbean states and the function of their structural integration within the world capitalist system." Rodney warned of the pitfalls of "romantic visions" about contemporary Africa. In stern terms, he declared, "We have allowed illusions to take the place of serious analysis of what actual struggles are taking place on the African continent; what social forces are represented in the government and what is the actual shape of society." For Rodney, therefore, Pan-Africanism "was a critical tool for analyzing revolutionary new forms for genuine African liberation." It ought to be directed not solely at some external foe but also at the neocolonial and domestic exploiters and perpetrators of the moral and political decadence that plagued Africa.[35] For Pan-Africanism to be effective, Rodney insisted, it had to move beyond race to class analysis. Consequently, Rodney advocated a Marxist perspective or class analysis in opposition to the racial perspective proposed by the American delegation. He wanted Pan-Africanism directed against the exploiter class, whoever exploited blacks and Africans and circumscribed their opportunities, regardless of race or color, both within Africa (that is, indigenous exploiters) and outside.[36]

A radical divergence on the definition of the basis of Pan-Africanism also surfaced in the deliberations of the Seventh Congress in Kampala in 1993. Regardless of the controversial, and increasingly complex, character of Pan-Africanism, the congress movement did underline the pervasiveness of the feeling of oneness unifying Diaspora blacks and Africans. The conviction of shared history, culture, and heritage supposedly joined the two in the congress tradition. The tradition itself activated the nationalist impulse and movements that eventually toppled colonialism in Africa and other parts of the world. This success had profound impact on the civil rights movement in the United States. As argued above, activists such as Malcolm X and Stokely Carmichael advocated "Pan-Africanizing" of the black American struggle. Malcolm saw Pan-Africanism as a means of injecting strength and vitality into a movement that was becoming increasingly localized and subverted within the United States. For Malcolm, unity between Africa and black America was needed for mutual development and redemption.[37] For Stokely Carmichael, Pan-Africanism was the "highest expression of Black Power." He urged black Americans to unite with Africans for greater strength and mutual liberation. Underlining the centrality of Africa, he declared, "We must make Africa our priority. We must deal clearly now with Africa and begin to support the movement for liberation on the continent."[38] There is no doubt therefore that a strong Pan-African consciousness pervaded the outlook of blacks in the Diaspora. Regardless of the harsh realities they confronted, black Americans did not forget their African ancestry. This Pan-African consciousness, however, remained "apolitical" and did not assume the character of an ideologically driven movement until the twentieth century.[39]

A critical examination of the history of Pan-Africanism, particularly of the strategies devised by leading black American nationalists for implementing the Pan-African ideal, reveals a deep cultural distance and alienation from Africa—a consequence, no doubt, of the acculturation process in the New World. There existed a critical cultural gulf between Africans and black Americans submerged beneath the veneer of Pan-Africanism; a gulf that widened with the passage of time. As indicated earlier, black leaders such as Paul Cuffee and Lott Cary acknowledged their African roots, expressed concern for Africa, and proposed schemes for the economic elevation of Africa. Cary once declared himself "an African," observing that "in this country (i.e., the United States), however meritorious my conduct, and respectable my character, I cannot receive the credit due to either. I wish to go to a country where I shall be estimated by my merits, not by my complexion; and I feel bound to labor for my suffering race." Here is a strong affirmation of his Pan-African consciousness; however, as suggested above, just before his trip to Africa, Cary delivered a farewell sermon at the First Baptist Church in Richmond in which he described his mission as a civilizing one, and expressed fear of finding "a grave . . . among the savage men . . . or wild beasts" that inhabit Africa.[40] These are loud echoes of the prevailing racist perceptions of Africa. Paul Cuffee also dedicated himself to the redemption of Africa. His ultimate objective was to establish a colony in Africa for the settlement of black Americans with a view to abolishing slavery, exploring Africa, and exposing Africans to civilized life. Though both men expressed pride in their African ancestry and felt a genuine desire to initiate contacts between black Americans and Africans, Cuffee and Cary also imbibed the prevailing paternalistic and racist culture and worldview that later unleashed the colonization impulse. However forceful their proclamation of interest in, sympathy for, and identity with Africa, these pioneer "Pan-Africanists" were equally products of a particular historical epoch, and their ideas reflected the prevailing cultural biases of that epoch.

From the birth of organized abolitionism in the early nineteenth century to the present, Africa had always served black Americans as a basis for articulating identity and inspiration in the struggle for freedom and survival. The tendency by Afrocentric scholars to inject some mutuality, or consensual ethos, into the historical relationship of Africans and blacks in Diaspora, however, misrepresents the reality. Such a tendency ignores the complexity of the relationship. A critical look at the crucial nineteenth century will illuminate the contradictions within black American nationalist and Pan-African thought.

While Diaspora blacks espoused Pan-African ideals and expressed a desire to identify with Africans, their activities betrayed their cultural alienation from Africa. Their expression of cultural identity was unambiguously Eurocentric; they sought to shape Africa according to the images of Europeans.

By the second half of the nineteenth century, black American nationalism had entered its "golden age," or what Wilson Moses calls the "classical age," a period characterized by the desire to create a black or African nationality outside the United States.[41] This emigrationist ethos, as Theodore Draper aptly noted, resulted from frustration over failure to achieve American nationality.[42] Emigrationists felt alienated from the United States. In very strong terms, the "militant" nationalists of the epoch rejected America and turned to Africa for the construction of an identity and nationality they had been denied. They expected this new nationality to function as the bulwark against a pervasive and ever-threatening Euro-American force. Given the depth of frustration and alienation from white Americans and European values and civilization, and the force and vehemence with which they defined their nationalist platform, it seems logical to expect an equally forceful and sustained declaration of identity and cooperation with Africa. Curiously, this Pan-African relationship did not materialize. As indicated above, all the leading black American nationalists of the classical epoch—Martin Delany, Alexander Crummell, and Henry McNeal Turner—began on a solid Pan-African theoretical platform only to relapse into a state of historical amnesia. They, especially Delany and Turner, set out on a strong anti-American and anti-European note, and declared a determination to unite with Africans in order to develop a black nationality. Both men drew the racial boundary line clearly, identifying Euro-Americans as threats to black cultural, emotional, and physical survival. Almost immediately, however, the two proceeded to contradict and subvert the goal they had defined. Instead of cooperation with Africans, they embraced European platforms and policies. They identified salvation for Africa with the programs of the European powers and seemed to have forgotten the threats Europeans and white Americans allegedly posed to blacks and Africans. In other words, they immersed themselves in the rising tide of imperialism and colonialism and embraced policies that were designed to effect the cultural alienation of Africans, the rape and pillage of the economic resources of the continent, and blatant violation and destruction of African sovereignty and territorial integrity.[43]

Late nineteenth-century black American nationalism was therefore not reflective of the true spirit of Pan-Africanism. The same blacks who expressed sympathy for Africa and initially declared a commitment to black and African development and liberation also harbored strong hegemonic aspirations toward Africa. They combined black nationalism and Pan-African ideals with hegemonic and imperialistic aspirations.[44] It is plausible, therefore, to contend that Pan-Africanism, if defined as a relationship of consanguinity, shared values, and aspirations, is not historically rooted as Afrocentric essentialists suggest. If Pan-Africanism is conceived not just as a statement of intent, an expression of desires and goals, but more in terms of the actual implantation of values and expressed desires and goals—that is, the praxis, as opposed to the theoretical postulations—then what nineteenth-century black nationalists espoused was Pan-African in name only. In other words, Pan-Africanism as "a political and cultural phenomenon that regards Africa, Africans, and African descendants abroad as a unit . . . (and) seeks to regenerate and unify Africa and promote a feeling of oneness among the people of the African world" is a twentieth-century phenomenon, more appropriately reflected in the congress movement. For example, the Seventh Pan-African Congress affirmed "a global calling to advance the cause of liberation, freedom and unity of African peoples at home and abroad," underscoring a relationship of mutuality between two or more peoples drawn together by shared experiences, and on the basis of which they construct a common platform of struggle for change.[45] Put succinctly, the conception of Pan-Africanism as a movement to "create a common identity between the Africans and Africans in Diaspora in order to achieve unity of purpose" was purely idealistic and visionary until the congress tradition.[46]

It is in the congress movement that we observe serious attempts to adhere faithfully to the mutuality ethos of Pan-Africanism. The most critical attribute of Pan-Africanism is the conviction that the shared cultural and historical experiences of Africans and Diaspora blacks constitute the basis of mutual struggle for advancement and development. In the past, especially in the second half of the nineteenth century, black American nationalists did not seriously consider indigenous Africans partners with whom they could engage in a common cause, their anti-European rhetoric notwithstanding. The notion of mutuality was rarely sustained to any great depth during the nineteenth century. Black American nationalism manifested a curious cultural fluidity and constantly shifted between admiration for, and revulsion against, both Africa and Euro-American cultural values. In essence, there has to be a distinction between the rhetoric of mutuality and the reality of contradiction and alienation that informed black American perception and treatment of Africa.

Acknowledgment of the role of black Americans in the ideological justification of imperialism has serious implications for the Pan-Africanism that is at the heart of Afrocentricity. It is necessary to reexamine the conceptual framework and acknowledge the historical limitations of Pan-Africanism. Those who define Pan-Africanism as a movement predicated historically on mutuality, consensus, shared identity, and interests between Africans and Diaspora blacks misrepresent and possibly misunderstand its history. The actual practicalization of the ideals of mutuality, shared identity, and cooperation between the two is a twentieth-century phenomenon inspired by colonialism and the global advance of imperialism. Colonialism made real unity and cooperation between Africans and Diaspora blacks possible and sustained that relationship through the anti-colonial phase to independence. Colonialism energized Pan-Africanism and strengthened Du Bois, George Padmore, Kwame Nkrumah, and others in their resolve and struggle. They stuck together, Africans and blacks in Diaspora, regardless of obvious cultural differences. In combination, they generated the force that ultimately toppled colonialism.

The demise of colonialism unfortunately also marked the beginning of the end of Pan-Africanism as a movement. When statesmen like Kwame Nkrumah of Ghana and Julius Nyerere of Tanzania tried to strengthen Pan-Africanism in the aftermath of independence, they came up against the forces of parochialism and national sovereignty. Other African countries, Nigeria included, refused to surrender their newly won sovereignty for a continental supra-sovereignty. The forces of regionalism, ethnocentrism, "tribalism," religious nationalism, and fanaticism have assumed preeminence in post-colonial Africa.

The belief in shared identity that some Diaspora blacks emphasized was based largely on shared experiences, struggles, and challenges, and not necessarily on shared ethnicity or culture. Black nationalists did acknowledge cultural distance from Africa. Cuffee and Cary lamented Africa's cultural decadence. They were prompted by a conviction of cultural difference from, indeed superiority over, Africans to initiate schemes designed to facilitate the economic development and cultural transformation of the continent. Later generations of black

nationalists would echo similar convictions, sometimes in a much
more forceful manner. The notion of shared identity, consequently,
derived purely from shared historical experience emanating from racism, marginalization, and domination, and not from any deep conviction of ethnic or cultural consanguinity. Even as they embraced
and uplifted Africa, and prioritized her problems and challenges,
nineteenth-century black American nationalists and Pan-Africanists
clearly did not regard Africans as culturally similar to themselves.
This fact played a greater role in shaping the ambivalence that black
American nationalists and Pan-Africanists of the epoch manifested
to a degree that rendered superfluous the whole notion of brotherliness and identity central to Pan-Africanism. The point is that Pan-Africanism was steeped in contradiction from its historical beginnings,
a contradiction that was perhaps most evident in the second half of
the nineteenth century. By the second decade of the twentieth century, however, the Congress movement, to a significant degree, had
minimized this contradiction. Africans became part of the Pan-African movement as partners of Diaspora blacks in ways the nineteenth-
century nationalist context and tradition did not permit. Although
they harbored equally condescending and Anglo-Saxon biases against
Africans, just as their nineteenth-century predecessors had, organizers of the Congress movement refused to embrace imperialism or engage it in any compromising manner. Du Bois, George Padmore, and
Henry Sylvester Williams embraced Africans as partners in a common
struggle and were unequivocal in their condemnation of colonialism
and imperialism, their intellectual and ideological ambivalence notwithstanding.

As it developed in the twentieth century, Pan-Africanism prioritized cooperation between Diaspora blacks and Africans for mutual advancement. The two were drawn together by consciousness of
shared historical experiences and identity. The combative outlook of
the twentieth-century Pan-Africanists was a reaction to the advancement and global trajectories of imperialism. The new breed of Pan-
Africanists were alarmed by the consolidation of colonialism in Africa
and the racial ramifications of imperialism. These developments has-
tened the transition of Pan-Africanism from consciousness to movement. The movement, and expression of mutuality and struggle built
on the notion of brotherliness, was indeed positive.

Modern proponents of Pan-Africanism in the Diaspora, Afrocentrists and others, ignore the state of decline and decadence in Africa

that is obviously detrimental to Pan-Africanism. Holding meetings and pronouncing lofty declarations are not enough if the foundations for realistically achieving the objective are nonexistent. How can black Americans and Africans revive Pan-Africanism as a weapon of struggle, survival, and advancement today if internally both are chronically dysfunctional and divided on the notion of identity? Black American advocates of Pan-Africanism ignore the existence of a conservative stream that is vehemently opposed to Pan-Africanism, one that sees black American problems as essentially internal and favors a solution that is localized. Douglass Turner Ward, the black American playwright, and Keith Richburg, former *Washington Post* Africa bureau chief, are among the many members of this group. In essence, there is a strong voice against essentializing the African connection even among black Americans.

As this study has shown, Pan-Africanism did at some point possess a noble history and goal, and manifested a certain degree of consistency. Africans and Diaspora blacks did come together, drawn by shared experience and a genuine sense of identity and mutual obligations to forge a common struggle. This was the Congress tradition (1900–1945) that accelerated the political decolonization of Africa. Indeed, this was perhaps the zenith of the Pan-African tradition. Pan-Africanism has since become a shadow of its former self. All talks about regenerating it have been rhetorical and intellectual posturing devoid of any serious attempts to grapple with its challenges and contradictions. The contradictions are of two dimensions. The first relates to the internal postcolonial realities of Africa. The second refers to the complex and problematic character of the identity problem in Africa and among black Americans. Though the movement was of Diaspora origin, Africa remained the centerpiece of Pan-Africanism. As Carmichael put it, "Although Pan-Africanism has its origin among the Africans of the Diaspora, Mother Africa is its *sine qua non*." He went on to argue, "Africans on both sides of the Atlantic contributed immensely to the ideology, but only in Africa will we see its fruition. *Unity of Africa is prerequisite for complete liberation of blacks*" (emphasis added).[47]

Pan-Africanism is about Diaspora blacks rallying to the defense of Africa. It is about continental Africans treating each other as one, and most important, as human beings. It is also about Africans and Diaspora blacks united in a common struggle. It is about a consciousness of identity, of Africans and peoples of African descent relating to each other on the basis of mutual respect. More than anything else, it is about conditions in Africa. A critical look at this African focus is crucial if present calls for reactivating Pan-Africanism are to be taken seriously. The African context is presently problematic, and until this is addressed, attempts to reactivate Pan-Africanism would remain essentially sloganeering. Pan-Africanism cannot be built on a truncated and dysfunctional foundation. A combination of circumstances renders the notion of shared experiences between Africans and black Americans problematic. Perpetrators of the ills plaguing Africa and black America—racism, ethnocentrism, corruption, unemployment, exploitation, marginalization, and poverty—are fundamentally different. There is no basis for unity on the grounds of shared problems, challenges, and enemies as was the case in the past. The problems may be similar, but the perpetrators, that is, the enemies, are not necessarily similar. The basis, therefore, for the kind of mutuality suggested by Afrocentric scholarship is nonexistent under present circumstances. Africans are being discriminated against, oppressed, denied basic human rights, killed, and maimed by fellow Africans. Many observers continue to perceive the ghosts of colonialism and neocolonialism in Africa's present predicament. They characterize the resilience of tribalism, the nagging cancer of ethnicity and ethnocentrism, and the undemocratic and destructive character of the military as enduring legacies of colonialism. While this is true to some degree, it is difficult to contend, as was fashionable in the immediate postindependent era, that all of Africa's problems are caused solely by colonialism and its relics or by indigenous leaders controlled by external interests. Many of the causes of the present dysfunctional state of many African countries are in fact direct consequences of the policies of the indigenous leadership. For example, the policies of the last Nigerian military junta, especially in the years under Ibrahim Babangida and his successor, Sani Abacha, had little to do with neo-colonialism. Neither of these men could be regarded as the internal stooge of a foreign power. In fact, Abacha perpetrated his reign of terror despite foreign opposition and condemnation.

There is need to see Pan-Africanism as a dynamic process, taking cognizance of changing historical time and space, and political contexts in both Africa and the Diaspora. The two critical factors of *time* and *space* ought to be reexamined. In the context of contemporary call for reactivation of Pan-Africanism, it is often forgotten that the historical context and time have changed. The historical circumstances that galvanized blacks in the nineteenth century—racism, colonialism—

have changed significantly. Blacks no longer confront a clear-cut racially definable "colonial enemy" around which to organize. Furthermore, though pertinent, racism has become more complex. The racial
enemy of the past—Europeans—is not the only racial enemy of today.
In other words, racism is no longer a subject of just black versus white,
as Delany put it in the nineteenth century, or as Du Bois concurred
half a century later in his "problem of the color line" assertion. The
essence of what critics call "tribalism" in Africa, and among Africans,
is as virulent, if not more virulent, than racism. It has all the hallmarks
and vestiges of racism, only this time, it is perpetrated by blacks upon,
and against, blacks. It is violent, sadistic, virulent, demeaning, and ob-
jectifying.

The two key rallying points of traditional Pan-Africanism, racism
and imperialism, are now much more complex. Imperialism itself has
changed. There are now in African countries mini-imperial or micro-
imperial designs reflected in regional hegemonic drives, and internal
Africa-on-Africa "colonial" subjugations that provoke cries for separation and independence. Furthermore, the role of Africa as a rallying
point of Pan-Africanism has become problematic. Nothing illustrates
this better than the recent failed efforts by leaders of the Africa Union,
successor to the Organization of African Unity (OAU), to agree on
a platform and program of continental unity beyond the rhetorical
framework of the Union. Prodded largely by Colonel Ghadafi of Lib-
ya, at their meeting in July 2007 in Accra, Ghana, which was chaired
by then President John Kuffour of Ghana, African leaders discussed
the need for a continental government for Africa. Some advocated a
kind of "United States of Africa." The goal of African nations speaking
with one voice and represented by one government was an imperative Kwame Nkrumah raised in the immediate aftermath of Ghana's
independence in 1957. Then, Nkrumah believed that Ghana's political
freedom was meaningless as long as other African countries were still
politically shackled. He envisioned a continent-wide political union
that would guarantee one political voice. But it failed, then, just as
now, largely because most other African political leaders were simply
unwilling to give up national sovereignties, and thus, their political
power bases, for a continental government. Put differently, the vision
of continental unity continues to falter because it conflicts with nationalism. The reality is that African political leaders who assembled
in Accra to discuss continental unity are ruling over dysfunctional
states—countries that are factionalized along ethnic, religious, linguis-

tic, and regional lines. Without first achieving national unity, without first successfully unifying and harmonizing the discordant elements and forces in their respective countries, it seems an illusion for the leaders to envision a continental union.

Africa is not ready for the kind of role required of a successful re-activation of Pan-Africanism. Furthermore, there is need to construct Pan-Africanism not just as a racialized framework, as has tradition-ally and historically been the case, but in the Rodneyan perspective, as a means of self-examination and interrogation of the internal cri-ses, challenges, and contradictions within Africa and among blacks in Diaspora. Reconceptualizing Pan-Africanism would also entail ac-knowledgment of the complexity of the African and black Diaspora worlds. There is no one African and black Diaspora experience. There are multiple global black experiences, with complex and divergent cultural and identitarian implications. Race has lost its value as a uni-fying construct. Any call for Pan-Africanism has to consider these re-alities, in addition to a new and global phenomenon that William Ack-ah alludes to in his study "Pan-African Americanism"—that is, how the changing political economy and dynamics of the black American condition itself renders any monolithic and essentialist construction of the black experience problematic.[48] While blacks may share racial identity, economic realities have injected a class dimension that belies racial essentialism. Those blacks who are economically successful, and many who are politically successful, do not embrace the essentialist model. The Michael Jordans, Michael Jacksons, Shaquille O'Neals, Kobe Bryants, Tiger Woods, Colin Powells, Condoleezza Rices, Oprah Winfreys, Whoopi Goldbergs, and Barack Obamas (to identify a few) who are living and reflecting the "American Dream" are manifestly opposed to, and reject racial and cultural essentialism. Furthermore, the realities of post-colonial Africa, and post-civil-rights America are complex and fundamentally different and do not allow clear identifi-cation of the enemy in strictly racial terms.

### The Identity Construct

The second critical dimension to Afrocentricity is the claim of Afri-can identity—that is, the insistence upon defining black Americans as Africans. The identity paradigm rejects any definition of black Ameri-cans other than as Africans, sometimes spelled with a "k." This conviction is based on the elements of African traditions and values (or what some scholars call "Africanism") found among blacks in Diaspora. The implication is that, centuries of enslavement and separation notwithstanding, blacks in Diaspora retain essential aspects of their African cultural identity. The identity paradigm defines black Americans, and indeed the entire black Diaspora population, as Africans, racially, ethnically, and culturally, centuries of exposure to, and acculturation in, Western/European values and civilization notwithstanding. At crucial moments in the history of the black American experience, the identity paradigm has been invoked by individuals and groups to advance the cause of freedom and upliftment.

Dona Marimba is a leading proponent of the African identity paradigm. In her *Let the Circle Be Unbroken* (1980) Marimba represents black Americans and blacks in the Caribbean and South America as Africans because they retained so much of indigenous African traditions in their music, religion, and lifestyles. According to her, Africans and blacks in Diaspora are united by the three essential ingredients of identity—spirituality, ethos, and worldview. These unifying African elements are supposedly immutable and should form the basis of reconstituting and reaffirming shared identity. As she contends,

> Until we learn that it serves our objectives to emphasize the similarities, the ties, the unifying principles, the common threads and themes that bind and identify us all as African we will continue to be politically and ideologically confused . . . Africa survives in our spiritual make-up; that it is the strength and depth of African spirituality and humanism that has allowed for the survival of African-Americans as a distinctive cultural entity in New Europe; that it is our spirituality and vitality that defines our response to European culture; and that that response is universally African.[49]

Thus, Afrocentric essentialism constructs a monolithic identity for all blacks regardless of geographical locations and historical experiences. As Algernon Austin argues,

> Afrocentrism . . . ideologically constructs a heritable essential difference among human populations. Within Afrocentric theory, people who are of the African Cultural system are presented as being fundamentally different from people outside this system. These differences are passed on to the descendants of people within this African Cultural System so that centuries

later the descendants of Africans are said to be culturally African. Because these cultural differences are not influenced by social forces, they remain present in the same form over millennia.[50]

The identity claim is based on historical linkage, heritage, and cultural retentions. The contention is that blacks in the United States are Africans and should vigorously and consciously exhibit this Africanness in their lives—modes of thought, dress, culture, and lifestyle.[51] This perspective deemphasizes the Du Boisean identity construct that asserts a complex black American identity. As argued above, in his epochal book, *The Souls of Black Folk* (1903), Du Bois described black Americans as peoples of dual identities who are constantly battling with, are in fact tormented by, the conflicting demands of their dual identities. This duality has formed a basis for critical discourses on black American identity. Many regard it as accurate and perceptive in its acknowledgement of the complexity of the nature and history of blacks. Du Bois insisted on validating both dimensions of the duality. According to him, in his quest for "self-conscious manhood" and attaining "'a better and truer self' blacks would not Africanize America, for America has too much to teach the world and Africa. He would not bleach his Negro soul in a flood of white Americanism, for he knows that Negro blood has a message for the world. He simply wishes to make it possible for a man to be both a Negro and an American."[52]

While acknowledging the American experience, Afrocentrists refuse to recognize it as a constituent element of black identity. Black Americans, Afrocentrists contend, remain essentially Africans, despite centuries of sojourn, experience, and enculturation in the New World. Black Americans were supposed to have come out of slavery and the American experience with their African identity intact. This is a direct contradiction of the Du Boisean perspective. It is my contention that Du Bois's insight was much more realistic. Regardless of the degree of African cultural retentions, regardless of how far black Americans went in changing their names and wearing African clothes, they remain, in large part, products of the American historical experience, an experience that significantly shaped their identity. This experience has left its mark indelibly on black American culture and identity. In essence, Du Bois's recognition of the dual historical and cultural experience is far more accurate.

The black experience in the Diaspora was culturally transformatory and revolutionary. It is impossible to ignore this complex historical reality, as leading Afrocentrists do in a bid to impose a superficial and problematic Pan-African identity. It is noteworthy that many black Americans remain skeptical of the potency, or even relevance, of a paradigm that situates their identity outside America. In fact, the debate among black American intellectuals on the pertinence of the African connection is heated. On the one extreme are the group identified in chapter 1, slavocentrists who argue that the black American identity should have America rather than Africa as its foundation. They identify slavery, rather than Africa, as the substantive force in the shaping of the black American experience and identity. For the slavocentrists, the experience of slavery was more potent than the fact of African ancestry. This is the antithesis of the Afrocentric perspective. A leading advocate of this view is the black American playwright, Douglass Turner Ward, who raised the issue in his keynote address delivered to the Southern Conference on Afro-American Studies in Baton Rouge, Louisiana. He distinguished between two identity paradigms, "slavocentric" and "Afrocentric." While acknowledging black American connections with Africa, Ward insisted that what shaped the black American identity was slavery rather than Africa, and since enslavement was essentially institutionalized here in America, the study of the black American experience and, consequently, the determination and definition of identity should focus on, and begin with, the American experience! Ward accorded preeminence to slavery and the American identity, in direct contradiction to the prevailing and increasingly popular Afrocentric paradigm. In other words, he supports deemphasizing the Pan-African paradigm. He is not alone in this conviction. Keith Richburg, also identified earlier, thanked God profusely that his ancestors "got out" of Africa. On identity, he wrote, "Thank God that I am an American." Furthermore, reflecting on his stay in Africa, "I know now that I am a stranger here. I am an American, a black American, and I feel no connection to this strange and violent place." Specifically on the concept "African-American", he emphasized, "You see? I just wrote 'black America.' I couldn't even bring myself to write 'African American.' It's a phrase that, for me, doesn't roll naturally off the tongue: 'African American.' Is that what we really are? Is there anything really 'African' left in the descendants of those slaves who made that torturous journey across the Atlantic?" Richburg prefers "black America," thus accenting race and slavery as the cornerstone of identity. He is puzzled why black "sons and daughters of America's soil" would "reaffirm an identity that . . . never existed in the first place."

Though many scholars, including this writer, disagree with Ward's and Richburg's nullification of the African background, they have little objection to acknowledging the Euro-American dimension of identity. Ward and Richburg represent an extreme position. Most critiques of the Afrocentric and Pan-African paradigms do not jettison the African background. They acknowledge its pertinence and object solely to the preeminence it is given. Many critics describe the tendency to overemphasize the African connection, at the expense of the complex American and Diaspora experience, as perhaps the most critical flaw of the Afrocentric and identity paradigms.[53]

Aside from the two polarities, there are other contending perspectives on the identity of black Americans. The Du Boisean perspective seems to be the most popular and current, since it acknowledges the pertinence of both experiences and underscores the complexities. This is the Afro-Americanist perspective. Another discernible perspective is the universalist. Universalists acknowledge both the African and American experiences but would exalt neither. They maintain that because blacks in Diaspora have been socialized among people of European ancestry, they inherited universal values, values that were neither distinctly African nor distinctly Euro-American. They suggest that black Americans share more in common with the broader humanity than with Africa and should identify themselves primarily as human beings. This group, however, tends to lean more toward the American identity. Members tend to be very critical and resentful of the Africanist/Afrocentric perspective. Reacting against what he termed "invented ethnicity," economist Glenn Loury affirms, "In my view, a personal identity wholly dependent on racial contingency falls tragically short of its potential because it embraces too parochial a conception of what is possible, and what is desirable."[54] Contending that blacks are only "partially" descended from Africa, cultural critic Stanley Crouch urged blacks to construct their identity within a much broader framework. He insisted that "Euro-American ancestry, far more than anything from Africa itself, also fuels the combination of ethnic nationalism and evangelical liberation politics domestic Negroes bring to high-pitched rhetoric over the issue of Nelson Mandela and his struggle."[55] In the same vein, actress and comedienne Whoopi Goldberg retorted, "CALL ME AN ASSHOLE, call me a blowhard, but don't call me an African American, please. It divides us, as a nation and as a people, and it kinda pisses me off. It diminishes everything I've accomplished and everything every other black person has accomplished on American soil."[56] In essence, there is a strong voice against essentializing the African connection among black Americans. This underscores a potent crisis of identity among Black Americans and negates the notion of a monolithic African identity.

Rhett Jones, former director of the Race and Ethnicity Research Center at Brown University, has addressed perhaps the most critical dimension of the problematic of identity: the absence, among black Americans, of an ethnic identity with Africa. He advanced what amounts to a neo-Frazierian position. According to him, slavery accomplished the total destruction of the ethnic identity of black Americans. The terrible experience of the Middle Passage and the brutal horrors of slavery eliminated any sense of ethnic identity among blacks. The rapid growth of the black American population meant that Africa was soon only a memory for the majority of black Americans. Knowledge of their ethnic affiliation and where they came from in Africa was soon lost. Perhaps the first batch of slaves brought in kept this knowledge; however, as the years progressed, such knowledge of language and culture became fuzzy and distant as the slaves became enmeshed in the reality of new sociocultural and ethnic formations. The loss of this ethnic identity consequently left black Americans clinging to the broader geographical construct "Africa." Unfortunately, there is no ethnic group called "African" in Africa. This is significant. The word "Africa" is a geographical construct and bears no ethnic connotation. There are thousands of ethnic/linguistic groups in Africa, among them Yoruba, Grebo, Hausa, Igbo, Xhosa, Zulu, Shona, Ewe, Fante, Asante, Hutu, Tutsi, and literally hundreds of others. Ethnicity is central to the construction of identity. In other words, the claim of identity is only validated on the basis of an ethnic affiliation. Underscoring the peculiarity of the black American condition, Jones argued that unlike in Brazil and Cuba, where the importation of African slaves continued well into the late nineteenth century, providing the strong force of African retentions in culture, music, and arts that is noticeable today, "comparatively few slaves were brought to the United States beyond the third quarter of the eighteenth century—the bulk of the slave population was, therefore, American not African born. By 1775 the vast majority of blacks in British North America were the grandchildren of persons born in the new world. As a result, few black Americans had a sense of African identity, although may identify with Africa." Consequently, Black Americans share *racial*, rather than *ethnic*, identity with Africa. Very often, however, racial identity is mistaken for, or used synonymously with, ethnic identity, and the emphasis given to racial identity often beclouds the lack of ethnic identity.[57]

In his *Racial Healing: Confronting the Fear Between Blacks and Whites* (1995) Harlon Dalton further underscores the centrality of ethnicity to the definition of identity. According to him, "Ethnicity is the bearer of culture. It describes that aspect of our heritage that provides us with a mother tongue and that shapes our values, our world view, our family structure, our morals, the food we eat, our mating behavior, our music. . . ."[58] If Dalton's contention is valid, and if one equally accepts Rhett Jones's claim that black Americans lack ethnic identity with Africa, then the Afrocentric claim of African identity becomes even more problematic. Black Americans have no mother tongue. Though African influences may reflect in their value systems, worldviews, family structure, music, or religion, the African essence and character is less dominant and pervasive than Dona Marimba and other Afrocentrists claim. The black American worldview and value system is an admixture of African and New World experiences. It is interesting to note that even among Afrocentric or "Africancentric" scholars, there is now a growing concern over the absolutist stance of Asante and Marimba on the subject of identity. In rejecting Asante's "100 percent African parentage" thesis, one "Africancentric" scholar contends, "To Asante all black people in this region of the world are Africans. . . . In Asante's Africancentric perception and philosophical or theoretical project, there are not significant distinctions between Africans and people of African descent . . . ignoring, or down-playing—and even suppressing—a lot of historical, cultural, and social reality." Essentially, he continues, Asante accepts "only an African parentage for blacks in America," while completely blacking out the Euro-American parentage.[59]

There is also unmistakable variance between the claim of African identity on the one hand and black American ability and willingness to reflect this "Africanism" in their lifestyles. In other words, there is much more to being African than simply changing one's names or dressing in African attire. Being African has to do with acknowledging the force and authority, and living according to the dictates, of African culture. Most blacks, especially Afrocentrists, are incapable of fully committing themselves to the power and authority of African culture. While they claim certain facets of African culture, they have yet to understand, yet alone acknowledge, the sovereign power of African culture. In laying claim to African identity, Afrocentrists merely emphasize the aesthetics of African culture—names, dress, festivals, even food—while ignoring perhaps the most significant factor in the making of the African identity, the "legislative" authority of African culture.

Culture is a powerful authority in Africa. It makes demands and imposes obligations that no man-made law can undermine or challenge. In fact, it is culture that shapes the most critical aspects of identity. A good example of this is the area of parental responsibility. It is tradition, not law, that defines and establishes the basis and extent of parental responsibility among Africans. Those raised in Western society may find this restrictive and oppressive. Child rearing among Africans is the responsibility of the family, both immediate and extended. This responsibility is perpetual, that is, until the child is able to assume a position of independence. Legal definitions of adulthood have no bearing on parental responsibility. As children grow up, they are socialized not only to recognize their place in the extended family network but also, and most important, to acknowledge that they equally owe a responsibility to the family, immediate and extended. The concept of responsibility is extended and perpetual. There is no point at which a parent or child can "legally" terminate this responsibility or relationship. This is what distinguishes the African ethos of responsibility and deepens and strengthens mutuality. Parents, children, the extended family network are all united and reassured by a strong sense of mutuality. Certain actions are consequently taboo in the African context—for example, acknowledging the legal determination of the limit of responsibility, sending the aged to retirement homes, and requiring children who should otherwise be in school to work in order to contribute to housekeeping expenses and pay their tuition while living with their parents. One is not suggesting that all black Americans subscribe to these practices. Undoubtedly, there are families, black American and even white, that replicate the African model. It is sufficient, however, to know that there are practices, both attitudinal and cultural, that are deemed normative and appropriate in American society to which blacks subscribe, that are inconceivable in an African cultural context. In other words, the American cultural context permits and normalizes tendencies that a true African would not embrace. That black Americans subscribe to Euro-American cultural patterns, even as they retain facets of African values, underscores the complexity of the identity problem. Though of African ancestry, black Americans are also Americans, and, consequently, they need to acknowledge and come to terms with the fact that it is impossible to turn their backs completely on the America experience and its cultural ramifications.

Reacting to the rising African and black consciousness movement in America in the 1960s, African nationalist Tom Mboya described black affirmation of African identity as superficial. "What makes it unrealistic," he argued, "is the thought that you can easily throw off American culture and become African. For example, some think that to identify with Africa means to wear a shaggy beard or a piece of cloth on one's head or a cheap garment on one's body. I find here a complete misunderstanding of what African culture really means." Mboya's definition of African culture is worth quoting at length: "Our culture is something much deeper. It is the sum of our personality and even our attitude toward life. The basic qualities that distinguish it are our extended family ties and the codes governing relations between old and young, our concept of mutual social responsibility and communal activities, our sense of humor, our belief in a superior being, and our ceremonies of birth, marriage and death. Those things have a deep meaning for us, and they pervade our culture, regardless of tribe or clan. They are qualities that shape our lives."[60]

Aside from the cultural problematic of black American affirmation of African identity, there is also the equally problematic character of identity among Africans. If there is a crisis of identity among black Americans, there is an even greater crisis of identity among Africans. Without resolving this crisis, talks of forging Pan-African linkage with blacks across the Atlantic are delusive. How can Africans talk seriously about shared identity with Diaspora blacks when they themselves do not wholly identify with their compatriots? How can Africans abroad talk about togetherness and identity with black Americans, when these Africans nurse mutual resentment toward each other based on ethnicity, religion, or some other primordial factor? Put differently, how can Pan-Africanism be revived in Africa where ethnocentrism and micro-nationalism have eroded the very foundation upon which Pan-Africanism could have thrived? It is no exaggeration to venture the suggestion that some Africans feel more at ease and comfortable with foreigners than with fellow Africans, particularly of a different ethnic background. This is a reality that black American advocates of Pan-Africanism, particularly Afrocentrists, have refused to acknowledge. There is consequently a far deeper crisis of identity among Africans than is acknowledged by Afrocentrists. Ethnic cleansing, the sort of barbaric human carnage witnessed in Rwanda, Burundi, Congo, Zaire, or Somalia, and the state of mass misery and impoverishment prevalent in Nigeria, Kenya, Liberia, Sierra Leone, and other African countries, are not manifestations of ethos of mutuality among Africans, nor are they indicative of a pervasive consciousness of shared identity, an essential attribute of Pan-Africanism.

The old romanticized perception of Africa that ignores the reality of ethnic, cultural, and linguistic divergence and contradictions (not just complexity) continues to shape the resurgence of Pan-African consciousness among black Americans. Black Americans acknowledge the complex nature of African society. What they have had difficulty coming to terms with is the fact that, besides the complexity, there are serious contradictions. The popular contention that Africa is peopled by complex cultures, languages, and ethnic groups who share underlying and unifying cultural attributes remains valid. Though Africans speak different languages and belong to different religious dominations and ethnic groups, they equally share certain common values. In other words, there are certain cultural traits that are indeed truly "African." Nevertheless, there is a more realistic perspective of looking at Africa today. Though Africans share certain unifying attributes, they remain a divergent and chronically divided people. The reality of Africa today does not justify the enthusiasm and faith of proponents of the Pan-African paradigm. Realistically, in its present condition, Africa cannot be a viable component of any Pan-African movement or tradition. Pan-Africanism essentializes brotherhood, cooperation, love, and togetherness. In other words, it engenders a mutuality defined by cultural identity, interests, ethos, and worldview.

In the 1920s, 1930s, and 1940s, Africa served as a rallying point of Pan-Africanism. During these times the whole continent was under colonial rule, and Jim Crow was on the rise in the United States. The problems that Africans and black Americans confronted were indeed identical and unambiguously clear: racism and colonialism. The enemy was easily identifiable. Everyone agreed on the definition and identity of the enemy—European imperialists and white Americans. Consequently, it was possible for Africans, black Americans, and West Indians to unite in the true spirit of Pan-Africanism. The situation in Africa today is different. Colonialism ended in most African countries over fifty years ago. It has been replaced by a new demon, however, an indigenous demon that is racially identifiable as black. The current state of political instability, economic decadence, corruption of epic proportions, systematic looting of state treasuries by the political elite, crisis of legitimacy reflected in the almost complete collapse of the nation-state, the ascendance of ethnocentric and micro-nationalistic sentiments are all perpetrated by indigenous leaders. Among the casualties are the concepts of nationhood and identity.

Political analysts agree that most black African states today are mere conglomerates of conflicting, diverse, and mutually resentful ethnic and linguistic groups and that loyalty has shifted from the nation-state to the ethnic or linguistic enclave. The State in Africa seems to have lost all legitimacy and is held together by the sheer force of terror and intimidation. In the last decade and half in Nigeria, Togo, Liberia, Sierra Leone, Somalia, Democratic Republic of the Congo, Kenya, Ethiopia, and Cameroon there have been persistent calls from alienated minority groups for greater autonomy and independence. Even in Nigeria, where a bloody civil war almost ripped the country apart in the 1960s, one hears loud echoes of secessionist aspirations, particularly from the southeastern part of the country. The genocidal policies and ethnic cleansing in Burundi, Rwanda, Somalia, Liberia, Zaire, and Ethiopia were, and in some places still are, perpetrated by Africans upon fellow Africans. Though some of these problems have their roots deeply buried in the colonial past, and may relate to the ghost of neo-colonialism, the intensity and degree of all these problems have been exacerbated by the policies of African leadership. An example is ethnicity, popularly known as tribalism, which has become perhaps the deadliest cancer to eat away at the very fiber of African nationhood. According to a leading authority, "In Africa [tribalism] has a colonial origin and its function was tied to the nature and purpose of colonialism." Though of colonial origin and contrived to facilitate domination and exploitation, ethnicity was soon perpetrated and developed by indigenous African leaders to facilitate the dominance and hegemony of one ethnic group or region over the others.[61] The result is the almost total meltdown of any bond holding the ethnic groups together. No one could have predicted the state of moral and political decadence in Africa today, much of it the result of the inept, ethnocentric, and selfish policies of its leadership. With the exception of a few countries, the entire continent is engulfed in some form of dictatorship, ethnic conflict, political persecution, instability, economic decay, and corruption of the worst kind. Africans are today perhaps the most oppressed and saddened peoples in the world. The revolution of rising expectations generated by independence has since given place to despair and nightmare. As George Ayittey, a leading author-ity on African political economy, surmised, "Various actors foreign as well as domestic, participated, wittingly or not, in the devastation of Africa. It is easy for African leaders to put the blame somewhere else, for example on western aid donors or on an allegedly hostile interna-tional economic environment. . . . Certainly, donor blunder and other external factors have contributed to the crisis in Africa, *but in my view the internal factors have played a far greater role than the external ones"* (emphasis added).[62]

Nobel laureate Wole Soyinka of Nigeria authored a scathing review of the state of political and moral decadence in Africa, with emphasis on Nigeria. His book, *The Open Sore of a Continent* (1996), should be read by anyone who professes an iota of interest in the future of Africa and in the relationship between Africa and blacks in Diaspora. La-menting the nonexistence of nationhood in Africa, Soyinka observes, "the essence of nationhood has gone underground and taken refuge in that primary constituency of human association, the cultural bastion. And the longer the dictatorship lasts, the more tenacious becomes the hold of that cultural nationalism, attracting to itself all the allegiance, social relevance and visceral identification that once belonged to the larger nation." "The African nation," Soyinka continues, "alas, is mostly viewed through the goggles of [rulership], in studied contrast to the far more organic, comprehensive apprehension of that word when ap-plied to entities like France, Sweden, Japan, Italy, South Korea." For Nigeria, he continued, "and this is certainly true of the Ghanaian, the Senegalese, the Malian, Kenyan, Malawian, and Zairois—the bound-aries of a communal identity are today set much more narrowly. The sights of the average nationalist are sadly contracted."[63]

Regardless of how much one reads about Africa, and the volume of information one acquires from the media, one can never fully un-derstand and appreciate, from the outside, the full extent of the trag-edy that Soyinka, Ayittey, and others highlight. Consequently, black Americans who advocate Pan-Africanism, believing that they con-front similar problems and challenges with Africans, and assuming that all is well with Africa, or that African problems are caused by external forces, are mistaken. They seem unwilling to confront the stark reality of internal structural violence and contradictions within Africa, realities that challenge and negate the concepts of harmony and consensus at the heart of Pan-Africanism. The fact is, Africans are not one and monolithic. They are not harmonious. Though Africans confront challenges that are not fundamentally dissimilar to those of black Americans, the sources are different. Acknowledging this reality is fundamental to developing a Pan-African relationship. The suggestion by the late Walter Rodney that Pan-Africanism be turned inward at the domestic despoilers of Africa remains even more relevant today. It would amount to self-delusion for black Americans and Africans to pretend that they share identical problems that are consistent with the traditional "black-against-white" framework, or that whatever problems they each confront could be easily resolved with a reactivated Pan-Africanism. The Seventh Pan-African Congress held in Kampala in December 1993 was largely a cooperative effort that involved representatives of blacks in Diaspora and Africans (from ordinary citizens to trade unionists, social critics, and political leaders). The deliberations and declarations of the Congress clearly betray a conservative orientation, the rhetoric of nationalism and Pan-Africanism notwithstanding. Delegates identified the goal of Pan-Africanism as "liberation of Africa from foreign exploitation, dispossession, and domination." They evoked the traditional Pan-African notion of a commonality of threat. According to a declaration of the Congress, "changes in the world political and economic structure pose threat to Africa and to African people scattered across the planet. Africa and her peoples are as a result confronted with new levels of violence, fascism, and re-colonization. Pan-Africanism has evolved and must continue to evolve as a movement for liberation and unity in these perilous times." This declaration underlines the resilience of the old romanticized view of Pan-Africanism and of the corporate conception of the relationship of black Americans and Africans. This suggests that the delegates remain unwilling to acknowledge the problematic and complexity of African and the black Diaspora nexus and challenges.[64]

Pan-Africanism cannot be meaningful if it is spearheaded and guided by the current African political leadership, those directly responsible for undermining the very foundation upon which a viable Pan-African tradition could have thrived. The policies of African political leadership since the dawn of independence have been demonstrably against the Pan-African spirit. Consequently, more than ever before in its history, Pan-Africanism needs to develop as an instrument of self-criticism, directed as well against internal and indigenous obstacles to African and black Diaspora unity, progress, and survival. Though the neocolonial and neoimperial external factors remain potent, it is equally significant to zero in on, and critically deal with, the indigenous factors. While from a distance, African problems may appear to black Americans as essentially neocolonial, those problems appear to Africans in their true domestic character and essence and are not consistent with the traditional racialized perspective. The reality is one of blacks against blacks, Africans against Africans. Though recolonization is certainly a threat to Africa's independence, contrary to the declaration of the Seventh Congress, it is not entirely an external threat. Paradoxically, recolonization as a possible solution to Africa's current crises is increasingly gaining currency even among Africans.

In the last three decades, Africans who are victims of and witnesses to corruption and violence, political instability, economic destruction, and cultural genocide, have engaged in debates on how to resolve the intractable African-on-African oppression. Many have come to the rather disturbing admission that perhaps political independence was premature. For instance, in the heat of the crises, corruption and moral decadence that punctuated the life span of Nigeria's Second Republic, a prominent politician and governor of one of the states lamented the state of moral and political decline and publicly expressed preference for the return of the British! Though few took him seriously, and many probably questioned his sanity, he expressed a feeling, albeit unpopular, that many other Nigerians identified with. While the notion of a return to classical colonialism is anachronistic, Africans have been known to express support for some form of "internal colonialism." During the 1994 African Studies Conference in Toronto, a special session was devoted to the subject of recolonization. The renowned Africanist Ali Mazrui suggested the possibility of some of the politically stable and economically viable countries in Africa recolonizing the weaker and poorer ones. Regardless of one's position on this subject, recolonization represents the antithesis of Pan-Africanism. It amounts to an acknowledgment of the demise and irrelevance of Pan-Africanism as a strategy. Some may detect in Mazrui's suggestion echoes of a Pan-African solidarity, akin to Nkrumah's advocacy of continental unity. This correlation is baseless. Nkrumah dedicated his life to the search for a political order that would safeguard the corporate existence of African states. He envisioned a "United States of Africa—great and powerful, in which the territorial boundaries which are the relics of colonialism will become obsolete and superfluous, working for the complete and total mobilization of the economic planning organization under a unified political direction." He called for the surrender of national sovereignty to a continental sovereignty. This Pan-African continental sovereignty would present a united front for Africa vis-à-vis external powers. It would generate the strength needed to protect all African states from external threats. The relationship was such that no state would dominate or exploit the others, in any form or manner.[65] Mazrui's suggestion is fundamentally different. He, in effect, called for the hegemony of some African states over others. He used the word "colonize," a construct, and an experience, that Nkrumah fought strenuously to deconstruct.

Advocates of the Pan-African construct also fail to acknowledge the reality of African and black American conflict, a reality that is often overlooked in the spirit of Pan-Africanism. The relationship between Africans and black Americans is informed by a growing distrust and resentment, exacerbated by the demographics and challenges of the new transplantation. Unlike the forced transplantation of the sixteenth, seventeenth, and eighteenth centuries, which brought Africans to the New World as slaves, the new transplantation is voluntary. It began rather imperceptibly, increasing in intensity in the last twenty-five years. This phenomenon involves Africans, mostly professionals—teachers, doctors, engineers, nurses, businessmen, and students—migrating into a relatively fluid, open, and inviting environment in search of employment, economic elevation, and higher education. The intensity of this migration has opened a new theater of conflict and tension, especially at a time when opportunities for black Americans appear to be shrinking in the wake of onslaughts upon, and the gradual erosion of, the gains of the civil rights movement. Black Americans perceive the new African migrants as potential rivals and beneficiaries of resources that, under affirmative action, would have gone strictly to black Americans. When implementing affirmative action, employers rarely distinguish between continental Africans and black Americans. Africans and black Americans become competitors for scarce resources, with the former assuming positions that the latter consider theirs by right. In other words, there is a growing nativist consciousness among black Americans directed against Africans. One reason this nativist consciousness has remained hidden or controlled is that those who harbor such convictions are often too scared to proclaim them openly. Many are afraid of being accused of undermining the "Pan-African" spirit. There are black Americans who espouse Afrocentric ideas and salute an African with "Hotep" and "brother," while at the same time exhibiting a nativist consciousness and questioning the appointment of Africans to positions they believe rightly belong to black Americans. One is not suggesting any degree of depth or universality to this consciousness. Suffice it to acknowledge that it does exist. The depth and pervasiveness of nativism among black Americans has not been, and may never be, accurately ascertained, given the cloud of hypocrisy that surrounds it. Nevertheless, it remains a disturbing reality that should be confronted and acknowledged rather than brushed aside and ignored.

The growth of anti-African feeling among black Americans has yet to attract any sustained scholarly interest, and this writer is mindful of its controversial and explosive nature. There is evidence, however, that this subject is now attracting both scholarly and popular interests. Godfrey Mwakikagile's recent massive historical interrogation of the relationship has ignited intense public debate and scrutiny of the subject.[66] My observations and contentions come from personal conversations with African and black American students and intellectuals in American colleges. My investigations reveal that many Africans are conscious of a growing resentment from black Americans, particularly over academic positions. Some black Americans have also quietly expressed concern, perhaps even alarm, at the challenges posed by the growing number of African intellectuals. What is particularly intriguing is that few are willing to express these concerns openly and confidently. I have therefore taken the responsibility of bringing this to the fore, knowing the hazards involved—the likelihood of being clobbered by both sides!

A few anonymous examples will suffice to corroborate this phenomenon. During my brief stay at a leading Black Studies Department in the Midwest, there was a search for a senior-level African historian. A continental African was invited for interview and eventually got the job. A senior black American faculty member who had earlier voted to invite the candidate for interview later expressed regret at the decision, explaining that he had endorsed the candidate because he thought his name sounded black American. This particular professor has been to Africa as a Fulbright scholar and was often quick to demonstrate, especially to Africans, pride in his African roots and connections. His objection and concern, this time around, he confided, was because the Black Studies Department already had too many Africans! More recently, at a major southern university, an African director of the African-American Studies Program was hounded out of the institution by persistent opposition, hostility, and pressure from the black American members of the program's advisory committee. Their hostile reactions to his appointment grounded the program and eventually compelled the African to resign. I witnessed the entire drama. These are not, and should not be treated as, isolated cases. Let me hasten to add that I am not unaware of the fact that there do exist harmonious relationships between the two groups in many other places and contexts. The point, however, is that the reality of hostility is often denied.

It has been customary to presume a certain harmony between Africans and black Americans. This seems a logical assumption and is largely behind the rise in Pan-African sentiments. Though no one has seriously looked at the phenomenon of discord between Africans and black Americans, studies on the experience of African emigrants in the United States clearly reveal the reality of perceptional discord between them. In his study, Kofi Apraku contends, "Obviously, the acculturation process and the experiences that black Americans have gone through in the United States accounts significantly for the perceived differences between them and Africans. These experiences may have shaped the differences in perceptions and attitudes between the two groups." Apraku's study reveals that this disharmony predated the civil rights epoch. African students have always encountered problems from black Americans. The relationship between them has not always been harmonious. There was some degree of mutual resentment. Apraku believes that the differences in their backgrounds account for the animosity. One, the black American, has been the product of enslavement, racism, oppression, and humiliation; the other, the African, was not. This distinction is not necessarily true of present-day African migrants, however. The African migrant of today appears to black Americans to be in a "favored" situation with whites and not subjected to the degree and intensity of the racism and degradation that the black American experiences. But this "favored" treatment is short-lived. According to Apraku, as soon as the situation of the African improves and he begins to manifest a desire to become domiciled here and goes after a share of the American dream, "he is no longer African but Black and must be treated as such. He is now exposed to precisely the problems and experiences of black Americans. He becomes the victim of discriminatory policies and derogatory remarks." Put differently, after a time, the African becomes exposed to the same negative experiences as the black American. He is no longer shielded from racism and other discriminatory experiences. "When it comes to racism in the United States," Apraku contends, "a real racist makes no

distinction between black Africans, Black Americans, or black Caribbean. To the racist, black is black, whether made in Africa, America or
the Caribbean."[67]

Serious limitations to the utilization of Africa as identity and Pan-
Africanism as medium of constructing a monolithic platform of struggle need to be acknowledged, as well as the complexities of the African
and black Diaspora contexts and experiences. When it comes to contemporary cultural nationalism, the relationship between continental
Africans and blacks in Diaspora is critical and is often invoked as the
basis for a common struggle. To solidify this linkage, cultural nationalists often infer a certain antiquity to this affinity. That is, they claim
that from time immemorial blacks in Diaspora evinced strong and
positive desires to be African and be identified with Africa, that they
manifested and harbored a strong "Afrocentric consciousness." It is
upon this claim of antiquity of "Afrocentric consciousness" on which
Afrocentric essentialists predicate their affirmation of the Afrocentric
paradigm and worldview.

# 4

# Afrocentric Consciousness and Historical Memory

Several scholars have documented and exhaustively analyzed the historical roots of Afrocentric consciousness.[1] Based on these studies, it is reasonable to suggest that Diaspora blacks had historically manifested strong African consciousness and professed strong affinity for Africa. Some scholars of the Afrocentric genre affirm not only the historical depth of "Afrocentric consciousness" but also a legitimacy derived from deeply rooted shared historical and cultural ethos of mutuality.[2] These scholars have often represented African consciousness among black Americans as positive and as a deep and authentic manifestation and representation of the consanguineous ethos that defined black American conceptions of, and relations to, Africa; molded and nurtured by a host of historical personalities, antecedents and traditions.[3] In other words, these scholars invoke history to validate Afrocentric consciousness. There is, however, some disagreement on the depth and sincerity of the African consciousness and professions of African identity. Consequently, I seek in this chapter to examine manifestations of Afrocentric consciousness among black Americans, with a view to ascertaining its depth, potency, and validity as an identitarian and unifying construct for Diaspora blacks and continental Africans. The conflicted and contradictory character of Afrocentric consciousness becomes evident when subjected to critical historical analysis.

Since Afrocentric identity is the product of Afrocentric consciousness, a working definition of Afrocentric consciousness is necessary. I define Afrocentric consciousness as a consciousness of affinity for Africa, sustained by, among others, subscription to African cultural values, advocacy and invocation of African ideals and idiosyncrasies, and the conception of existential realities within an African cosmological framework. Affirmation of African identity derives logically from this Afrocentric consciousness. Africa becomes the basis of self-knowledge and identity, the quintessence of one's being. This Afrocentric consciousness, and concomitant identity formation, has increasingly gained popularity among black Americans, especially in consequence of a deep and pervasive sense of alienation. Afrocentric consciousness, and the African identity that it advances, are constituents of a very strong ideological and combative movement that has both intellectual and popular dimensions. The intellectual is the corpus of scholarship that defines the structure, essence, strategies, and utility of Afrocentricity. The popular dimension, spurned largely by the rhetoric of the intellectual, is exemplified by symbolic and aesthetic manifestations of Afrocentric identity among black youths, many of whom lack informed knowledge and understanding of the ideology. They embrace Afrocentricity as a protest countercultural weapon. Ironically, despite its popularity among blacks, Afrocentricity has a weak and fragile historical foundation. As this chapter will demonstrate, the Afrocentric genre was neither consistently defended by nor deeply rooted in the consciousness of black Americans, its present combative and domineering character notwithstanding.

### Underlying Premises

First, the Afrocentric identity construct is to some degree superficial. This superficiality derives partly from the fact that the unifying or underpinning element/factor in black American proclamation of African identity is race, that is, the fact of being black. Unfortunately, race is a weak and unreliable construct for identity owing to its socially and politically constructed nature. Race was the invention of the plantation economy. It unified all slaves for the purpose of efficient and effective enslavement. Historically, being black attracted scorn and alienation. All blacks were linked by the fact of shared oppression to a common identity, an identity distinguished by the key sociopolitical construct: race. Consequently, what united blacks was the fact of being black, and the negative cognitive values and experiences that it engendered.

Second, since all blacks originated from the landmass Europeans called "Africa" and since, collectively, blacks were referred to as "Africans," the word "Africa" has naturally been adopted as a unifying and identifying construct. There is, however, a problem with the term "Africa." Its essential artificiality and complexity render "Africa" an ineffective identitarian construct. Emerging historiography of the black Diaspora underscores something that had always been known but had never been seriously analyzed—the superficiality of race and Africa as identity constructs. Africa now appears the weakest of bases for

identity construction for Diaspora blacks. First, it has no ethnic significance, even though many scholars erroneously suggest otherwise.
Second, Africa is a Eurocentric-imposed identity construct. Europeans referred to transplanted slaves collectively as Africans. European
colonialists referred to those in the continent they appropriated and
occupied collectively as Africans.[4] In fact, according to renowned African scholar Ali Mazrui, "the term Africa, the consciousness of being African which united Africans was a colonial creation." The late
Julius Nyerere of Tanzania once argued that "the sentiment of Africa,
the sense of fellowship between Africans, was something which came
from outside." It was colonialism that generated among Africans "a
sentiment of oneness." Mazrui elaborates further,

> Carried to its logical conclusion this says that it took colonialism to inform
> Africans that they were Africans. I do not mean this merely in the sense
> that in colonial schools young Bakongo, Taita and Ewe suddenly learned
> that the rest of the world had a collective name for the inhabitants of the
> landmass of which their area formed a part—though this was certainly one
> medium by which Africans were informed by colonialism that they were
> Africans. A more important medium was the reaction against colonialism
> leading, as it did, to a new awareness of the geographical contiguities . . .
> and the new responses that this called out.[5]

In a recent publication, James Sidbury corroborates Nyerere's and
Mazrui's contentions. According to him, "The terms 'Africa' and 'Africans' and the perception that the continent of Africa (or the sub-
Saharan portion of it) comprises a united cultural and/or 'racial' unit
are European in origin." They are both products of plantation slavery
in the New World. Furthermore, he argues, "Britons in England and
America used 'Africans' interchangeably with 'Negroes' and 'blacks' to
refer to the people they purchased and imported into the Americas, as
well as to the American-born (or Creole) descendants of those victims
of the slave trade."[6] Thus, Nyerere, Mazrui, and, more recently, Sidbury all underscore the importance of deconstructing the historically
untenable practice of essentializing and historicizing Africa, on the
basis of which monolithic African identity has been constructed for all
blacks, thus deemphasizing and obscuring the complex, ambivalent,
and diverse nature of the identity problem. As another scholar argues,
the Africa from where the slaves were taken was a far more complex

entity than Europe. Slaves represented extraordinary ethnic, regional, and cultural diversity. Modern researchers continue to underscore the complexity and diversity of Africa.[7] In fact, according to Sidbury, blacks accepted this imposed "African" identity, and, despite its association with negative and pejorative images, they strove to develop and construct a countervailing and empowering image of Africa that would enhance self-esteem. They succeeded in constructing a new diasporic identity (African) that was, however, radically different from the ethnic identities in Africa. Their new diasporic identity reflected the racist context within which they functioned and "was founded on emerging European perceptions that residents of Africa shared a 'racial' essence."[8] However, as another scholar argues, there is now a "growing awareness of the diversity of Africa's peoples and cultures (which) has rendered the term African as problematic as European. Indeed it powerfully suggested that the diverse peoples brought to the Americas as slaves from the Gold Coast, the Congo, or Angola (themselves rather crude modern analytical constructs) became African only after they were jumbled together in America."[9] The concept of Africa is the creation of what Ali Mazrui terms "tyranny of the map maker."[10] In other words, what gave "Africa" a character was its geographical framework, and many scholars and politicians acknowledge this fact by referring to Africa as "geographical designation," "geographical fiction," or "geographical expression."[11]

There is another problematic dimension to the concept of Africa. Along with race, Africa is the center-point of the Afrocentric genre, which accords it both geographical and ethnic connotations. In other words, in Afrocentrism, Africa is the unifying construct that binds Diaspora blacks and continental Africans as one people.[12] Yet, historically, as this study underscores, Diaspora blacks did not always feel good about Africa. Since it shared with race the distinction of being a major consideration for enslavement, many blacks felt alienated from, and uncomfortable identifying with, Africa. In pro-slavery ideology, being black (race) was the mark of inferiority; being of African ancestry meant a person without civilizational and cultural heritage. In combination, race and Africa legitimized black subordination.[13] This reality evoked conflicting responses among blacks. Those able and willing, through the "blessing" of miscegenation, took the opportunity to "pass" for whites and affected a distance from being black and African. For the many that are unable to "pass," being black and of African ancestry became an imposed identity over which they had little choice. Others still stood up to the challenge and embraced Africa, espousing cooperation and unity.

A third underlying premise of this chapter is that, throughout black American history, the claim of African identity was more utilitarian than substantive. That is, there was always a function that Africa was supposed to serve, a goal it was supposed to aid in achieving. This utilitarian underpinning of Africanism among black Americans has largely been ignored. In times of dire distress and alienation, many black Americans turned toward Africa for succor. This utilitarian function of Africa can be traced to the very dawn of slavery. As several studies reveal, slaves managed to subvert the debilitating and dehumanizing impact of enslavement by invoking African cultural values and idiosyncrasies. Slaves developed a world of their own, whose realities were shaped more by African than European values. It is this African-derived primary world that enabled the slaves to survive the destructive force of the secondary world of the masters.[14] Beyond this, throughout the nineteenth century, as this study shows, black leaders frequently invoked Africa as the source of solutions to critical problems of adjustment, accommodation, and resistance.

Fourth, the professions of African consciousness by black Americans, and of interest in and concerns for the plight of continental Africans, have historically evolved in reaction to what I call the all-encompassing and all-embracing character of the Eurocentric worldview, particularly its characterization of all blacks (Diaspora and continental Africa alike) as primitive and inherently inferior. That is, the lack of distinction between the "primitivism" of continental Africans and the cultural transformation and ipso facto "superiority" of Diaspora blacks. Judged inferior by association, or ancestral entrapment, many black Americans sought escape by affirming their superiority over Africa or by distancing themselves from Africans, while emphasizing their Euro-American cultural identity.

Affirming their superiority over Africa was achieved implicitly, if not explicitly, by acknowledging the "primitivism" of Africans and advocating paternalistic and missionary solutions to the problems of Africa's alleged backwardness. As discussed above, some of the pioneers of the black nationalist and Pan-Africanist traditions derived their ideas and schemes from the prevailing Eurocentric/racist idiosyncrasies of the age. For example, Paul Cuffee and Lott Cary, both of them acclaimed black nationalists and Pan-Africanists, embraced the colonization scheme that was premised on the conviction that Africa was backward and primitive. As colonizationists, these blacks envisioned themselves as missionaries responsible for the transfer of progress and civilization to backward Africa.[15] Thus, they were able to distance themselves from "primitive Africa," becoming culturally superior to, and alienated from, Africans.

Many of the leading black American nationalists identified in this study underscored their disdain for Africa's primitive nature and proclivities by proclaiming their Euro-American cultural essence and affiliations. They endeavored to convince themselves, and the Europeans, of their cultural superiority over continental Africans.[16]

A fifth underlying premise of this chapter is that there was a certain utilitarian consideration to the Pan-African identity schemes that leading black American nationalists proposed. These schemes were driven by the conviction that fundamental changes in the black Diaspora condition depended on substantive transformations of the African condition. The underlying impulse for this "Pan-African" consciousness, this acclaimed ethos of trans-Atlantic mutuality, therefore, derived from a desire to reform the black Diaspora condition, an essentially utilitarian consideration. Transform Africa, civilize the indigenous people, and create strong political and economic entities; these changes would reflect positively upon blacks worldwide and thereby compel recognition for the rights and privileges of black Americans and, in the process, radically transform the domestic realities of the United States. Pan-Africanism, in part, was meant to serve as a platform for the eventual realization of the elusive American identity. This domestic American dynamic of Pan-Africanism was not always obvious. A strong desire for American identity informed the rhetoric of Pan-Africanism. No individual manifested this as unambiguously as Martin Delany, the acclaimed ideological guru of Pan-Africanism. In the concluding section of his seminal publication, *The Condition, Elevation, Emigration and Destiny of the Colored People of the United States* (1852), a book that many have described as his definitive testament on emigration, Delany qualified his call for emigration with a strong affirmation of love for his native United States. Underlining his reluctant endorsement of emigration and the fragility of his African nationalism, Delany characterized the relationship between black American migrants and their host country in Africa in adoptive terms. As he lamented, "We love our country, dearly love her, but she don't (sic) love us . . . she despises us, and bids us begone, driving us from her embraces; . . . but when we do go, whatever love we have for her, we shall love the country none the less that receives us as her adopted children."[17] More important, Delany's scheme for an independent black nationality in Africa was designed ultimately for the transformation of the domestic American order. The political and economic success of an independent black state in Africa, would, Delany hoped, debunk the racist ideas that had justified the enslavement and subordination of blacks and help shape world opinion in favor of conceding the rights and privileges of black Americans.[18] Other black nationalists such as Henry Garnet and Henry McNeal Turner advanced similar schemes.[19] In other words, the underlying impulse of the nineteenth-century Pan-African scheme was to transform Africa for the primary purpose of effecting a greater transformation of the American order. This utilitarian character of Pan-Africanism was evident in the "nationalist" ideas and schemes of Paul Cuffee, Lott Cary, and David Walker. In his famous *APPEAL*, a book lauded for its supposedly militant Pan-Africanist slant, David Walker espoused strong nationalist aspirations that were undoubtedly and unmistakably American. Although he also espoused strong "Pan-African" ideals, Walker's Pan-Africanism had an equally strong utilitarian underpinning. What nudged him toward Pan-Africanism was the brutal and debilitating condition of black America. What he sought the most for blacks was the realization of the American identity.[20]

The utilitarian dimension is also evident in the early black protest tradition. For example, the struggles of free blacks in Philadelphia, New York, and other northern states from the late eighteenth to the early nineteenth centuries reflected a utilitarian conception of Africa. These blacks identified Africa with their institutions and structures as part of a protest tradition of affirming an identity in response to the threat of being forced into an identitarian void by the pro-slavery and racist culture. Another example is the efforts of Absalom Jones and Richard Allen that laid the foundation for the rise of the African Methodist Episcopal Church in Philadelphia and other institutions with the African nomenclature. Rejected by the racist establishment and denied access to its institutions and structures, blacks invoked Africa in protest.

A sixth premise is that to essentialize the African identity, as Afrocentric scholars do, is ahistorical, precisely because it ignores the historical and transformatory character of the transplantation experience. This in no way denies the existence of African cultural retentions. The point, however, is that the African retentions, in whatever form or shape, are only partially African in essence. There is an equally compelling Euro-American, Anglo-Saxon component in the character and totality of the cultural identity of Diaspora blacks. This hybridism and complexity is often deemphasized in Afrocentric essentialist discourse.

Seventh, applied to black Americans, two of the cardinal components of identity among Africans are problematic: culture and ethnicity. While there is noticeably a black American culture, which is only partially African, the black American has, however, been almost completely cleansed of any trace of African ethnicity. The concept "African-American" possessed more geopolitical and nationalist than ethnocultural utility. The prefix "African," as earlier argued, is more of a geographical construct, delineating Americans of African ancestry, born of a growing sense of alienation from the American establishment. The claim of African identity, therefore, is premised on a weak foundation—race (being black) or being of African ancestry (geographically)—and is not necessarily based on culture and ethnicity. Race, as already indicated, is too weak a foundation for constructing identity, especially since it is a social and political construct. There is nothing particularly inherent or genetic about being black. Being black acquired importance in history primarily because some people chose to use pigmentation as the basis of dealing with others. In other words, race assumed significance only because of a conscious and deliberate effort by a group of humans to adopt it as a platform for hegemony and exploitation.

### The Utility of Africa

The utilization of race as a weapon of hegemony by whites provoked conflicting and ambivalent reactions from blacks. First, there was a tradition of negative reaction to, and outright rejection of, Africa. One of the earliest manifestations of this occurred during the first organized efforts by black leaders to deal with the challenges posed by prosecution, alienation, dehumanization, and outright denial of American identity in the wake of the Cincinnati race riots of 1829. These riots inspired organized black abolitionism and the convention movement. It is revealing to note that African identity and consciousness was relegated to the background in the National Negro conventions that were held between 1831 and 1835. Positive affirmation of

African identity was never a consideration among organizers of the convention movement. Black American consciousness was unmistakably American. Attaining American identity was the overarching goal of the conventions. In the ensuing debates and deliberations of the conventions, black leaders concentrated efforts on how best to ensure the realization of American identity. They displayed remarkable optimism in the face of rejection and brutalization. They wanted American citizenship. To achieve this, many black leaders advocated deemphasizing race in favor of universalism. At the 1835 national Negro convention in Philadelphia, William Whipper introduced a motion, which was seconded by Robert Purvis, that resolved, "That we recommend as far as possible, to our people to abandon the use of the word 'Colored', when either speaking or writing concerning themselves; and especially to remove the title of 'African' from their institutions, marbles of churches, etc." The resolution was unanimously adopted. Whipper's motion underscored a growing concern over the separatist and troubling character of the appellation "African." Whipper was perhaps the leading advocate of the universalist ideology, which failed to win mass appeal among blacks. Yet, in the ensuing State conventions of the 1840s, blacks adopted "Colored" rather than "Africa" as identifying construct; referring to themselves as "people of color." This choice of color should not be misconstrued to suggest that these leaders cherished separatism. Integration was the ultimate goal, although many came to the conclusion that perhaps the best strategy for achieving integration was for blacks to reform themselves through racially distinctive institutions and strategies.[21]

The threat that the word "Africa" constituted led to efforts to remove it from identifying structures and institutions. In the late 1830s, the African Baptist Church of Boston, founded in 1806, changed its name to the "First Independent Church of the People of Color." The members justified this action thus: "for the very good reason that the name African is ill-applied to a church composed of American citizens." Samuel Cornish, editor of the *Colored American* provided the following justification for this name change; "Many would rob us of the endeared name, 'American,' a distinction more emphatically belonging to us than five-sixths of this nation, one that we will never yield. In complexion, in blood and nativity, we are decidedly more exclusively American than our white brethren; hence the propriety of the name of our people, Colored Americans, and of identifying the name with all our institutions, in spite of our enemies, who would rob us of our nationality and reproach us as exotics."[22]

The above represents rejection of "Africa" on the grounds that it compromised being "American." To acknowledge being African was seen as tantamount to relinquishing being American. The name "African" had become an albatross that had to be jettisoned. In later years, especially in the second half of the nineteenth century, the same rejection of and feeling of discomfort with Africa shaped black nationalist ideas and schemes. Even when Africa was later accepted and acknowledged as part of the repertoire of deconstructing Eurocentric historiography, it served more as the basis of claims for inclusion and integration in America. As discussed elsewhere, the emigration movements of the late nineteenth century were very much utilitarian. The motivating impulse was not so much love for Africa but rejection by America. These nationalists left few in doubt as to their most cherished identity.[23]

In fact, the choice in the 1830s and 1840s was between two contending conceptions of identity, neither of which represented a positive attitude toward Africa—universalism and race. These two perspectives shaped the black abolitionist crusade during its first two decades (1830–1850). As discussed in chapter 1, the universalists, led by Whipper, advanced the notion of one humanity. The racialists, led by the "radical" Samuel Cornish, editor of the *Colored American*, embraced race as the dividing line and the basis of identity construction. Regardless of their disagreement, each conceived of its ideology as potentially the route to American identity. It should be noted that black affirmation of American identity, and rejection of Africa, predated the convention movement. As earlier argued, blacks reacted to the colonization threat of the early nineteenth century with strong affirmation of American identity and an equally strong rejection of Africa. The struggle of black abolitionists against colonization and displacement, and demand for full citizenship, according to one scholar, "led to a subtle alteration in black self-presentation after 1830." Convinced that colonization meant repatriation to Africa and mortgaging of their American identity, black abolitionist leaders sought to jettison "Africa" from their institutions and self-identification. Race now became the preferred basis of self-definition. According to Horton, to use the word "African" in connection with the identity of American blacks seemed to reinforce the argument of the increasingly powerful group in the American Colonization Society who would use African colonization as a forum for free colored removal. The term "colored" was more acceptable. The concept "colored American" became the preferred identity. As in "We are Americans—colored Americans."[24]

At a meeting in Bethel Church, Philadelphia, in January of 1817, blacks resolved; "Whereas our ancestors (not of choice) were the first successful cultivators of the wilds of America, we their descendants feel ourselves entitled to participate in the blessings of her luxuriant soil, which their blood and sweat manured; and that any measures or system of measures, having a tendency to banish us from her bosom, would not only be cruel, but in direct violation of those principles, which have been the boast of this republic." At this same meeting, these blacks established further grounds for distancing themselves from Africa and in the process provided one of the earliest articulations of the myth of savage and primitive Africa among Diaspora blacks. This is unambiguously represented in the following resolution: "that without arts, without science, without a proper knowledge of government, to cast into the savage wilds of Africa the free people of color, seems to us the circuitous route through which they must return to perpetual bondage."[25]

On January 25, 1831, blacks in New York gathered to protest colonization. They affirmed their American identity, invoking both the Declaration of Independence and ancestral contributions. According to them, "The time must come when the Declaration of Independence will be felt in the heart, as well as uttered from the mouth, and when the rights of all shall be properly acknowledged and appreciated. God hasten that time. This is our home, and this is our country. Beneath its soil lie the bones of our fathers; for it, some of them fought, bled, and died. Here we were born, and here we will die."[26]

At a state convention held October 26–27, 1843, in Detroit, Michigan, blacks vehemently protested colonization and rejected the notion of inherent inferiority. They designed a positive rendition of Africa primarily as a weapon of protest. These blacks portrayed Africa as an enlightened and civilized continent, a fountain of knowledge from which Europeans drank. This exalted Africa was designed to negate claims of black inferiority. As they declared:

> Our condition as a people in ancient times, was far from indicating intellectual or moral inferiority. For, we were informed by the writings of Herodotus, Pindar, Aeschylus, and many other ancient historians, that Egypt and Ethiopia held the most conspicuous places among the nations of the

earth. Their princes were wealthy and powerful, and their people distinguished for their profound learning and wisdom. Two thousand years ago people flocked from all parts of the known world, down into Africa, to receive instructions from those woolly haired and black skinned Ethiopians and Egyptians. Yes, even the proudest of the Grecian philosophers, historians and poets, among whom were Solon, Pythagoras, Plato, Herodotus, Homer, Lycurgus, and many others, all went down into Africa, and sat at the feet of our ancestors, and drank in wisdom, until they were taught in all the arts and sciences of those ancient African nations.

Furthermore, they proclaimed, "The sun of civilization rose from the center of Africa, and like the bright luminary of the celestial regions, it casts its light into the most remote corners of the earth, giving arts, science and intellectual improvement, to all that lay beneath its elevating rays. . . . Therefore, fellow citizens, proscribe us no longer, by holding us in a degraded light, on account of natural inferiority; but rather extend to us our free born rights, the elective franchise, which invigorate the soul and expands the mental powers of a free and independent people." The statement was clearly a positive portrayal of Africa as a weapon of debunking the myth of inherent inferiority and justifying claims of political equality and rights.[27]

In 1852, blacks in Maryland gathered to discuss the prospect of Liberia as a possible place of relocation. In support of colonization, they adduced two contradictory images of Africa. The first was a positive elevating image of a rich, wealthy, and industrious place, with institutions and facilities of greatness that surpassed America, Asia, and Europe. As they contended,

Asia could not exceed the variety of the productions of Africa. Europe with her numerous manufactories and eternal resources, could not cope with her in physical greatness—America with her noble institutions of power, facilities of improvement, promises of greatness and high hopes of immortality, was this day far, very far behind her in natural resources. Nothing can excel the value of her productions—sugarcane grows rapidly, cotton a native plant, corn and hemp flourish in great perfections, oranges, coffee, wild honey, lemons, mahogany . . . abound there, mules, horses, oxen, sheep, hogs, fowls of all kinds, are in the greatest abundance. She holds out a rich temptation to commerce and a strong inducement to emigration.[28]

The second image was of a wretched place controlled by a destructive barbarous people, desperately in need of the infusion of civilized values. These blacks saw themselves as missionaries of progress, Africa's own children, returning after a sojourn of cultural transformation in the Diaspora. According to them, "On the lap of American civilization and around the altars of this Christian land, have been born the moral elements of civil and Christian power, ordained by heaven [for] the redemption of Africa. For the last 2000 years, that wretched land of mystery and crime has been abandoned to the cupidity of the most cruel barbarism. This makes us bold in saying that emigration is the only medium by which the long closed doors of that continent are to be opened; by her own children's returning, bearing social and moral elements of civil and religious power."[29] These paternalistic and missionary conceptions shaped professions of African consciousness and identity among black Americans for much of the nineteenth century. As argued elsewhere, providentialism was a critical ideology of the colonization movement. God supposedly sanctioned the enslavement of some Africans so that they would be civilized through contacts with Europeans and, after regaining freedom, would return to help civilize and redeem the rest of the continent.[30]

In New England in 1859, blacks strongly affirmed their American identity while distancing themselves from Africa. In proclaiming their right to American identity, these blacks defined themselves as the true Americans, who embodied quintessentially American ideals. Realizing American identity would amount to fulfilling of America's ideals and vision. As they declared,

> Our old enemy the colonization society has taken advantage of the present state of feeling among us, and is doing all in its power to persuade us to go to Africa; the emigration scheme has new life, and another enemy, under the name of the African civilization Society has sprung into existence, and beckons us to a home in a foreign land . . . Our right to live here is as good as the white man's, and is incorporated in the Declaration of Independence, in the passage which declares, That all men are created equal, and endowed by their creator with certain inalienable rights; that among these are life, liberty and the pursuit of happiness. Then let us remain here, and claim our rights upon the soil where our fathers fought side by side with the white man for freedom. Let us remain here and labor to remove the chains from the limbs of our brethren . . . Yes, let us stay here, and vindicate our right to citizenship, and pledge ourselves to aid in completing the Revolution for human freedom, commenced by the patriots of 1776. We must take our stand in defiance of the FSL and Dred Scot.[31]

In his presidential address to the New England convention, George T. Downing of Rhode Island reiterated the claims of blacks to American identity. He described the Negro as the nerve center of American ideals and existence. As he put it,

> We have . . . an inseparable, providential identity with this country; with its institutions, with the ideas connected with its formation, which were the uplifting of man—universal brotherhood . . . We are the life of the nation's existence; a nation must have issues to exhibit vitality. All of the great principles of the land are brought out and discussed in connection with the Negro. But for him, there would be a sameness; the great principles, the great ethical school of the times, would be closed for the want of a subject. We are the alphabet, upon us, all are constructed . . . Blacks represented elements for the fulfillment of American mission and destiny—the fraternal unity of man.[32]

As blacks became acculturated in America, Africa assumed an essentially utilitarian function and space in black consciousness. No longer in a realistic position to claim African identity, blacks nonetheless found assertions of African identity a useful part of their repertoire of cultural resistance, and as the years progressed, that African identity became the foundation for establishing claims to the American identity. In the 1850s, during this onset of the "golden age" of black nationalism, we observe a very powerful anti-American and anti-establishment nationalism that exalted African culture and identity. Yet, as argued above, even this forceful Africanist nationalism was driven by strong Americentric/Eurocentric aspirations and consciousness. Traditionally, scholars have overemphasized the anti-American, and supposedly countercultural, essence of black nationalism to the neglect of the Eurocentric and Americentric underpinnings. It is necessary, however, to distinguish between real and manifest identities. What blacks projected in response to alienation and rejection in America was the African identity as a counteridentity. Africa served to balance the denial of American identity (a utilitarian role). Many blacks advanced a positive African identity as part of the intellectual repertoire of resistance to Eurocentric historiography. This Africa served as a protest weapon and platform for exposing the fallacies of Eurocentric historiography. Proclaiming African identity, backed by proofs of African historical and cultural wealth, became a potent protest weapon. As Amos Wilson unabashedly admitted, Africa served as a useful and effective protest weapon, providing a convenient platform for revolutionary posturing. Being "Afrikan" reinforced him "against the impossible odds of being Black in America!"[33] Identifying with Africa became the terrain upon which blacks attempted to construct their American identity. As James Campbell surmised, "As paradoxical as it may sound, Africa has served historically as one of the chief terrains on which African Americans have negotiated their relationship to American society. To put the matter more poetically, when an African American asks 'what is Africa to me?' he or she is also asking 'What is America to me?'"[34]

Nineteenth-century black nationalists constructed a dual cultural space within which they attempted to rationalize their ambivalent location between Europe and Africa. First, they advanced a positive image of Africa—as a culturally and historically vibrant and wealthy continent to negate Eurocentric historiography and as a counterhegemonic platform. Second, they portrayed Africa as backward and primitive, which enabled them to claim and affirm affinity with Euro-America. This dual cultural space allowed them to accomplish the theatrics of attacking Europe's hegemonic claim while emphasizing their African identity, and acknowledging Africa's primitive nature while distancing themselves from the continent. It amounted to deconstructing Eurocentric worldview while acknowledging a critical aspect of that worldview that sustained Europe's hegemony—the alleged barbarism of Africa. The dual cultural space allowed black nationalists, therefore, to condemn Europe's cultural arrogance while forcefully seeking to situate themselves within that same cultural world. It was a cry for acceptance and for the conferment of American identity. Acknowledging Africa's barbaric nature distanced blacks from the alleged backwardness and civilizational primitivism of Africa, thus establishing affinity to Europe, at least culturally, and establishing their claim to Euro-American identity. The dual cultural space implies acknowledging the transformatory character of the transplantation experience, at least culturally, a dimension modern Afrocentric scholars deemphasize. In this instance, the simultaneous exaltation and relegation of Africa served utilitarian purposes. The exaltation debunked the hegemonic claims of Europe. The relegation served to enhance the appeal of blacks for acceptance and inclusion into the Euro-American cultural world.[35]

Furthermore, early-twentieth-century intellectual challenge to Eurocentric historiography launched by Du Bois, Carter Woodson, and others, though predicated on acknowledgment of African ancestry, was itself driven by utilitarian aspirations: to establish grounds for integration. Proving the historicity of Africa was designed to challenge the hegemonic Eurocentric order and establish the claims of blacks to American identity. Put simply, the underlying rationale reads thus: we are denied American identity, rights, and privileges of American citizenship largely because our African heritage is maligned, misrepresented; to overturn this, it is necessary for us to demonstrate the true nature and character of our heritage. Rehabilitating African history, therefore, became a weapon of protest, of deconstructing Eurocentric historiography and establishing the claims of blacks to American citizenship.

This protest and utilitarian function of Africa became especially pronounced during the civil rights struggles. Being black and being proud of it became not just an affirmation of racial identity but also a slogan of protest against exclusion and segregation. Afrocentricity combines African cultural appurtenance, molded within a broader cultural space that defines and, more realistically, exemplifies real identity and aspirations that are fundamentally Americentric, its bold and combative professions of African identity notwithstanding. There is, therefore, a need for a clear distinction between verbal and rhetorical assertions of African identity and emulation of African cultural and aesthetics ideals, on the one hand, and subscription to cultural, sociological, and behavioral values and tendencies that are essentially Americentric, on the other. This distinction will establish, first, that African cultural and aesthetic patterns were utilized essentially as protest weapons against a hegemonic and culturally threatening mainstream and, second, that black American culture is in essence partially African, partially Euro-American, essentially American, tangentially African.

The Afrocentric identity is rendered even more tenuous as a monolithic, all-embracing identity construct for Diaspora blacks by new studies that reveal complex and multiple levels and layers of black Diaspora experiences across historical space and time. Some blacks had positive and endearing experiences within a particular Diaspora space and time and manifested integrative identity consciousness, whereas for others, within the same geographical space and historical time, the experiences and responses were negative and alienating, inducing separatist identity consciousness. For others still, the experience may not be as clear-cut as to induce certainty on identity.[36]

Explanation of the utilitarian and fragile nature of Afrocentric identity lies in part in something that contemporary cultural nationalists who insist on identifying Diaspora blacks as African are reluctant to admit: the transformatory nature of the transplantation experience. As Michael Gomez contends, "with the African antecedent in view, it becomes possible to more fully comprehend the change, the transition from a socially stratified, ethnically based identity directly tied to a specific land, to an identity predicated on the concept of race. There were specific mechanisms in each phase of the African's experience— initial capture and barracoon, transatlantic trek and seasoning— through which he was increasingly nudged toward reassessment of identity. The experience of enslavement resulted in the restructuring of the slave's identity."[37]

Torn away from Africa, denied American identity, suspended between two identities—a distant and increasingly fuzzy African one and a cherished but elusive American one—blacks responded in various ways, pursuing policies and activities that clearly revealed how they defined themselves. Their responses to Africa were informed by profound ambivalence and complexity. The ambivalence toward Africa and the utilitarian, ephemeral, and shallow African consciousness underscore the problematic of identity. An increasing number of scholars are now focusing attention on the transformatory nature of the Diaspora experience. As W. D. Wright argued, "when black Africans moved to other parts of the world, they not only moved into different geographical areas but also into different time and spatial zones, and into different historical, cultural, and social contexts. In each geographical and time and spatial zone, they took their original African culture with them, and it also became modified."[38] This modification underscores a complex global Diaspora history. We need to acknowledge not just different levels and layers of the African Diaspora—America, Europe, Asia, the Caribbean, Latin America, and the Pacific—but also their complexities. There are profound differences, historically and culturally, in the global experiences of blacks. Yet, the growing realization of the complexities of Africa and the black Diaspora has not stopped Afrocentric essentialists from extending their monolithic perspective to the global arena.

# 5

# Afrocentric Essentialism
# and Globalization

The last two decades have witnessed a deepening of the crisis of black American alienation. Reacting to the conservative upsurge that continues to erode significant gains of the civil rights movement, black cultural nationalism, according to some scholars, has assumed a heavily "hyper-politicized" character, extending black alienation beyond the boundaries of the United States into the global arena. Leading black cultural nationalists portray globalization as a force for perpetuating the hegemonic aspirations of Europeans, and thus inimical to the racial and cultural survival of blacks. They are consequently suspicious of, and opposed to, the prospect of a global cultural citizenship. Against globalization, they counterpoise cultural isolationism, constructing the ideal identity for blacks in distinct racial and cultural terms and proffering what essentially is a global extension of Afrocentrism.

As I have argued consistently, Afrocentricity is premised on a conflict conception of society and social change. The combination of political powerlessness, economic impoverishment, and systematic erosion of the gains of the civil rights struggles has pushed blacks to the depth of social misery and alienation, and, in the judgment of Afrocentric scholars, provides proof of the continuing relevance and potency of race and ethnicity as unifying identitarian constructs. The crux of Asante's ideas is the identification of Eurocentrism as the major threat to both Africans and blacks in Diaspora. According to him, this problem has been with blacks since the dawn of history and has remained intractable in spite of emancipation and the gains of the civil rights movement.[1]

The Afrocentric response to globalization entails the use of African consciousness to build a racial and cultural monolithic Africa–black Diaspora world, the creation and envisioning of a unified black world against the cultural onslaughts of global European hegemony. Molefi Asante, Maulana Karenga, and other scholars of the Afrocentric School view the United States as "a hegemonic society, in which the relatively powerful members trace their ways of thinking, their philosophical foundations, and their canons of knowledge to the cultures of Western Europe. These people, over the generations, have used societal institutions and resources to glorify their Western European cultural heritage while, at the same time, devaluing through processes of omission, distortion, and misrepresentation knowledge centred in the cultures of others in the same society who do not trace their origins to Western Europe."[2] To combat this hegemonic force, Afrocentric scholars advocate advancing knowledge of African history and culture among blacks as a defensive weapon against what is characterized and perceived as a pervasive and domineering Eurocentric worldview.

Asante's concepts of *centering* and *location* are culturally defined. In terms of epistemology and pedagogy, the black person or scholar has to be *located* and *centered* within African culture. Knowledge and its contents and purveyors are validated *only* within the African cultural context.[3] The end result is a model of identity rescued from the cultural/historical stranglehold of Eurocentric socialization. A black person is thus socialized to be suspicious of, and in antagonism against, western ideas and values. This underscores the continuing relevance of the color line.

The color line has been a constituent part of, and basis for, Afrocentric identity and consciousness from the start. Afrocentricity united Africans and blacks in Diaspora, regardless of historical experiences, circumstances, and contexts as peoples of one identity and culture. Their shared experiences of slavery and colonialism derived from another shared identity—blackness. Consequently, race became the unifying element, the basis of confraternity, the solid foundation for constructing a Pan-African framework of struggle, and the common platform against an enemy that was similarly conceived in essentially racial terms—Caucasian and Eurocentric. The color line thus upholds a Manichean depiction of society as a theatre of perpetual conflict between two irreconcilable foes, each distinguished by racial characteristics—black and white.

Despite its centrality to Afrocentricity, the color line, as suggested earlier, is rooted in an earlier phase of black history. Prominent black leaders of the nineteenth and early twentieth centuries advanced the color line as the platform for constructing an effective defense against European domination. Delany's 1854 address before the Negro National Emigration Convention in Cleveland, Ohio, contained perhaps the most forceful and articulate projection and defense of this strategy. Although Delany would later contradict his own injunction and endorse European activities in Africa, the color line retained its appeal as a dynamic force in black-white relations. Many critics identify race as the central problem of the twentieth century and, some would argue, a central problem of the twenty-first century as well.⁴ This growing ascendance and privileging of race compels interrogation of the global dynamics and implications of Afrocentric essentialism.

Globalization has been identified as among the major dynamics of change in twenty-first-century history. Although few doubt its reality, many are very apprehensive of its broader implication for human interactions. Responses to globalization have consequently been mixed. Some are apprehensive of its perceived economic and political threats to the livelihood of millions of workers. Others dread the economic and political implications of a world order in which the leading industrialized European nations exercise hegemonic control and influence.⁵ But there are also those who welcome globalization as a force that would lead inexorably to greater human interdependence and interactions, with the attendant shrinkage of spatial distance and separation. Enthusiasts foresee and predict the imminence of a global civilization—"a discrete world order with shared values, processes and structures." Globalization thus portends a world economy, greater international migrational pattern, and the eventual disappearance of "permanent settlement and the exclusive adoption of the citizenship of a destination country." Global cities would emerge from "intensification of transactions and interactions between the different segments of the world," and the "de-territorialization of social identity challenging the hegemonizing nation-states' claim to an exclusive citizenship a defining focus of allegiance and fidelity in favor of overlapping, permeable and multiple forms of identification."⁶

The global context of cultural citizenship suggests the possibility of transcending the limitations of national citizenship, ethnicity, or other primordial constructions of identity. Affirmations of sovereignty and political independence, national distinctiveness, and citizenship are all attributes of the emergent nation-state. Robin Cohen identifies as a critical feature of modernity the attempt by leaders of homogenizing nation-states to make citizenship an exclusive claim to identity. This exclusivity is challenged in the postmodernist context. As Cohen further argues, "the scope for multiple affiliations and associations that has been opened up outside and beyond the nation-state has also allowed a diasporic allegiance to become both more open and more acceptable. There is no longer any stability in the *points of origin*, no finality in *the points of destination* and no necessary coincidence between social and national identities."[7] This is particularly troubling for a paradigm (such as Afrocentricity) that essentializes *points of origin* and *destination* and insists on absolute coincidence between race, culture, and identity.

The essence of globalization, therefore, is the expansion of the spatial parameters of human encounters. This expansive development effects profound transformation in the hermeneutics of human experience as we come to emphasize *interactions, impacts, exchanges,* and *shared experiences*, values that render the rigidity, isolation, and insularity of a racialized worldview problematic. Globalization entails acknowledging *engagements, contacts, interactions,* and *encounters* as key historical dynamics of human development, forces that have hitherto been overshadowed by negative responses and reactions to the destructive and negative characteristics of the encounters. There is a widespread belief that the world is becoming one global village and that technology is breaking down and shrinking spatial distance and barriers, with the implication that as we get to know more of each other and as we interact more, we are inexorably led to discover that *commonalities, shared experiences*, rather than *differences*, define the human experience. Afrocentrists, however, consider this expansion in the parameters of human encounters pregnant with hegemonic implication that would render the global system one of unequal relationships. In other words, they discern the spectre of a "colonial situation" within this global framework, where European and superpower dominance would constitute an ever-threatening force to the survival of weaker nations and peoples.

If Robin Cohen is right that globalization could potentially circumscribe the political and cultural authority of the nation-state, then Afrocentric scholars view the resultant supra-cultural and cosmopolitan order as the global trajectory of Eurocentrism. This conjures the image of a supra-European hegemonic cultural force, with the same devastating impact that many see in the political-economy of globalization. The Afrocentric paradigm relies heavily on a monolithic and hegemonic construction of European culture. Europeans, according to this perspective, have used, and would continue to use, culture as a weapon of domination. By denying and denigrating African culture and history, Europeans succeeded in constructing a hegemonic world order. Afrocentric scholars therefore see nothing in the new global cultural order to inspire optimism. To the Afrocentric mindset, Europe's cultural threat to blacks is perpetual and absolute. Therefore, a critical problematic of globalization from the Afrocentric essentialist perspective is the move toward global cultural citizenship. The global gravitation toward the evolution of cultural citizenship has strengthened the suspicion of Afrocentric scholars. It should be acknowledged, however, that the global projection of Eurocentric hegemony is not of Afrocentric origin but rooted in black American history. As discussed in previous chapters, leading nineteenth-century black nationalists such as Martin Delany and Henry McNeal Turner advocated a racialized platform of struggle against what they perceived as a global scheme by American whites and those Delany identified as their European "cousins" to keep Africans and blacks in Diaspora in perpetual subordination.[8]

The conception of cultural citizenship implies human capacity and willingness to deemphasize or even transcend national or some other primordial construction of citizenship and identity—be it race, ethnicity, or religion—coupled with familiarity with, and the capacity to engage, multiple cultural experiences without being boxed in, or restrained, by one's *original* cultural identity. Afrocentric scholars who advocate an absolutist and monolithic construction of African and black Diaspora identity are opposed to, and deeply suspicious of, any global cosmopolitan construction of identity. From the Afrocentric perspective, the global context itself is problematic, since it is perceived as an extension of the hegemonic domestic American reality that is deemed detrimental to black identity and consciousness. Thus, the cultural implications of globalization have given an added urgency and poignancy to the Afrocentric notion of cultural threat, since culture is perceived as a critical front in the war against Eurocentric hegemony. The cultural agenda of Afrocentricity is to socialize blacks to recognize the dangers of white American and European cultural values, and regard any notion of intercultural dialogue with deep suspicion, while developing strong affection for African culture and privileging it as the essential basis of identity.

Thus, globalization and its implications have compelled Afrocentric essentialist scholars to invoke a countervailing racialized ideology for survival against what they perceive as the hegemonic character and implications of a European-dominated world order. The racial underpinnings and construction of the black struggle are problematic in the context of the global expansion of the boundaries of human encounters and the attendant shrinkage of traditional patterns of distinctiveness. Afrocentrists deem the global context problematic and troubling, especially as it impacts the utility of race as both weapon of struggle and framework for understanding reality. In their judgment, globalization has rendered blacks more susceptible to western and European hegemonic interests. To counteract this, they advocate strengthening and expanding the global parameters of the color line.

Although studies in the last decade and a half underscore the complexity of the African and black Diaspora historical and cultural experiences, Afrocentric scholars persist in essentializing African cosmology as the only legitimate and true basis of culture and identity for all blacks, and therefore the most effective weapon for survival against Eurocentric threat. In the Afrocentric genre, therefore, globalization is identified essentially as a disguised European imperialistic force, a postmodern metamorphosis of nineteenth-century imperialism. The difference, however, is that this new global imperialism has not assumed the blatantly racist arrogance and ideological and militaristic characters of the past. Instead, it is cleverly disguised as an internationalist, worldwide phenomenon that potentially could benefit all of humankind, by shrinking traditional parameters and patterns of differences, alienation, distinctiveness, and separation. Although Afrocentric essentialist consciousness had existed among blacks from the dawn of black American history, the projection of racial essentialism as a weapon of direct struggle and as a countervailing force against Eurocentric essentialism and influences is a product of the cultural nationalist slant of late-twentieth-century black nationalism. Though not all Afrocentric scholars espouse racial essentialism, the core values of Afrocentrism have inspired and nurtured racial essentialist consciousness and convictions (pan-blackism). The "pan-blackists," therefore, are also *gloracialists* who essentialize blackness as both a global unifying force and a formidable weapon of struggle against what they perceive and characterize as an equally unified, and racially constructed and culturally particularistic, European-dominated global order.

The origins of "pan-blackism," the ideological embodiment of *gloracialized* consciousness, can be traced to the early nineteenth century efforts by black leaders to use both slavery and racism as unifying constructs. The tradition became much more pronounced in the mid-nineteenth-century black nationalism and back-to-Africa schemes of Martin R. Delany, Henry H. Garnet, and others. Frustrated and alienated, these leaders gave up on integration, convinced that racism was deeply entrenched, invincible, and unconquerable. Martin Delany's writings in the 1850s underscored the global threat that white Americans and Europeans posed to blacks. His analysis of the global threat and black predicament derived from the dismal and gloomy domestic American realities.[9] These writings established Delany's enduring historical reputation as a racial essentialist. Marcus Garvey would develop this racial essentialism and global construction of the black struggle further in the 1920s.[10] This historical depth notwithstanding, Afrocentrism exemplifies modern amplification and global projection of racial essentialism. From its inception, Afrocentricity had relied for its appeal on the color line. Color occupies a central location in Afrocentric construction and analysis of the problems and challenges confronting blacks in Africa and the Diaspora. Afrocentric scholars advocate absolute adherence to the color line as the best guarantee of the physical and cultural survival of blacks in both the national and global contexts of white hegemony. In the last ten years, however, with the growth of globalization, and imminent shrinkage of traditional parameters of differentiation, Afrocentric scholars have become almost schizophrenic in their opposition to the cultural impact of globalization on the black experience.

Several scholars, including the late Chancellor Williams and John Henrik Clarke laid the groundwork for the cultural projection of a racialized Manichean global order. In his critically acclaimed study of how the West "destroyed Black Civilization," Williams urged the creation of a "race organization," which he described as "a nation-wide organization of Blacks only." He called on blacks to begin "building step by step, a race organization so great that it will not only be the voice of a united people but will carry on *efficiently* an economic development program to assist their advance on all fronts."[11] Molefi Asante is undoubtedly the leading modern philosophical advocate of this genre. His Afrocentric paradigm embodied the separatist vision in Williams's "organization." As already established, the paradigm within which Asante envisions the black struggle is unambiguously and essentially culturally constructed upon African historical and cosmological foundations. He calls for cultural vigilance and unity against an ever-threatening Eurocentric force. Based essentially on race and culture, such unity, Asante insists, was critical to black survival and eventual triumph in a world order still dominated by Europeans.[12]

In his own study, Haki Madhubuti underlines the ever-present threat of "white world supremacy" and the need for blacks to strive toward "total separation." He defines this "white world supremacy" as "the supremacy of whites worldwide *finally* and *undiluted*." Madhubuti enjoins blacks to limit contacts with whites in a social and cultural context and presents a litany of reasons. Primarily, whites have proven themselves to "be traditionally and historically enemies of black people." Looking toward the twenty-first century, he urges blacks to organize themselves "for a future not dependent on the concepts and visions of others who do not have our best interests in mind."[13] Thus, these Afrocentric scholars articulate a *gloracialized* and "pan-blackist" framework in response to their perception of a disguised global Eurocentric threat to black cultural survival. In their judgment, the emergence of globalization requires a countervailing racially constructed global force if blacks were to survive its cultural hegemonic essence.

Perhaps no other Afrocentric scholar has defended the paradigm and condemned the global hegemonic character of Eurocentrism as fervently and scathingly as Marimba Ani (aka Dona Marimba Richards), whose seminal publication *Yurugu* (1996) is a devastating critique and deconstruction of the hegemonic character of Eurocentric history and culture.[14] She is also one of the most powerful defenders of the absolutist construction of African identity for blacks in Africa and the Diaspora. Her study of identity deemphasizes the impact of New World transplantation and acculturation on black culture and identity. In her analysis, blacks retain their African essence and identity, centuries of transplantation in the New World notwithstanding.[15] In *Yurugu* she reaffirms a cardinal Afrocentric conviction: the inherent and absolute hegemonic character of Eurocentric culture. She calls for the "de-Europeanizing" of culture. This would render culture much more relevant to the political needs of blacks. Her book emphasizes the urgency of racial and cultural vigilance in a global context in which, she contends, blacks continue, more than ever before, to be threatened by Eurocentric values and cultural contacts.[16]

More than any other Afrocentric scholar, Ani underscores the global, or what she calls the international, character of the Eurocentric threat. In a rather tragic misrepresentation of European culture as monolithic, Ani discerns a unified and homogeneous European world order. According to her, Europeans are driven by the urge to dominate and fraudulently invoke "universalism" and "internationalism" as weapons for expansion into, and domination of, other societies. She warns blacks against embracing "internationalism" of any kind, particularly one spearheaded by and involving Europeans. Since European culture is inherently expansionistic and hegemonic, she urges black cultural unity and vigilance. In her analysis, two culturally monolithic worlds confront, and have always confronted, each other: African and Eurocentric, inherently and diametrically opposed. One, the white, represents the death and destruction of the other, black. "Europe," she writes, "is a culturally homogeneous" entity and thus threatening to blacks. She wants to dispel any illusions of cultural harmony. Culture, she insists, is ideological, political, and hegemonic. Furthermore, she argues, European culture is also "extremely cohesive and well-integrated" with a deceptive veneer of heterogeneity.[17] The world order, in Ani's perception, is an arena of perpetual cultural antagonism and conflict. Black survival is conceivable only in the context of perpetual opposition to, and vigilance against, and not in association with, Eurocentric values and influences.

Given the above convictions, Afrocentric scholars are deeply suspicious of a "global context"; especially one in which, as H. V. Perlmutter suggests, "multiple cultures are being syncretized in a complex way. The elements of particular cultures can be drawn from a global array, but they will mix and match differently in each setting."[18] It is precisely the "mixing" and "matching" that, according to Afrocentric scholars, could potentially destroy black cultural originality. The call for "pan-blackist" cultural vigilance and unity, and the projection of a monolithic African cultural world and identity, therefore, represent a response to the cultural implications of globalization. In the Afrocentric worldview, culture is an arena of irreconcilable conflict and antagonism between blacks and whites. Blacks are expected to maintain a respectable distance from, and vigilance against, white cultural contacts. In Afrocentricity, the notion of "cultural citizenship" suggests distinct antagonistic cultural zones, in perpetual conflict, with no grounds for discourses, exchanges, encounters, and influence. Instead of cultural understandings, Afrocentric cultural worldview underlines a world of cultural isolation, suspicion, and antagonism, one in which citizenship is defined not by cultural connectedness or attempts to discover such connections, but by cultural disharmony and disengagement, foreclosing dialogue and communication across cultural spaces. It becomes imperative, therefore, for Africans and blacks in Diaspora to maintain cultural vigilance. This posture undermines intercultural communication and dialogue. In the judgment of Afrocentric scholars, therefore, globalization represents internationalization of the domestic American cultural war. The probability of a global cultural citizenship deepens Afrocentric distrust of Eurocentric culture. Such citizenry is emblematic of European hegemony and, therefore, inimical to black interests.

Afrocentricity is, therefore, vehemently anti-globalization, preferring an isolationist posture for blacks. Advocates emphasize race, ethnicity, and a monolithic black identity. Afrocentric response to globalization betrays paranoia and provincialism. Afrocentric scholars are convinced that embracing globalization would jeopardize and compromise black cultural distinctiveness and lure blacks into a false sense of security, while subjecting them to European cultural hegemony. This is logical because, in the Afrocentric worldview, the global context is an expanded terrain of the racial and cultural war.[19] Globalization is thus a euphemism for Eurocentric hegemony. Survival for blacks in the context of this overarching global hegemony mandates the adoption of separate and isolationist disposition. As Asante elaborates in a recent publication, "Eurocentrism in its most extreme form has generated an entire cacophony of voices that have been arrayed against the best interests of international cooperation and mutuality. It has generated a view toward the world of domination, hegemony, and control. Every aspect of the gross Eurocentrism seems articulated toward this end, ultimately the subverting of international relationships."[20]

Although he acknowledges that "all people of Europe are not racists and imperialists," Asante insists that "it is very difficult for Europeans to escape the conditions of their historical realities. They are like passengers on a giant balloon that contains a captain who is intent on destruction." Given this construction of Europe, Asante concludes, "So let me hasten to say that, for Africa, Europe is dangerous; it is five hundred years of danger for Africans—and I am not talking of physical or ecological danger (although that history is severe enough), but psychological and cultural danger. One knows, I surmise, that a people's soul is dead when it can no longer breathe its own philosophical air and when the air of another culture seems to dominate every aspect of conscious life."[21]

In opposition to the intercultural implications of globalization, Afrocentric scholars advocate racial distinctiveness, a distinctiveness preserved through a strict observance of the color line on a global scale, in which blacks, regardless of sociopolitical experiences and geographical locations are drawn together to forge a strong global united *gloracialized* front. Of course, the emblematic factor besides

race is culture—the assertion that blacks in Diaspora are culturally African. Though some Afrocentrists deemphasize *race* as an identitarian
construct, due to its problematic character, they embrace and highlight *culture*, arguing essentially that centuries of transplantation had
not fundamentally altered the original African culture. This cultural
*continuum* therefore constitutes the basis of unity between Africans
and peoples of African descent in the Diaspora who are threatened by
European global domination. Both should expect nothing but cultural
annihilation from any transcultural engagement on the global arena.
But then, culture is as confining and restrictive as race in defining a
monolithic identity for all blacks. In other words, the cultural paradigm within Afrocentricity is as confining and restrictive as the racial
one. The cultural line depicts African cultural experience as a unique,
distinct, and original experience that is threatened by Eurocentric
cultural influence. It becomes imperative, therefore, for Africans and
blacks in Diaspora to maintain cultural antagonism and vigilance. The
cultural line consequently erodes any grounds for intercultural communication and dialogue. The configuration of the cultural line emphasizes the enduring character of Eurocentric cultural threat. The
spectre of a global cultural citizenship deepens Afrocentric distrust of
Eurocentric culture.

## Transformative and Neo-Afrocentricity

In the last decade and half, a historiographical movement within African American studies has developed that acknowledges the global
imperative and attempts to move black Americans away from an isola-
tive paradigm to one that could potentially facilitate coming to terms
with globalization. While the appeal of Afrocentricity remains strong
within the general black population, it is waning among intellectual
elites in institutions of higher education. Emerging counter-Afrocen-
tric and neo-Afrocentric studies in the last decade underscore the
complexity of the African and black Diaspora experiences, eroding
the force of the racial and cultural lines.[22] This transformational paradigm, as some scholars characterize it, is associated with the bour-
geoning black Atlantic or black Diaspora perspective. This approach
acknowledges the complexity of the black Diaspora experience, arguing that a monolithic, racialized, and conflict-driven paradigm could
not adequately represent the gamut of the African and black Diaspora
experiences.[23]

There is also a growing awareness of the social character of human beings and the need to accommodate cross-cultural communication, engagement, and dialogue. Recent studies present a much more interactive and complex view of historical encounters, defined by harmony as well as conflict—encounters within and between ecological, geo-political, and historical spaces that engender both distinctiveness and shared attributes. Such views inspire a growing awareness of the greater connectedness of human beings, transcending traditional boundaries of race, ethnicity, and culture. The language of communication is no longer defined by distinct historical and national experiences, but by transnational experiences and cross-cultural encounters and exchanges. In Rebecca Martusewicz's view, "Human beings are fundamentally social creatures. We come together from unique places and histories . . . As we enter into social relations, into a socially and discursively organized world or culture; we are shaped and modelled by it. The meanings, beliefs, and structures that pre-exist us have been made historically by just such engagement . . . Our understanding of ourselves and of the community and the larger world is shaped by this relational context of meaning and the ways that it is exchanged or imposed."[24] Essentially, Martusewicz underscores an interactive and intersubjective relational system. In other words, the human historical experience is, to a far greater degree, shaped by cultural encounters and exchanges than many are willing to acknowledge. This position is particularly problematic for black Americans of the Afrocentric persuasion, whose worldview is defined by antagonism, and for whom culture is a weapon of perpetual conflict.

The emerging transformational historiography challenges Afrocentric homogenization. The historiography is spearheaded by scholars who also acknowledge the centrality of the African heritage while depicting the black Diaspora as a world of profound transformations, of complex and conflicting experiences and reactions. Consequently, instead of a monolithic black Diaspora world, the transformative paradigm acknowledges spheres of complex, conflicting, and at times overlapping Diaspora experiences, at the same time underscoring the inherent shortcoming of the traditional practice of isolating the black Diaspora experience into distinct national and geographical zones—North America, South, Central and Latin America, Europe, Asia, Africa, and the Caribbean. They offer a macro-Atlantic-and-Diaspora framework as a more effective theoretical model for highlighting shared attributes and discovering distinctiveness and complexities.[25]

This new paradigm has other far-reaching implications, perhaps the most revolutionary of which is the deconstruction of the prevailing monolithic construction of African and black Diaspora history and culture. But perhaps most telling is the deessentializing of racialized and monolithic perspectives. As Dwayne Williams urges, we need "to acknowledge that there is no one idea of 'blackness' or 'African' which could or should control how the histories of the peoples of African descent are studied . . . It is impossible to fully capture the complex and varied histories of African people with any one definition of Blackness/African identity."[26]

This perspective represents a move away from distinctiveness toward transformation, from narrow cultural provincialism to cosmopolitanism, revealing a complex black Diaspora world that invalidates monolithic constructs of history and identity. The transformational model for global dynamics facilitates the recognition of historical discourses, interactions, and exchanges, making it difficult to posit a distinct, separatist, and isolationist construction of identity. Rather, it locates identity within a wider context of global interaction that reflects shared attributes and differences for all, including blacks, thus underscoring the complexities of African and black Diaspora history and culture.

Although critical of Afrocentricity, the postmodernist transformational paradigm affirms the imperative of validating the historical heritage of Africa and blacks while at the same time acknowledging the transformative and complex character of the transplantation experience. According to Earl Lewis, this entails historicizing "the processes of racial formation and identity construction. Race . . . is viewed as historically contingent and relational, with full understanding of that process dependent on our abilities to see African Americans living and working in a world of overlapping diasporas (dispersed communities)."[27] It is thus powerfully driven by racial transcendentalism. It deessentializes race, suggesting the necessity of deconstructing and jettisoning prevailing racialized constructions of reality. This transformative paradigm, according to Stuart Hall, "is defined not by essence or purity, but by the recognition of necessary heterogeneity and diversity; by a conception of 'identity,' which lives with and through, not despite, difference; by hybridity. Diaspora identities are those which are constantly producing and reproducing themselves anew, through transformation and difference."[28]

Jack Greene argues that the transformational approach emphasizes "the flow and mixture of peoples and cultures and implied a process of social and cultural formation that, far from being imposed from the top-down, derived from a continuing process of negotiation or exchange among the various peoples and cultures involved."[29] Perhaps the most revolutionary implication of this historiography is its paradigmatic shift and reformulation, replacing the nation-state with the much broader Atlantic or Diaspora construct as the more substantive framework for analyzing the black experience. Like Afrocentricity, this captures and highlights shared negative historical experiences (slavery, colonialism, racism); however, unlike the combative Afrocentric paradigm, it acknowledges experiential variations and complexities, and situates Africa among other contending historical and cultural factors in the construction of black Diaspora identity. The emphasis here is on the growing complexity of the Diaspora. It is no longer just in the United States, Latin America, Europe, and the Caribbean. It is imperative that we begin to interrogate the complexity of the black experience even within these regions. The experiences of blacks in Germany cannot be deemed identical to those of blacks in Scandinavia, Austria, Russia, France, Australia, the Middle East, and Asia. In fact, more recent studies of the Diaspora point toward an even broader conceptualization beyond the tradition homogeneity-heterogeneity discourse. The paradigm shift is toward micro-analytical case studies that investigate new forms of Diasporas within and without Africa, Diasporas that grew out of what Leif Manger and Munzoul A. M. Assal describe as "the decay in the contemporary African post-colonial state."[30] These case studies focus on Eritrean refugees in Germany, southern Sudanese in the United States, and Somali and Sudanese refugees in Norway, among many others.[31] The global black landscape is complex and multilayered, the product of what Ruth Hamilton and others call "proliferations of departures across time and space, conditioned by, and within, a changing global culture and political economy." Undoubtedly, there are shared experiences relating to "persistence of oppression, racialization, prejudice and discrimination, political disenfranchisement, and hostile social environment." But, as Ruth Hamilton and others insist, "Such *continuity* should not be interpreted to mean *fixed*. Collective identities are contested, negotiated, conflictual and dynamic. They are paradoxical and contradictory, generating internal 'differences...' Thus we deliberately use terms such as social identities, social identity formation, and social identifications to emphasize that the significance and meaning of group membership are ongoing, and transient, relational to others and therefore comparative."[32]

The black Diaspora is neither monolithic nor culturally isolated and distinct. Afrocentric construction of an isolationist black world is inherently contradictory. The construction of a distinct community "We" is itself a relational construct. "We" cannot exist without "They." As Ruth Hamilton underscores, "Even the extent to which the mobilized actions of a people can be conceptualized as 'acts for itself' implies a contradiction: people stand (act) in opposition to the forces that have conditioned their existential reality and material circumstances . . . At the general and specific levels of African Diaspora formation, there is variation by geographical location, by generations, by material and institutional conditions, and by socio-economic and demographic patterns."[33] Underlining the situational and contextual underpinnings of identity and culture, Anthony Smith writes, "The obstinate fact is that national cultures, like all cultures before the modern epoch, are *particular, timebound* and *expressive*, and their eclecticism operates within strict cultural constraints." Furthermore, he continues, "The concept of 'identity' . . . implies the subjective feelings and valuations of any population which possesses common experiences and one or more shared cultural characteristics (usually customs, language or religion). These feelings and values refer to three components of their shared experience: 1. a sense of continuity between the experiences of succeeding generations of the unit of population; 2. shared memories of specific events and personages which have been turning-points of a collective history; and 3. a sense of common destiny." Afrocentric essentialist scholars ignore these critical cultural and experiential criteria in their attempts to construct a uniform and monolithic black world. A major challenge "in any project to construct a global identity and hence a global culture," Smith contends, "is that collective identity, like imagery and culture, is always historically specific because it is based on shared memories and a sense of continuity between generations."[34] This generational continuity should not be construed in isolation from the broader human experiences. It does not, and should not be construed to, privilege isolation, cultural purity, and specificity. Afrocentric essentialism is an attempt to build a transnational identity within a fundamentally flawed, ill-defined, ill-conceived, and problematic context. In the context of globalization, transnational identities have to come to terms with, embrace, and accommodate multiple, multifaceted, and complex experiences that may not necessarily be culturally compatible. Thus, an Afrocentric essentialist attempt to construct an isolationist black world is inherently problematic and dysfunctional. Blacks could never exist in isolation, however strong the bond of "shared memories and . . . continuity" and however strong their "oppositional consciousness."

The second critical challenge, neo-Afrocentricity, is internal to the Afrocentric paradigm and developed from efforts by Afrocentric scholars to respond to some of its critics by broadening its appeal. Among the most innovative studies is C. Tsehloane Keto's *Vision, Identity and Time: The Afrocentric Paradigm and the Study of the Past* (1995). In this revisionist study, Keto, a onetime member of the Temple School of Afrocentricity, proposes a framework that acknowledges the interactive and contributory character of the human experience instead of the traditional Afrocentric conflict theory. He envisions a truly global and "multi-centred" perspective that allows for greater intercultural discourses on a non-hegemonic basis. He represents his paradigm as "a constituent aspect of a global intellectual movement of liberation and a step toward the creation of a 'multi-centred' and diversity affirming perspective for all the peoples of the world of the future." This would allow for greater engagement since it would accommodate all perspectives (including African, European) without privileging any. Underlining the global imperative of his perspective, Keto writes:

> The African Centred perspective which is an outcome of the Afrocentric paradigm is a vital **contributor** to a holistic approach in the study of the world and its heterogeneous peoples. An African centred perspective should not be confused with an apologia, or a chauvinist posture tied to an exclusivist principle that encourages analytical dichotomy of studying "them" versus studying "us." Properly applied, the African centred perspective liberates all minds and sets an important **foundation** for a global perspective that does not peripheralize the peoples of Africa, of Europe, of Asia, of the Americas or of the Pacific.[35]

Keto proposes a nonhegemonic point of intersection of heterogeneous experiences and paradigms. This paradigm represents not just one hegemonic cultural group but the intersection of many groups of equal importance, each contributing to, and participating in, a common pool or tradition of historical encounters.[36] This framework therefore enables Afrocentric and other culturally centered experiences to come together in a context that acknowledges contributions, differences, distinctiveness, as well as commonalities. It shifts Afrocentricity away from separatist and oppositional to interactive and relational conceptions of culture and identity. This shift has the potential to facilitate intercultural dialogue, a process that enhances mutual awareness of, and appreciation for, the wealth, diversity, and complexity of the human experience.

Although a modest beginning, his paradigm is significant nonetheless in recognizing the interactive and contributory character of the human experience. Keto's reformulation is based on the recognition that no one group or perspective can claim cultural distinction and preeminence but that all contribute to enriching a common pool of culture and knowledge. This reformulation, without compromising the African-centeredness, also opens up the possibility of developing a paradigm that would command respect and recognition across racial and cultural and ethnic lines. As he explains,

> An Afrocentric paradigm therefore asserts itself in the study and reconstruction of the past in two ways. First, it establishes the continent of Africa as the primary historical core area or center on which to build narrative about, and to undertake the analysis of, the experiences of peoples of African descent in Africa itself, Eurasia, the Americas and elsewhere . . . At a more inclusive dimension, the African centered perspective that emerges from the Afrocentric paradigms seeks to interpret and understand global events by infusing into the "recognized" conventional guidelines extrapolated from the experience of the "East" (Asia) and that of the "West" (Europe), those additional ingredients whose history is traceable, in part or in whole, to the African experience.[37]

Thus, Keto advances Afrocentricity as "a vital *contributor* to a holistic approach in the study of the world and its heterogeneous people." This suggests some compatibility with the emerging global order. According to him, "The concern about the humanity of all people is (or should be) an essential value element in the cosmovision that undergirds an African centered perspective. The historical pain of oppression should not blind anyone to the central principle of respect for all humanity as a guide to theories of interpersonal relations and the study of the human past."[38]

Keto's framework facilitates the kind of cross-cultural or intercultural discourse that some scholars advocate. For example, in a keynote address at an international conference on "Cultural Citizenship and the Challenges of Globalization" in Melbourne, Australia, in 2002, Inta Allegritti suggested interculturalism as the more appropriate representative paradigm for a postliberal construction of cultural citizenship in the context of globalization. She envisions interculturalism as a pedagogy that mediates between, and facilitates discourses across, cultures. The intercultural perspective, as defined by Allegritti, constructs humans as members of cultures that interact and overlap, thus facilitating, she contends, transcendence of inherited and imposed cultural boundaries, instead of isolation in distinct homogeneous cultural zones. It emphasizes inclusion and recognizes cultural differences, while inculcating a sense of belonging. This encourages, according to Allegritti, "the ethical challenge of living with others."[39]

If Afrocentricity is indeed compatible with globalization, as Keto's study seems to imply, and could be reformulated to align with other perspectives, a major obstacle is cleared for a more representative and truly multifaceted paradigm that mirrors the interactive, complex, and complementary character of the new global reality. The human historical drama entails encounters, cultural exchanges, and transformations. A viable and productive pedagogy is one that reflects this multilevel process and educates people to identify with this larger and broader human family and experience, manifesting greater knowledge of and appreciation for each other's unique roles and contributions. Keto's reformulation of Afrocentricity is a step in this direction.

The attempt to construct a monolithic racial and cultural identity for all blacks regardless of historical contexts and experiences has thus far failed, underscoring the difficulty of homogenizing complex historical and cultural consciousness and experiences. What makes the notion of a monolithic and uniform African and black Diaspora culture problematic is the failure to acknowledge the complexity of this experience and culture. There is a globalizing trend within black experience. Regardless of what Afrocentric essentialists say or wish, there is a divide, an economic and class divide, among blacks, leading some to embrace and become immersed in the global economic force that many others see as threatening to blacks. The Afrocentric projection of cultural uniformity and the construction of battle lines at the cultural level entail inherent contradictions. As William Ackah suggests in his revisionist study, such monolithic construction ignores the growing cosmopolitanism and internationalism of black American culture. This culture, he argues, is intimately tied to, and reflective of, the broader American culture, which nourishes and fosters its growth and development. Ackah refers specifically to the arenas of sports, entertainment, economics, and popular culture. Black American athletes, entertainers, and comedians now exercise considerable cultural, social, and economic influences abroad, transforming, and even obliterating, indigenous cultural institutions and values in black communities across Africa and the Caribbean. He refers to this phenomenon as "Pan-African-Americanism." This force is essentially commercial in character and orientation, and, like its parent American capitalist culture, on whose wings it is transported, it is hegemonic, and its ultimate impact on black societies and cultures in Africa and the Caribbean is exploitative and destructive.[40]

Thus "Pan-African Americanism" exemplifies a shift, "wherein African American culture (assumes) a prominence in relation to other black cultures globally." Ackah refers specifically to Africa and the English-speaking Caribbean, where African American arts, music, dance, drama, and sports figures are imported through the media of satellite and television. Bill Cosby, Michael Jackson, Michael Jordan, and Oprah Winfrey have become iconic household names in these societies and are used to sell and promote a range of products and cultural artefacts that have "no positive impact on these societies." This spread of African American culture has "unforeseen and negative consequences in relation to the range of diversity of African derived cultural influences globally."[41] Indigenous arts, music, drama, and sports give way and lose ground to the models represented and promoted by black Americans. It is ironic, therefore, that while Afrocentric scholars would have us believe that there is a uniform black American culture in opposition to American and Eurocentric culture, a variant of that culture (that is, black American) is actually intimately tied to the apron string of mainstream American culture.

The invocation of the aesthetics of black and African culture to build a monolithic anti-establishment black culture ignores what could rightly be characterized as the "moral economy" of black culture—a potent force as Ackah describes it in his study. He demonstrates how difficult it is to isolate black culture from the broader capitalist dynamics of American society and culture. He thus underlines a dimension to black American culture that ties it intimately to mainstream American culture. This dimension is cosmopolitan in orientation and intertwined with the global economic and political fortunes of the United States. It seems contradictory for Afrocentric scholars to affirm black cultural distinctiveness and alienation while that same black culture manifests the essential defining character of mainstream American culture.

The notion of cultural citizenship is central to Afrocentricity. The unique and distinct character of African culture and its survival in the New World give blacks an equally unique and distinct cultural identity. The alienation of blacks from mainstream America reinforces this cultural distinction, a distinction that was soon extended beyond the boundaries of the United States. They construct a racially and culturally antagonistic Afrocentric citizenry with a pathological disdain for Eurocentric values. Afrocentricity envisions the black American as a cultural citizen but one who is not socialized to embrace the expanded, transnational, and transcultural context of globalization. He or she is an Afrocentric cultural citizen who perceives European culture as monolithic, driven by the single goal of black subordination. The rebuilding and preservation of black culture is therefore conceivable only in the context of isolation from the threatening Eurocentric influence. Afrocentric scholars reject the interpretation of black culture as reflective of the larger American experience. The implication is that blacks in America went through centuries of transplantation with their original African identity and culture intact. The revisionist perspective proposed by Keto suggests a shift toward a more inclusive construction of the human experience. In this paradigm, the Afrocentric is no longer a distinctive, isolated perspective but part of a complex conglomeration of perspectives and experiences, which acknowledges interactions, exchanges, and influences.

Globalization is, however, threatening to circumscribe and render superfluous the underlying considerations for Afrocentric essentialism. On the expanded terrain of global encounters, cultural contacts become fundamental in ordering human affairs. Culture has become the playing field of human relations. Afrocentric essentialists are apprehensive of the homogenizing prospects of globalization. Cultural homogeneity, they fear, would erode and possibly obliterate black distinctiveness. In my judgment, this concern is overblown. Whether or not globalization results in cultural citizenship upstaging national citizenship is debatable. Cultural citizenship is certainly a possibility. Cultural homogeneity, on the other hand, seems far-fetched. What globalization portends is a broadening of the spatial boundaries of intercultural, cross-cultural, or transcultural discourses and engagements. This is precisely the kind of scenario that, according to H. V. Perlmutter, multiple cultures would mix and match.[42] There is no doubt, however, that as the arena of human encounter expands beyond the restrictive boundaries of the nation-state, culture would play a major role in shaping and defining peoples' interactions and constructions of identity. The notion of cultural citizenship denotes possibilities beyond the geographical delineation of the nation-state—a transnational landscape, and a transnational citizenry that is familiar with, able to engage, and comfortable with complex and multiple cultural experiences. Citizens of this transnational landscape would, one hopes, be able to engage in transcultural dialogue within and across national boundaries. They would imbibe what Allegritti describes as "the ethical challenge of living with others."[43] Within the Afrocentric worldview, however, this transnational and transcultural landscape is greeted with deep and abiding skepticism.

# Conclusion

The use of Africa by blacks in America to construct an essentialist ideological worldview is grounded in their historical experiences. It is a reflection of, and a legitimate response to, alienation. It is a historical and existential quest for validation in the context of objectification and negation. It resulted in the construction and affirmation of a countervailing monolithic protest identity. Unfortunately, the identity is one-dimensional and ahistorical and is more reflective of the alienation of blacks in America than a true representation of the historical process. That black Americans are of African ancestry is undeniable; however, that they remain essentially *African* despite centuries of separation from Africa is historically flawed. Defenders of Afrocentric essentialism are reluctant to acknowledge this fact, largely because it accents the historical essence and cultural relevance of the American experience. In the Afrocentric essentialist worldview, the American context is considered fundamentally inconsequential to the making of black America. Yet, the centralization of Africa notwithstanding, its role and functions, as this study has shown, have historically been essentially utilitarian.

Afrocentric essentialism constructs black American relations with Africa within a monolithic, one-dimensional framework that underscores underlying mutuality and shared values. Drawn together by the exigencies of history, continental Africans and black Americans became unified by an existential ethos of shared racial and "ethnic" identity and experiences. These unifying experiential factors are grounded in alienation and white hegemony and thus mandate a relationship characterized by monolithic and homogeneous values and idiosyncrasies. Yet, despite this mutuality and homogeneity, the historical relationship has largely been defined by paternalism and utilitarianism, a reflection of the racist and hegemonic character of black American acculturation. Furthermore, Afrocentric emphasis on the African identity accents only a dimension of a complex identity. As Du Bois rightly underscored, New World acculturation resulted in a new and complex personality and identity that included the American. By denying or deemphasizing the significance of black American metropolitan, New World acculturation, Afrocentric essentialism presents blacks with a grossly distorted construction of the self, history, and experience that problematizes and further complicates the crisis of identity. Consequently, the decision by Afrocentric scholars to validate and privilege the African identity mirrors their frustrations and alienation. More important, it satisfies the need for existential validation. The late Amos Wilson unabashedly established this utilitarian construction of African identity. For Wilson, being African was empowering. It was the utmost expression and manifestation of counter-hegemonic disposition. Few Afrocentric scholars are willing to go this far in boldly acknowledging this cynical character of the utilitarian nature of African identity. Wilson was unambiguous that *feeling*, and *being*, African exemplified rebellious disposition and validated one's essence as a countercultural and counterestablishment character.

The global "Pan-African" projection of Afrocentric essentialism reflects nostalgia for a tradition that once had relevance at a critical historical moment—from the early to the mid-twentieth century when Africans and blacks in Diaspora struggled against vestiges of colonialism, imperialism, and racism. They were drawn together and galvanized by this global, trans-Atlantic experiential linkage. Race was a critical unifying element largely because the enemy was identifiable in racial terms—whites/Europeans. Whether in Africa, North America, or the Caribbean, blacks shared common challenges of racism, segregation, and imperial domination. But that was then. Modern-day calls for reactivating Pan-Africanism and the many summit meetings held are only symbolic and could never evolve into a truly Pan-African relationship. Advocates of reactivating Pan-Africanism fail to take into consideration historical developments over the last sixty years. The unifying experiential factors have become too complex. The geographical boundaries of imperialism and racism are no longer just "external" and racially exclusive. The challenges are now *within* Africa, *within* black America, and *within* black Diaspora. In other words, the racist and imperial enemy or challenge is no longer just the old, hegemonic white and European enemy. For Africa, it is also the indigenous enemy within. For black Americans, it is the internal complexities and conflicted constructions of America, as well as conflicted responses to Africa. For the entire black Diaspora, it is the growing globalization and complexity of the Diaspora context and experiences. Any call to revive Pan-Africanism that does not take these critical dimensions into consideration is futile. Pan-Africanism has to deal with the complex, complicated, and conflicted nature of the African, black American, and black Diaspora experiences and contexts.

Throughout black history, Africa played and assumed multiple roles and functions. At times, blacks found Africa fascinating and endearing. At other times, they resented Africa and wanted very little to do with the continent and her peoples. But most important, the roles and functions black Americans assigned to Africa have largely been utilitarian: Africa was the instrumentality for realizing equality and freedom in America. Contrary to contemporary Afrocentric essentialist claims, black American did not always view Africa positively. Unifying and shared ethos of mutuality did not always exist. The bond and the relationship had not always been close-knit and positive. Black American understanding of, and relation to, Africa had often been determined and driven by the values they had imbibed in their socialization in the New World. Their conceptions of Africa shaped their construction of identity, and the debate on identity itself reveals how profoundly their New World experiences had impacted their vision of Africa. Furthermore, Africa was not the only significant historical "other" for blacks in Diaspora. Both the moral suasion and emigration phases clearly show that although blacks harbored deep and complex consciousness of identity, they reflected an underlying desire and quest to belong and be identified not necessarily to and with Africa but culturally and politically with the United States. In the moral suasion epoch, being "colored" and of African ancestry was a unifying experiential and existential factor. Acknowledging African ancestry was a historical fact that did not always invoke endearing emotions and consciousness. Moral suasion was more about how to actualize fully the American identity. For those who emphasized race, being "colored" suggested not necessarily positive affirmation of African identity but a means of galvanizing the struggle toward becoming fully American. The mid-nineteenth-century emigration/nationalism phase was unambiguous in its rhetorical affirmation of the African nationality imperative. Yet this "African consciousness" illuminated a deeply felt desire for American identity. Africa was a utilitarian tool for actualizing this most cherished of identities. Delany, Turner, Garnet, and Crummell did not embrace Africa with the intention of becoming fully immersed in African culture, and fully assuming African identity, but positioned themselves as exemplars of what Africa was not and could and ought to be—polished, civilized. They envisioned themselves in close proximity to the metropolitan culture from which they had been alienated. Tom Mboya provided this apt summation of the utilitarian character of the Africanist consciousness of black Diaspora nationalism:

> There is a reason for this movement which has far less to do with the Negro's relations to Africa than to America. The "Back to Africa" and separatist tendencies are always strongest at the very time when the Negro is most intensely dissatisfied with his lot in America. It is when the Negro has lost hope in America—and has lost his identity as an American—that he seeks to re-establish his identity and his roots as an African . . . The combination of progress, aroused hopes, frustration and despair has caused many Negroes to withdraw into separatism and to yearn for Africa.[1]

The construction of Afrocentric essentialist ethos today rests on a deliberate refusal to confront the complexities and paradoxes of African, black American, and black Diaspora history and relations. The reality is that Afrocentric scholars use race and ethnicity (Africanness) to construct a problematic, countervailing, and counterhegemonic world. But, as Debra Dickerson suggests, it is time to come out of this restrictive world of "blackness" and embrace the challenges and complexities of modernity. Afrocentric essentialism nourishes a constraining, conspiratorial conception of reality that imprisons blacks behind a wall of "blackness," a racialized order whose foundation is becoming increasingly porous and fragile. There are profound and compelling considerations for constructing black history not as an isolated stream, a narrow stream that flows in one direction, but as part of a larger ocean fed by numerous tributaries. For blacks to transcend the narrow and suffocating confines of Afrocentric essentialism requires a willingness to confront the complexities of the black experience, especially in relation to both Africa and the black Diaspora. In other words, there is need for critical interrogation of the ethos of mutuality. As Laduna Anise contends, "'the ultimate expression of collective identity,' the claim that 'all black people are African' . . . fails to consider the impact of socialization in different geographical settings. Collective black identity does not mean all blacks everywhere share the same values, goals and destinies. All may share in the struggle for liberation and freedom, but the content of these are most likely to vary from one social system to another. Black peoples of the world live in different planes of consciousness as well as environmental and existential necessities."[2] This does not absolutely nullify the notion of mutuality. There is no doubt that Africans and Diaspora blacks share a collective identity based on race and ancestry; however, the intervention of history has significantly altered this reality. This intervention and attendant cultural transformations underline profound discontinuities that mandate a qualified affirmation of collective identity. From the nineteenth century to the present, as this study has demonstrated, black Americans who have been drawn physically to Africa by the lure of racial identity have often quickly confronted the reality of cultural divergence and distance.

In the second half of the twentieth century, black American nationalism became, according to some critics, hyperpoliticized.[3] This hyperpoliticization underscores a deepening of the state of black alienation in consequence of the upsurge of right-wing conservative onslaughts on the gains of the civil rights movement. The growth of the "prison industrial complex," the crisis of black impoverishment and marginalization, and the ever-widening gap between the American Dream and black American aspirations, all contribute to the engine dynamo of hyperpoliticization, which is reflected in hip-hop, gangster rap, and other countercultural expressions of black popular culture. Nowhere is this state of hyperpoliticization more evident and pronounced than in the development and advancement of Afrocentric essentialism as the ideological expression and representation of both alienation from America and a defiant affirmation of a countervailing worldview. At critical moments in American history, black nationalist consciousness had developed around essentialist ethos of race, ethnicity, or culture. Regardless of which ethos assumed dominance, Africa was the nucleus. Blackness, ethnicity, and culture all derived from the African heritage. From Martin Delany through Marcus Garvey down to Malcolm X, Stokely Carmichael, Molefi Asante, and Maulana Karenga, Africa was the centerpiece of response to what some characterize as "American Apartheid." Although the centrality of Africa is widely acknowledged, the essentially utilitarian and problematic nature and implications of Africa's location is not.

In an age when many are amplifying the complex and multidimensional character of black and African history and experiences, Afrocentric essentialists advance and defend an isolated ahistorism that both misrepresents and overtly simplifies the complex history and experiences of both peoples. Emphasis on identity politics in Afrocentric essentialism reflects the state of alienation of blacks from the American socioeconomic and political realities. This condition became particularly pronounced under the Reagan-Bush counter-civil-rights initiatives of the 1980s and 1990s, coupled with onslaughts of ultra-conservative, right-wing Republicans on Affirmative Action and other social policies that benefit blacks. Despite the vigor with which Afrocentric scholars defend the African identity, the fact remains that it is more of a protest identity for the vast majority who embrace it. It functions more as a utilitarian weapon of resistance and not necessarily an expression of genuine desire to become fully African.

As contended in this study, the identity debate and crisis among black Americans is historically rooted in the emergence of organized black abolitionism in the early nineteenth century. Despite the claims of defenders of Afrocentric essentialism, the focus of the identity search has remained consistent through the ages. From the moral suasion beginning, to the Thirteenth Amendment that abolished slavery, through the Fourteenth that conferred citizenship on blacks and promised them equal protection of the law, to the gains of the twentieth-century civil rights movement (particularly the Voting and Civil Rights Acts), blacks have consistently affirmed preference for the American identity.

The question "Who are we?" remains unresolved, and precisely because of its seemingly problematic character, opinions remain sharply divided among black Americans. Racism and other manifestations of anti-black consciousness and policies have helped to make the identity problem even more contentious. This not withstanding, the record does show a utilitarian construction of Africa. Although blacks manifested African consciousness from the dawn of enslavement, once they evolved organized structures and movement for concerted struggles, Africa's role became largely utilitarian. Even the New York "radicals" of the moral suasion epoch did not wholly embrace Africa. They chose instead to adopt race/color as a medium both of protest and of facilitating the goal of integration—American citizenship. It was only *after* the failure of moral suasion that some blacks adopted Africa and pushed vigorously for an African nationality and identity. But, as this study has demonstrated, even this adoption was not total. It was purely utilitarian—the adoption of an African identity as a "protest identity" to underscore the frustrations of blacks with the elusive character of American citizenship.

Black Americans have not passionately and consistently embraced the African identity. What they cherished the most was the American identity. The nullification of the Euro-American cultural influence suggested by Afrocentric essentialist epistemology is not corroborated by the historical records. Though nineteenth-century black nationalists articulated and manifested the Du Boisean duality complex, their preferred and cherished identity was unambiguously Euro-American. History underscores a much more complex and ambivalent response to Africa. At the point of alienation, some blacks embraced Africa, manifesting "Afrocentric consciousness." Slavocentrism, on the other hand, assumed dominance among the hopefuls, those who had cause to be optimistic. These optimists proudly displayed Americentric consciousness of identity. Universalism, the espousal of neutralist conception of identity, represents an affirmation of affinity with, and subscription to, values that are supposedly universal and color-blind. Of the contending identity strands, "Afrocentrism" is the most frail and fragile, the least consistently defended and the most utilitarian, designed as a means of verbalizing protest against denial of the most desired and cherished of identities—American identity. It is therefore imperative to distinguish between embracing and advocating African identity as a reaction to alienation and marginalization, and an indirect cry for acceptance, on the one hand, and actually *desiring* to be African, on the other. Put differently, we need to distinguish between the *critical factor* in the black American quest for, and construction of, identity and the *incidental/utilitarian factor*. The former was undoubtedly the American; the latter was the African. The depth and historicity of the "African consciousness" and identity accented in Afrocentric epistemology is, therefore, misleading.

The nineteenth-century emigration phase shows that blacks acknowledged their African ancestry (affirmation of racial identity, that is, being black), while at the same time loudly and clearly exhibited preference for Euro-American cultural and national identity. The moral suasion phase was clearly dominated and influenced by strong integrationist aspirations and values. The underlying objective of moral suasion was the attainment of American citizenship. Consequently, the adoption of "color" (race) as a strategy by the likes of Samuel Cornish and Thomas Sidney did not suggest a total rejection or renunciation of American identity. Separatism was a strategic option designed to facilitate integration.

The advancement of African identity served more as a protest factor—a means of fighting back, of registering a protest against the denial of the desired American identity. As Laduna Anise suggests, we need to analyze black American identity within the discourse of alienation. Do black Americans really want to be African? Or is affirmation of African identity an expression of frustration and alienation? According to Anise, "It is not easy to escape the ambivalence of the black American. His experiences tend to compel him to disown the only land and culture he has known. And it is not certain that he really does not love America. It seems that it is his alienation from her he really hates."[4] It is precisely this alienation that elevated African identity to the utilitarian role it performs. Amos Wilson's declaration, noted earlier, is a clear acknowledgment of this utilitarian character of the African identity. It is therefore reasonable to suggest that all the identity strands identified in this study grew out of integrationist aspirations. Experience of rejection and marginalization induced alienation, compelling many blacks, rather reluctantly, to embrace the African identity and manifest colorphobic Afrocentric essentialist consciousness and disposition. On the other hand, blacks who felt optimistic and hopeful manifested integrationist aspirations and advanced the American identity. Regardless of the conflicting configurations of the identity consciousness, and regardless of the antagonistic positions of the Afrocentric essentialist school, one fact stands out: black American consciousness and constructions of identity have historically been conceived within an integrationist *weltanschauung*.

This interrogation of Afrocentric essentialism, especially the location and utility of Africa, should not be construed to suggest a complete negation or rejection of the claim of shared experiences and mutuality between Africa and blacks in Diaspora. There are indeed shared historical, social, and cultural experiences; however, as Ruth Hamilton underscores, "To recognize the existence of common and particular features does not imply cultural unity or the existence of only one culture of the black diaspora." It is imperative to accent those profound differences and complexities. The terrain of history is dynamic and complex, and participants experience complex and profoundly transforming experiences. Consequently, we need to adopt what Hamilton calls "a non-essentialist" view of the Diaspora, one that accents and acknowledges the contextual, situational, and historical specificities of identity and culture.[5] Few understood these "contextual and historical specificities" better than the late African revolutionary Amilcar Cabral. "The value of culture as an element of resistance," he once argued, "lies in the fact that culture is the vigorous manifestation, on the ideological or idealist level, of *the material and historical reality of the society that is dominated . . .* culture is simultaneously *the fruit of a people's history* and a determinant of history." Furthermore, Cabral emphasized, "Culture, as the fruit of history, reflects at all times the material and spiritual reality *of the society* . . . is a social reality independently of men's will" (emphasis added).[6] Cabral's conception of culture underlines complexity and relativism. The accenting and acknowledgment of the imperative of the historical and material specificities of Africa and black Diaspora are glaringly missing in Afrocentric attempts to construct a uniform global black world.

It is imperative to view Pan-Africanism as a dynamic construct that changes with time and space. At some point in the nineteenth and early twentieth centuries, Africans and blacks in Diaspora shared certain historical and cultural experiences that transcended geographical space and historical time and made constructing a Pan-African relationship and cooperation possible. This is no longer the case today. The historical contexts, the culture, economic, political, and social experiences of blacks in the Diaspora and Africans are too complex and even conflicting. Though there are shared vestiges of racism, Jim Crow, and neocolonialism, crucial divergent elements also exist. A successful revival of Pan-Africanism has to take these into consideration. On the subject of Pan-African and global black unity, Afrocentric essentialists confront two critical choices. The first choice—to acknowledge both the problematic, complex, and conflicted nature of Africa and the black Diaspora, and the fact that a revival and reactivation of Pan-Africanism under those circumstances seems improbable—mandates jettisoning an essentialist worldview. The second option is to ignore these realities and pretend that they do not exist, or that they are inconsequential, and thus continue to construct a Pan-African and global monolithic black world, as essentially a psychological and therapeutic feel-good-together philosophy.

The analysis in this study is not intended as a total nullification of the Pan-African and identity paradigms. Though it is difficult for a revamped Pan-African movement to materialize under present circumstances, the Pan-African spirit is presently kept alive by organizations such as PAMUSA and Randall Robinson's Washington, D.C.-based black lobbying group, TransAfrica. They testify to the fact that though a reactivation of the old tradition may presently seem inconceivable, organizations and individuals can still function to perpetuate Pan-African values and advance the interests of African and peoples of African descent abroad. This can continue while acknowledging the problematic of both the Pan-African and identity paradigms and working diligently to confront and deal with the myriad and complex manifestations.

The deconstruction of *race* has compelled some Afrocentric scholars to deemphasize the construct and reconsider its centrality in the black struggle. In the place of race, many now substitute *culture* as the key factor, the defining and unifying block for a Pan-African identity and consciousness. Instead of blackness, African culture became the essential defining and unifying element for the construction of a monolithic African and black Diaspora identity and platform of struggle. The implication is that centuries of transplantation had not changed or transformed the cultural heritage of blacks. The presumed indestructibility of African culture sustains an Afrocentric Manichean construction of reality and reinforces its combative, isolationist and separatist character. Given the importance of race in American history, it is not surprising that Afrocentric scholars advance a racial conception of the black experience. Yet race has thus far failed to unify all blacks, its preeminence in the black experience notwithstanding. The use of race as a unifying construct has thus far proven problematic and indefensible.

In both Africa and the black Diaspora, the black experience is much too complex to support homogeneous and monolithic constructions of identity and struggles. The Afrocentric essentialist worldview remains grounded theoretically and historically in a discourse of alienation that forecloses possibilities of engaging the complexities of the African and black Diaspora experiences. It is a response to alienation and hegemony. It seeks to impose a monolithic cultural and historical experiential paradigm on all blacks. The essential defining and unifying elements of Afrocentric essentialism—identity, race, culture, ethnicity—are all derived from Africa. Historically, Africa has served, and continues to function, as a utilitarian, counterhegemonic identifying construct. To be African, to claim and affirm African identity, has become an effective expression of protest against alienation and rejection in America; however, contrary to Afrocentric essentialist thinking, such disposition is not indicative of a desire to be fully African. Even those who claim to be African still must deal with the obvious and glaring contradictions and conflicts that their lived experiences in America embody. Furthermore, to be African is much more than just affirming it. There is a cultural dimension that is often not understood. The claim and affirmation of geographical identification (African American) has often been misconstrued to entail cultural identification. Black Americans share geographical identification through ancestral connection with Africans. Yet the black American is a composite and complex cultural amalgam of both Old and New World experiences. He is only *partially* African. Taban Lo Liyong's apt summation of the complexity of black identity is worth quoting at length:

> The Negro is a unique creature. He is of Africa; and yet not quite. He is of Europe; and yet not quite. He is of America; and yet not quite. But he combines these three disparate strands in his constitution. The confusion which ensues from this combination is the root of all his problems ... For, although African slaves were transported to America three or four hundred years ago, the moment they left the African coast, they were no longer African entirely. Europe, America and the sea determined their fates ... Hence the Negro is the joint product of Africa and Europe, in America. If he calls Africa "motherland," he must also call Europe "motherland"—or more appropriately, "fatherland." He has the right to be proud of the old African empires of Ghana and Songai [sic]. Equally, he must take pride in French civilization, in English empire, in German greatness, in the Spanish Golden Age, in classical Italy and classical Greece. Those are the homes of his other parents. Culturally, he is sub-American and extremely little African.[7]

Vehemently opposing a proposed plan of mass emigration of black Americans to Africa, Tom Mboya conceded to a Harlem audience in 1960 that Africans and black Americans do indeed share experiences and challenges. Both are engaged in a universal struggle for equality and human dignity. But he also drew attention to fundamental and profound differences. African nationalism sought integration, that is, the molding of diverse ethnic groups into national entities. As he told the audience, "just as the African must reconcile the differences between his tribal and his national identity, so too must the black American realize to the fullest extent his potential as a black man and as an American." In his view, the tension and conflict within black America between racial and national identities (that is, between Black Nationalism and American nationalism) has induced blacks to adopt a racialized view of reality that turned them toward Africa. Thus, their desire to identify with Africa was primarily racial and therefore unrealistic, since their identity is much more complex. They simply could not escape the American heritage. Identifying with Africa on the basis of race would not actualize the freedom they seek. As he emphasized, freedom should not be seen "as an act of withdrawal" but as "a major step in asserting the rights of black people and their place as equals among nations and peoples of the world." He urged the black American to "merge his blackness with his citizenship as an American, and the result will be dignity and liberation."[8]

The distinction Du Bois made between the Self (Negro) and the Other (America) is a more accurate reflection of the reality, and blacks must take seriously the Du Boisean admonition not to privilege one identity over the other but to seek the *disruption* of the Self-Other binary through merging of the Negro and the American. The ideal is for the "Self" and the "Other," "the two warring ideals," to merge and attain "self-conscious manhood," with neither sacrificing its essential character. Africa can continue to serve utilitarian and protest functions; however, this neither constitutes nor validates claims of cultural affinity and identity. Identity is much too complex. It is a product of complex historical process. Black American identity is a product of a complex New World acculturation. It should be noted that acknowledging this is not a denial of African cultural survivals and retentions. No doubt, African ethos and values survived the transplantation. But not in their original forms. The black American is a product of a complex cultural formative process in the New World. Afrocentric essentialism as expressive of black alienation and protest is justified; however, it becomes problematic in its larger and broader existential affirmations that limit and circumscribe black capacity to reflect, engage, and come to grips with the complexities of the black experience. Black Americans and blacks in Diaspora do not exist and function in cultural isolation. They live in an ever-changing, ever-expanding world. Their capacity to function effectively in this context depends on their adaptability to changing circumstances. Afrocentric essentialism, as presently constructed, does not accommodate adaptation. It obscures and simplifies the nuances of black history and imposes a narrow, utilitarian historically and culturally skewed racialized identity and worldview on blacks, ignoring complex historical and cultural transformations. It constructs a monolithic and homogeneous African/black world on a rather simplified and simplistic representation of both Africa and Europe that deemphasizes complexities, contradictions, and conflicted realities.

This interrogation of racial essentialism should neither be construed to suggest a denial of the relevance or saliency of racism nor a validation of America as a deracinated nation. On the contrary, the problematic and troubling America that Andrew Hacker analyzed in his iconoclastic study, characterized by alienation and deep racial antagonism, remains very much a reality. He described America as "Two Nations, Black and White: Separate, Hostile and Unequal."[9] Afrocentric scholars regard Hacker's analysis as true reflection of past, present, and future realities of America. Others, however, disagree and diminish the import of race, insisting not only that racism has ended but also that blacks could be, and are in fact being, judged according to the "contents of their character."[10] Afrocentric scholars reject the notion that race is on the decline. America, they insist, is very much a color-driven nation. They view attacks on Affirmative Action and other civil rights initiatives as symptomatic of the depth of racism in America. Given this reality, Afrocentric scholars argue, homogeneous and monolithic constructions of African and black Diaspora historical and cultural experiences become sine qua non for survival. In their judgment, racism is so entrenched that blacks had no choice but to respond with an equally forceful racially constructed worldview. Race becomes a countervailing and utilitarian construct for struggle and survival.

For race to be eradicated or transcended, Afrocentric essentialist scholars believe there has to be, a priori, an acknowledgment by whites of the role race has played, and continues to play, in creating and sustaining the historical and systemic structures of white hegemony. They object vehemently to what they perceive as a deceptive representation of whiteness as a neutral, universal, and normative category. They insist on accenting whiteness as the embodiment of immense power and privileges. This focus on the political and "cultural dynamics of whiteness" is due largely to what J. L. Kincheloe and Shirley Steinberg describe as whiteness's "phenomenal ability to camouflage itself to the point it can deny its own existence. Whiteness presents itself not only as a cultural force or norm by which all other cultures are measured, but as positionality beyond history and culture, a non-ethnic space. Thus in a culture where whiteness as ethnicity is erased, critical multiculturalists receive strange looks when they refer to their analysis of white culture."[11] Thus far, they contend, race has been analyzed as having little to do with white people. Instead, race is presented as a problem of nonwhites and ethnics and problems caused by their difference—that is, their difference from white people.

Afrocentric scholars concur with Kincheloe and Steinberg and view the deracializing of whiteness and camouflaging and deemphasizing of race as designed to mask societal structural imbalances and project a false and dubious neutralist construction of reality. They regard as hypocritical the affirmation of a neutral or objective, color-blind social order in the face of glaring racially configured differentiations.

Thus, despite its growing scholarly deconstruction, Afrocentric scholars continue to invoke race as a potent intellectual and ideological force, the anchor for existential validation. It seems ironic that such an artificial factor (race) has become for these scholars a unifying experiential construct and basis for constructing boundaries and frameworks for existential struggles. The focus of these scholars on race seems validated by a growing scholarship on the increasing significance of race in America and its growing appeal among blacks as a medium not just of validation but of signifying a much more realistic portrait of America. The general consensus is that America is further from being race neutral and color-blind, that race indeed remains a major defining factor in American society despite the proclamation of its apparent demise or invisibility by some critics. In a recent iconoclastic study, Joe R. Feagin and Leslie H. Picca attribute this apparent demise or invisibility of racism to a shift in the theatre of racial performance from the *frontstage* to the *backstage* where whites seem more comfortable, among their own, to share racist jokes and innuendos without public scrutiny and recriminations.[12] In another study, Feagin and Hernan Vera contend, "In the United States white racism is a centuries-old system intentionally designed to exclude Americans of color from full participation in the economy, polity, and society. Today, racial prejudice and ideologies still undergird and rationalize widespread white discrimination against people of color."[13] In a more recent study, Feagin analyzes the depth of what he terms systemic racism. According to him, "In the United States racism is structured into the rhythms of everyday life. It is lived, concrete, advantageous to whites, and painful for those who are not white. Each major part of a black and white person's life is shaped by racism."[14] Corroborating the above, Farai Chideya writes, "Race is probably the most tangible and subjective force in our lives." Citing statistic from the Census Bureau and other sources, she underlines the racial divide in resources and opportunity—higher education, employment, income, and life expectancy.[15] Echoing Andrew Hacker, Chideya argues, "Black America and white America still live separately. Most whites live in predominantly white neighborhoods; most blacks live in majority-black ones. Americans of different races still tend not to live together, socialize together, or chart their paths in this society together."[16] What does this gloomy social analysis and pessimistic worldview portend for the future of race relations in the United States? Is the Afrocentric essentialist worldview immutable? Is essentialism, be it racial or cultural, the permanent solution for addressing the challenges of blacks in America and the Diaspora? Is there a possibility of moving beyond and transcending race and the essentialist worldview, or is this approach the one and only viable strategy for blacks?

Richard Payne believes that it is possible to get beyond race and suggests the following strategies. First, he urges focusing on the positive as opposed to the failures of American society. This, he suggests, would encourage and motivate Americans to strive for improved understanding of each other and common ground. The problem with this is the temptation to presume a progressive history. Emphasizing success may create the impression that things have always been good—the progressive myth. Payne suggests that getting beyond race would, over time, erode emphasis on racial identity and categories as people treat each other regardless of color. Second, he advocates a "bottom-up" approach to improving race relations, placing greater responsibility on individuals to move beyond race. This prescription is problematic. Many prefer the "top-down" approach since racism is systemic-induced, sustained, and protected from top-down. Third, Payne urges more attention to how the growing complexity of American society erodes the force of race. This is a presumption based on the notion that increasing opportunities to and rise in socioeconomic status of blacks would obliterate the need to identify with one's race, and thus racial identity and consciousness would equally diminish. In other words, improvements in the social and economic status of blacks would result in *class* supplanting *race*.[17] Unfortunately, history belies this assumption. The problem is that, historically, class has never been potent enough to upstage race in America. Regardless of improved and elevated economic status, the black middle class has never been able to completely overcome, experientially, the overarching, pervasive, and negative effects of race. For blacks, race remains the nondiscriminatory unifier! Deracination from the bottom up seems far-fetched. But radical socioeconomic reforms that clearly show broad-based equalizing tendencies, instead of token cooptation of a few, could create conditions that would predispose some blacks to think less about race. Payne would seem to concur with the school represented by Debra Dickerson that I discussed in the introductory chapter. This school regards race as burdensome and destructive. Dickerson advocates deemphasizing or completely jettisoning *blackness* as an identitarian and existential ethos. She urges the "black powers that be" to move beyond *blackness*. Moving "beyond blackness" is not as simple as Dickerson assumes. In order for blacks to move beyond *blackness*, there has to be a corresponding move on the part of the dominant white society. Deemphasizing race has to be culturally rooted, pervasive, and universal. The prospects are presently nonexistent. Another dimension of class, albeit beyond the scope of this study, ought to be mentioned: the almost total neglect of class analysis in Afrocentric essentialist epistemology. The explanation for this is not far-fetched. Afrocentric essentialist scholars are predominantly middle class. It would have been extremely difficult to construct an essentialist worldview rooted in economic analysis without risking self-implication. Race, ethnicity, and "culture" have become the only practical and "safe" unifying ethos for Afrocentric essentialist scholars to invoke without illuminating their "class" culpability in the socioeconomic malaise of the ordinary people.

On the prospect of overcoming race, Leonard Steinhorn and Barbara Diggs-Brown are not optimistic. The best we can hope for, they suggest, is some form of "racial coexistence" that acknowledges the preeminence of race while striving to confront and challenge the stereotypes and images that impede cooperation. This "racial honesty" could, in their view, lead to "mutual understanding and respect" and eventually to "coexistence marked by reciprocity, trust, and a genuine commitment to common cause," out of which presumably a genuine intercultural model would evolve. Thus, this school considers the continued quest for integration an illusion. Urging blacks and whites to abandon integration and pursue the more realistic option of racial coexistence, Steinhorn and Diggs-Brown write, "Unless there is a profound and remarkable transformation in this country, however, unless the peculiar nature of race relations undergoes fundamental changes, let us not have any illusions that the vast majority of Americans will ever become truly color-blind. The sooner we acknowledge the permanence of the color line in American life, the sooner we strip away the fictional integration behind which the majority hides, the sooner we can begin an honest accounting of our racial divide and develop an alternative vision of our collective future."[18]

They describe integration as a myth that actually "thwarts progress, particularly when the very success of promoting the myth becomes a convenient way to avoid addressing the real problem." The real problem, they suggest, is an endemic racism and segregation. Blacks and whites may interact, "but rarely do they integrate. Blacks and whites maintain different neighborhoods, schools, work, faith, entertainment and social life . . . In these areas we go separate ways, or when forced together, follow what seems like a shadow dance of polite interaction. This by no means denies the real and meaningful contacts between some blacks and whites, but these instances are infrequent enough to be the conspicuous exceptions that prove the rule."[19]

Furthermore, they contend, "Black and white Americans wake up in separate neighborhoods; send their kids off to separate schools, listen to different radio stations during the morning commute, briefly interact on the job but rarely as equals, return to their own communities after work, socialize in separate environments, and watch different television shows. This is a day in the life of two Americas." The solution, therefore, is racial coexistence. Accepting the racial reality, Steinhorn and Diggs-Brown argue, may turn out to be very liberating: "if we stop pursuing an impossible ideal, blacks may be able to focus more on the realistic one . . . No longer would our leaders be able to find refuge in integration symbolism and color-blind rhetoric."[20]

More recent studies, however, tend to underscore the permanence of racism and thus reinforce Afrocentric skepticism and, ipso facto, seem to validate Afrocentric essentialism. Those who celebrate the demise of racism tend to ignore or underestimate its transformative and transmogrified nature. According to Eduardo Bonilla-Silva, a new powerful racial ideology has emerged that combines elements of liberalism with culturally based anti-minority views to justify the contemporary racial order. He calls this color-blind racism, and its defining elements include abstract liberalism, cultural racism, naturalization, and minimization of racism.[21] There can never be any meaningful integrative and harmonious order in America, he suggests, unless and until there is demonstrable willingness by everyone to acknowledge the continuing relevance of race. In other words, to overcome race and affect cooperation across cultures within a framework that promotes mutual interaction, communication, and exchanges, there has to be, a priori, universal acknowledgment of the potency of race. It is not possible, Afrocentric scholars contend, to presume a racially neutral paradigm within a context that glaringly underscores the relevance of race.

The corroborative contexts and circumstances notwithstanding, Afrocentric essentialism remains fundamentally a backward-looking paradigm that, in the postmodern context, seeks to limit and foreclose the boundaries of human engagement and transcultural discourses and understanding. Undeniably, Afrocentric essentialism has a role in offering blacks a countervailing, counterhegemonic alternative to negative, demeaning, and degrading experiences in America. This should be constructed not as a zero-sum paradigm, however, but more practically as a possibility among possibilities, a dynamic paradigm that reflects and responds to the changing and complex dynamics of the human experience. The challenges of Afrocentric essentialism highlighted in this study—the use of race as the underpinning of African and black Diaspora experiences, the attempt to impose a monolithic identity on all blacks, the utilitarian and problematic usages of Africa, the homogenization of African and black Diaspora experiences, and the advancement of a zero-sum racialized ethos of mutuality that subverts critical intraracial discourses—are all reflective of the inherent ambivalence and, ipso facto, crises of black nationalism and Pan-Africanism.

# Notes

## Introduction

1. Delany, "Political Destiny," 327–67.
2. Ibid., 337–38.
3. Ibid. See also Delany, "Political Aspect"; Delany to Professor M. H. Freeman; Delany, "Political Events."
4. Delany, "Political Events."
5. Du Bois, *Souls of Black Folk*, 13.
6. Holt, *Problem of Race in the 21st Century*. Barndt, *Understanding and Dismantling Racism*.
7. Ibid., 3–4.
8. Ibid.
9. Stampp, *Peculiar Institution*; Elkins, *Slavery*; Davis, *Inhuman Bondage*.
10. Delany, "Political Aspect," "Political Events." See also his "The International Policy of the World Towards the African Race."
11. Delany, "Important Movement."
12. Adeleke, "Color Line as Confining and Restraining Paradigm." See also Adeleke, "Black Americans and Africa."
13. Richburg, *Out of America*.
14. "Richburg Firestorm," 51.
15. *Journal of Black Studies*, September 1997, 129, 130–32. Also, Sackeytio, "For a Self-Denying 'African'-American Journalist," 53; Egbo, "Self-Denial and Retribution," 52.
16. Mohammed, *Fall of America*, 17.
17. Eure and Jerome, *Back Where We Belong*, 247.
18. Asante, *Afrocentricity* and *The Afrocentric Idea*; Kemet, *Afrocentricity and Knowledge*.
19. Asante, *Afrocentricity*, 30.
20. Ibid., 39.
21. Shavit, *History in Black*; Howe, *Afrocentrism*; Lefkowitz, *Not Out of Africa*.
22. Blaut, *Colonizer's Model of the World*.
23. Morris and Braine, "Social Movements and Oppositional Consciousness."
24. Shavit, *History In Black*; Howe, *Afrocentrism*. See also Walker, *We Can't Go Home Again*; Moses, *Afrotopia*; Ziegler, *Molefi Kete Asante and Afrocentricity*.
25. Austin, *Achieving Blackness*, 12–13.
26. Ibid., 128.
27. Shavit, *History in Black*; Walker, *We Can't Go Home Again*; Howe, *Afrocentrism*.
28. James, *Stolen Legacy*.

29. Rodney, "African History in the Service of Black Revolution," 51. See also Adeleke, "Guerilla Intellectualism."

30. Shavit, *History in Black*; Stowe, *Afrocentrism*; Lefkowitz, *Not Out of Africa*.

31. Asante, "Racism, Consciousness and Afrocentricity."

32. Ani, *Yurugu*.

33. Adeleke, "Gloracialization."

34. Adeleke, "Moral Suasion and the Negro Anti-Slavery Crusade."

35. Adeleke, *UnAfrican Americans*. See also his "Constructing a Dual Cultural Space."

36. Dickerson, *The End of Blackness*, "Introduction," 3.

37. Ibid., 4–5.

38. Graves, *Myth of Race*.

## Chapter 1

1. Bethel, *Roots of African-American Identity*, 82.

2. Ibid., 81–82.

3. Ibid., 81.

4. Ibid., 82.

5. Ibid.

6. Du Bois, *Souls of Black Folk*, 3.

7. Ibid., 3–4.

8. Early, *Lure and Loathing*.

9. Bethel, *Roots of African American Identity*, 25–27.

10. Asante, *Afrocentricity*. See also his *Afrocentric Idea* and *Kemet*. Richards, *Let the Circle Be Unbroken*.

11. Howe, *Afrocentrism*, 233.

12. Richards, *Let The Circle Be Unbroken*, 1.

13. Wilson, *Falsification of Afrikan Consciousness*, 40–41.

14. Wright, *Black Intellectuals*.

15. Richburg, *Out of America*.

16. Early, *Lure and Loathing*.

17. Bell, "American Moral Reform Society." McCormick, "William Whipper."

18. Miller, *Search for a Black Nationality*; Kinshasa, *Emigration vs. Assimilation*; Moses, *Golden Age of Black Nationalism*.

19. Eyerman, *Cultural Trauma*.

20. Stampp, *Peculiar Institution*, 141.

21. Andrews and McFeely, *Narrative of the Life of Frederick Douglass*.

22. Berlin, "From Creole to Africa," 19.

23. Ibid.

24. Ibid., 19.

25. Ibid., 20.

26. Ibid.

27. Edwards, *Equiano's Travels*.

28. Campbell, *Middle Passages*.

29. Magubane, *Ties That Bind*, 15–88. Walvin, *Questioning Slavery*, 49–95. Oakes, *Ruling Race*, 3–34.

30. Tise, *Proslavery*. See also Genovese, *World the Slaveholders Made*.

31. Reed, *Platform for Change*, ch. 3. See also Horton, *Free People of Color*, 152–53. Nash, *Forging Freedom*, ch. 4.

32. Cook, " Tragic Conception of Negro History," 225–31.

33. Lincoln, *Coming Through the Fire*, 101.

34. Curry, *Free Black in Urban America*, 81.

35. Walvin, *Questioning Slavery*. Oakes, *Ruling Race*. Jones, *Born a Child of Freedom*, ch. 1.

36. Mills, *Racial Contract*, 13–14.

37. Ibid., 16.

38. Kolchin, *American Slavery*, 133. Also, Walvin, *Questioning Slavery*, 64–71.

39. Stampp, *Peculiar Institution*. Also, Kolchin, *American Slavery*; Walvin, *Questioning Slavery*.

40. Aptheker, *American Negro Slave Revolts*. See also his "Consciousness of Negro Nationality to 1900."

41. Adeleke, "Primacy of Condition."

42. Sorin, *Abolitionism*, 17–37, ch. 3. Mabee, *Black Freedom*. Stewart, *Holy Warriors*. Gienapp, "Abolitionism and the Nature of Ante-Bellum Reform."

43. Ibid.

44. Sorin, *Abolitionism*, 44

45. Ibid., ch. 3. Mabee, *Black Freedom*, 1–111. Gienapp, "Abolitionism."

46. Mabee, *Black Freedom*. Also, Simmons, "Ideologies and Programs of the Negro Anti-Slavery Movement."

47. Horton, *Free People of Color*, 158.

48. Aptheker, *Documentary History of the Negro People in the United States*, vol. 1, 82.

49. Bethel, *Roots of African American Identity*, 119–26.

50. Ibid. See also Curry, *Free Black*, 96–111.

51. Bell, *Survey of the Negro Convention Movement*. Pease and Pease, "The Negro Convention Movement," in Nathan I. Huggins, ed., *Key Issues in the Afro-American Experience*.

52. Bethel, *Roots of African American Identity*, 120, 130. Horton, *Free People of Color*, 158. Reed, *Platform for Change*, ch. 5.

53. Wright, *White Man Listen!* 16.

54. Bell, *Survey*. Reed, *Platform for Change*, ch. 4. Pease and Pease, "Negro Convention Movement." Quarles, *Black Abolitionists*. Horton, *Free People of Color*.

55. Nash, *Forging Freedom*, 103.

56. Bell, *Minutes of the Proceedings*, 34.

57. Tise, *Proslavery*, chs. 6, 10, 13. Walvin, *Questioning Slavery*, chs. 4–5.

58. Bell, *Minutes of the Proceedings*.

59. Ibid. See also Simmons, "Ideologies and Programs," ch. 2.

60. McCormick, "William Whipper."

61. Ibid.

62. *The Colored American*, July 29, 1837, 3.

63. Ibid., September 9, 1837, 3.

64. Whipper, "Address on Non-Resistance," 3.

65. Ibid.

66. Ibid.

67. *The Colored American*, March 29, 1838, 2.

68. Ibid., March 13, 1841, 3.

69. Ibid.

70. Ibid., September 9, 16, 1837, 3; February 10, 1838, 3; March 17, 1838, 3.

71. Ibid., September 9, 1837, 2; March 13, 1841, 3.

72. Ibid., March 6, 13, 1841.

73. Ibid., December 2, 9, 1837; January 13, 27, 1838; February 10, 1838.

74. Ibid., November 3, 1837, 2.

75. Ibid., February 16, 1839, 3.

76. Ibid.

77. Woodson, "West," *Colored American*, February 17, May 3, 1838; January 15, February 5, March 2, 16, July 15, August 31, 1839.

78. Ibid., January 15, June 15, August 31, 1839, 3.

79. Ibid.

80. Litwack, *North of Slavery*, ch. 5. Curry, *Free Black*, 37–48.

81. Laurie, *Working People of Philadelphia*, 53–66.

82. Litwack, *North of Slavery*, ch. 5. Richards, *"Gentlemen of Property and Standing,"* ch. 2. Curry, *Free Black*, ch. 6.

83. Simmons, "Ideologies and Programs," 34.

84. Foner and Walker, *Proceedings of the Black State Conventions, 1840–1865*, vol. 1, 124.

85. Foner and Walker, *Proceedings of the Black State Conventions*. Bell, *Minutes of the Proceedings*.

86. Ofari, *"Let Your Motto Be RESISTANCE,"* 133–34, 149.

87. Foner and Walker, *Proceedings of the Black State Conventions*, vol. 1, 39.

88. Adeleke, "Race and Ethnicity in Martin R. Delany's Struggle."

89. Delany, *Condition, Elevation, Emigration and Destiny*, ch. 17, 154.

90. Ibid. See also Delany, "Political Destiny."

91. Rollin, *Life and Public Services*, 335.

92. Adeleke, "Race and Ethnicity."

93. Ofari, *Let Your Motto Be RESISTANCE*, chs. 6–7.

94. Foner, *Life and Writings of Frederick Douglass*, 202.

95. Adeleke, "Race and Ethnicity."

96. Ibid.

97. Sterling, *Making of an Afro-American*, chs. 20–22.

98. Coulter, "Henry M. Turner." Redkey, "Bishop Turner's African Dream."

99. Turner, "American Colonization Society," 44, 52–59, 83–84.

100. Redkey, "Flowering of Black Nationalism." Also, Redkey, "Bishop Turner's African Dream."

101. Rigsby, *Alexander Crummell.*

102. Delany, "Official Report of the Niger Valley Exploring Party," 102–6, 133–34.

103. Turner, "Emigration to Africa," 55, and his "American Colonization Society," 44.

104. Crummell, "Relations and Duty of the Free Colored Men," 215–84. See also his "Duty of a Rising Christian State," 87; "Progress of Civilization Along the West Coast of Africa," 107; "Our National Mistakes, and the Remedy for Them."

105. Adeleke, *UnAfrican Americans.*

106. Rollin, *Life and Public Services,* 351–56.

107. Rigsby, *Alexander Crummell,* 113.

108. Turner, "Question of Race," 74.

109. Turner, "Emigration Convention," 147.

110. Adeleke, *UnAfrican Americans,* ch. 6. See also his "Religion in Martin R. Delany's Struggle."

111. Ibid., 570–76, 580, 583.

## Chapter 2

1. Walvin, *Questioning Slavery,* 79–80.

2. Ibid., 80.

3. Ibid., 85.

4. Ibid., 92.

5. Frederickson, *Black Image in the White Mind,* 43.

6. Ibid., 49, 52.

7. Walvin, *Questioning Slavery,* chs. 4, 5; Frederickson, *Black Image;* Eze, *Race and Enlightenment;* Okoye, *American Image of Africa;* Genovese, *World the Slaveholders Made.*

8. Blaut, *Colonizer's Model of the World.* Also, Eze, *Race and Enlightenment.* See also Isaacs, "American Negro and Africa"; Friedman, "Africa and the Afro-American."

9. Kinshasa, *Emigration vs. Assimilation,* 35–37. Stewart, *Holy Warriors.*

10. Kinshasa, *Emigration vs. Assimilation,* 36–45.

11. Sherwood, "Paul Cuffee," 167.

12. Ibid., 195–96. See also Sherwood, "Paul Cuffee and His Contribution to the American Colonization Society."

13. Fisher, "Lott Cary," 385–89, 391.

14. Bruce, "Reasons Why the Colored American Should Go to Africa," 489–90.

15. Williams, "Slavery and Colonization" 59, 60.

16. Moses, *Golden Age of Black Nationalism.* See also Adeleke, *UnAfrican Americans.*

17. Foner and Walker, *Proceedings of the Black State Conventions, 1840–1865,* vol. 1, 193–94.

18. Whipper, "Eulogy on William Wilberforce," 73.

19. Thorpe, *Black Historians*, 33, 35, 46–55.

20. Delany, "International Policy of the World Towards the African Race," 323, 324, 326, 289–92.

21. Blyden, "African Problem and the Methods of its Solution," 575, 576.

22. Crummell, "Civilization as a Collateral and Indispensable Instrumentality."

23. Turner, "Afro-American Future," 188.

24. Sherwood, "Paul Cuffee," 194–95.

25. Adeleke, *UnAfrican Americans*, ch. 3, p. 59, ch. 4.

26. Delany, *Condition, Elevation, Emigration and Destiny*, 12.

27. Ofari, *Let Your Motto Be RESISTANCE*, 79.

28. Ibid., 71–102, 183–84.

29. Delany, *Condition*. See also his "Political Destiny of the Colored Race on the American Continent"; "International Policy"; Delany letter to Dr. James McCune Smith; Delany to Professor M. H. Freeman.

30. Redkey, "Bishop Turner's African Dream"; see also his *Respect Black*. Scruggs, "We the Children of Africa in This Land"; Rigsby, *Alexander Crummell*.

31. Bruce, "Reasons Why the Colored American Should Go to Africa," 489.

32. Ibid., 489–90. For more on Bruce Grit, see Seraile, *Bruce Grit*. Crowder, *John Edward Bruce*.

33. Lewis and Warner-Lewis, *Garvey*. Lewis and Bryan, *Garvey*. Jacques-Garvey, *Philosophy and Opinions of Marcus Garvey*.

34. Von Eschen, *Race Against Empire*, 10.

35. Esedebe, *Pan-Africanism*; Langley, *Pan-Africanism and Nationalism in West Africa*; Thompson, *Africa and Unity*.

36. Du Bois, "To the Nations of the World."

37. Thorpe, *Black Historians*, 101.

38. Bracey, Meier, and Rudwick, *Afro-Americans*, 389.

39. Esedebe, *Pan-Africanism*; Langley, *Pan-Africanism and Nationalism*.

40. Magubane, *Ties That Bind*; Johnson, *Black Globalism*.

41. Shabazz, *Malcolm X on Afro-American History*, 63, 65, 55, 73.

42. Carmichael, *Stokely Speaks*, 183–220, 222, 223.

43. Ofari, *Let Your Motto Be*, 76.

44. Ibid., 74–79, 162–63.

45. Ernest, *Liberation Historiography*; Quarles, *Black Mosaic*; Harding, "Beyond Chaos"; Harris, "Coming of Age."

46. Delany, "International Policy," 323, 324.

47. Grisham, "Functions of the Negro Scholar," 629, 630, 632–33.

48. Ofari, *Let Your Motto Be*, 76.

49. Thorpe, *Black Historians*, 129; Woodson, *Mis-education of the Negro*, 110.

50. Meier and Rudwick, *Black History*, 1–72. Franklin, "On the Evolution of Scholarship in Afro-American History."

51. Jacques-Garvey, *Philosophy and Opinions*, 77.

52. Ibid., 68, 13. For a more critical interrogation of Garvey, see Walker, "Virtuoso Illusionist."

53. Meier and Rudwick, *Black History*, 73–238.

54. Rodney, "African History in the Service of Black Revolution," 51

55. Ibid.

56. Rodney, *History of the Upper Guinea Coast*.

57. Rodney, *How Europe Underdeveloped Africa*, 58.

58. Asante, *Afrocentric Idea* and *Afrocentricity*; Keto, *Vision, Identity and Time*.

59. Asante, *Malcolm X As Cultural Hero*, 18, 48.

60. Akbar, "Africentric Social Sciences for Human Liberation."

61. Walker, *We Can't Go Home Again*; Howe, *Afrocentrism*; Shavit, *History in Black*.

62. Diop, *African Origin of Civilization*. See also his *Civilization or Barbarism*, 3; "Africa: Cradle of Humanity"; "Origins of the Ancient Egyptians," 27–57.

63. Asante, *Afrocentric Idea*, 9.

64. Wilson, *Falsification of Afrikan Consciousness*, 25.

65. Howe, *Afrocentrism*; Shavit, *History in Black*; Walker, *We Can't Go Home Again*; Moses, *Afrotopia*; Lefkowitz, *Not Out of Africa*.

66. Quoted in Walker, *We Can't Go Home*, xix–xx.

67. Shavit, *History in Black*, chs. 6–7. See also Lefkowitz, "Origins of the 'Stolen Legacy.'"

68. Du Bois, *Souls of Black Folk*, 3–4.

69. Asante, "Racism, Consciousness and Afrocentricity."

70. Shavit, *History in Black*, chs. 1–2.

71. Ibid., 3.

72. Berger, "Professor's Theories on Race ." Also quoted in Schlesinger, *Disuniting of America*, 73.

73. Shavit, *History in Black*, 23.

74. Ibid., 29.

75. Ibid., 38. Also chs. 4–5. Although not counted among the Afrocentrists, leading Afrocentric scholars advance Martin Bernal's work as incontrovertible intellectual corroboration of the Greek Dependency theory. Bernal's work on Egyptian influence on Greece has become a standard reference source on the Afrocentric genre. See his *Black Athena*, vols. 1 and 2, and *Black Athena Writes Back*.

76. Walker, *We Can't Go Home*, 40–41, 44, 46–50.

## Chapter 3

1. Ajayi, "Black Heritage Summit."

2. Harris, "Jamaica Pre-Summit."

3. Ani, *Yurugu*; Asante, *Painful Demise of Eurocentrism*.

4. Richards, *Let the Circle Be Unbroken*, 52.

5. Asante, *Painful Demise of Eurocentrism*.

6. Asante, *Afrocentricity*, ch. 2, pp. 2, 43, 67. It is noteworthy that Asante did not acknowledge the "European" as part of this new composite ethnic identity.

7. Wright, *Crisis of the Black Intellectual*, 106.

8. Asante, *Afrocentricity*. See also his *Afrocentric Idea*.

9. See also Asante, *Kemet, Afrocentricity and Knowledge*.

10. Asante, "Afrocentric Idea in Education," 171. See also his "On Historical Interpretations" and "On Afrocentric Metatheory."

11. Karenga, *Introduction to African American Studies*. See also his "Corrective History"; *Kawaida Theory*; *Kwanza*.

12. Wilson, *Falsification of Afrikan Consciousness*.

13. Marimba, *Yurugu*. Also see her *Let the Circle Be Unbroken*.

14. Akbar, *Chains and Images of Psychological Slavery*; Wright, *Psychopathic Racial Personality*.

15. Lemelle, "Politics of Cultural Existence," 335.

16. Gordon, *Black Women, Feminism and Black Liberation*.

17. Asante, *Afrocentricity* and *Kemet, Afrocentricity and Knowledge*.

18. See also T'Shaka, *Art of Leadership*.

19. Asante, *Afrocentricity*, chs. 3, 4, pp. 65–69, 26, 30.

20. Hickey and Wylie, *Enchanting Darkness*, 308–18; Walker, "Distortions of Afrocentric History"; Lemelle, "Politics of Cultural Existence," 334–36.

21. Ibid. See also Howe, *Afrocentrism*; Shavit, *History in Black*; Walker, *We Can't Go Home Again*.

22. Lemelle, "Politics of Cultural Existence," 336.

23. Esedebe, *Pan-Africanism*, 4, 5.

24. Sherwood, "Paul Cuffee."

25. Fisher, "Lott Cary."

26. Wiltse, *David Walker's Appeal*.

27. Delany, "Political Destiny of the Colored Race on the American Continent"; Miller, *Search for a Black Nationality*; Griffith, *African Dream*.

28. Delany, "Political Destiny," 335.

29. Miller, *Search for a Black Nationality*; Griffith, *African Dream*. See also Delany and Campbell, *Search for a Place*; Delany, *Condition, Elevation, Emigration and Destiny*.

30. Adeleke, *UnAfrican Americans*.

31. Lewis, *Marcus Garvey*; Lewis and Beyan, *Garvey*.

32. Hine, *State of Afro-American History*; Meier and Rudwick, *Black History and the Historical Profession*; Thorpe, *Black Historians*; Stuckey, "Twilight of Our Past."

33. Esedebe, *Pan-Africanism*; Langley, *Pan-Africanism and Nationalism in West Africa*.

34. Madhubuti, *Enemies*, 70.

35. Hill, "Walter Rodney and the Restatement of Pan-Africanism in Theory and Practice," 85.

36. "Black Scholar Interviews: Walter Rodney."

37. T'Shaka, *Political Legacy of Malcolm X*; Malcolm X, *Malcolm X on Afro-American History*; Breitman, *Malcolm X*; Alkalimat, *Perspectives on Black Liberation and Social Revolution.*

38. Carmichael, *Stokely Speaks*, 202, 205.

39. Drake, "Diaspora Studies and Pan-Africanism," 341–402.

40. Fisher, "Lott Cary," 389, 391.

41. Moses, *Golden Age*; see also his *Classical Black Nationalism.*

42. Draper, "Father of Black American Nationalism."

43. Adeleke, *UnAfrican Americans.*

44. Ibid. See also McAdoo, *Pre-Civil War Black Nationalism.*

45. Esedebe, *Pan-Africanism*, 5; Lemelle and Kelley, *Imagining Home*, 361.

46. Olusanya, "African Historians and the Pan-Africanist Tradition," 10.

47. Carmichael, *Stokely Speaks*, 223.

48. Ackah, *Pan-Africanism.*

49. Richards, *Let the Circle Be Unbroken, 1.*

50. Austin, *Achieving Blackness*, 128.

51. Ibid. Asante, *Afrocentricity.* See also Asante's "Racism, Consciousness and Afrocentricity."

52. Du Bois, *Souls of Black Folk*, 3.

53. Richburg, *Out of America*, 227–28.

54. Loury, "Free At Last?"

55. Crouch, "Who Are We? Where Did We Come From? Where Are We Going?" 80–94. See also Crouch's *All-American Skin Game*, 45–57.

56. Goldberg, *Book*, 105.

57. Jones, "Why Pan-Africanism Failed," 54–61.

58. Dalton, *Racial Healing*, 107.

59. Wright, *Black Intellectuals, Black Cognition, and a Black Aesthetic*, 38–39.

60. Mboya, "American Negro Cannot Look to Africa for an Escape," 410, 412. See also Mboya, "Africa and Afro-American," 246–57.

61. Nnoli, *Ethnic Politics in Nigeria*, 1, 35–97, 140–214.

62. Ayittey, *Africa Betrayed*, 335–36.

63. Soyinka, *Open Sore of a Continent*, 139, 120, 128.

64. "Resist Recolonization!" 364, 357.

65. Mutiso and Rohio, *Readings in African Political Thought*, 346. Also, Nkrumah, *Some Essential Features of Nkrumaism.*

66. Mwakikagile, Relations *Between Africans and African-Americans.* See also his *Relations Between Africans, African Americans and Afro-Caribbeans.* Johnson, *Why Blacks Left America for Africa*; Magubene, *Ties That Bind: Afro-American Consciousness of Africa*; Meriwether, *Proudly We Can Be African.* Also Ohaegbulam, "Continental Africans and Africans in America"; Campbell, *Middle Passages*; Gaines, *African Americans in Ghana*; Wamba, *Kinship.*

67. Apraku, *Outside Looking In*, 112, 113, 114, 101, 115.

## Chapter 4

1. Moses, *Afrotopia*; Howe, *Afrocentrism;* Asante, *Afrocentric Idea* and *Afrocentricity.*

2. Asante, *Afrocentric Idea* and *Afrocentricity* . See also Richards, *Let the Circle Be Unbroken.*

3. Asante, *Afrocentric Idea* and *Afrocentricity.* See also his *Kemet, Afrocentricity and Knowledge.* Richards, *Let the Circle Be Unbroken.* See also her *Yurugu.*

4. Hine and McLeod, *Crossing Boundaries;* Wright, *Black Intellectuals, Black Cognition, and a Black Aesthetic;* Ackah, *Pan-Africanism.*

5. Mazrui, "On the Concept of 'We are all Africans,'" 89, 90. Also Wright, *Black Intellectuals,* 41.

6. Sidbury, *Becoming African in America,* 6.

7. Hine and McLeod, *Crossing Boundaries.*

8. Sidbury, *Becoming African in America,* 6–7.

9. Greene, "Beyond Power," 332–33.

10. Mazrui, "On The Concept of 'We are all Africans,'" 88.

11. Ibid. See also Awolowo, *Awo,* 27.

12. Asante, *Afrocentric Idea;* Richards, *Let The Circle Be Unbroken.*

13. Walvin, *Questioning Slavery;* Frederickson, *Black Image in the White Mind.*

14. Blassingame, *Slave Community;* Rawick, *From Sundown to Sunup.*

15. Sherwood, "Paul Cuffee" and "Paul Cuffee and His Contributions to the American Colonization Society"; Fisher, "Lott Cary."

16. Adeleke, *UnAfrican Americans.*

17. Delany, *Condition, Elevation, Emigration and Destiny,* 203.

18. Ibid. See also his "Political Destiny of the Colored Race on the American Continent."

19. Ofari, *Let Your Motto Be;* Redkey, "Bishop Turner's African Dream" and *Black Exodus.*

20. Wiltse, *David Walker's Appeal.*

21. Bell, *Minutes of the Proceedings of the Colored National Negro Conventions;* Aptheker, *Documentary History of the Negro People in the United States,* vol. 1. Also Horton and Horton, *In Hope of Liberty,* 201. Adeleke, "Afro-Americans and Moral Suasion."

22. Horton and Horton, *In Hope of Liberty,* 201. Also *Colored American,* March 4, 1837.

23. Adeleke, *UnAfrican Americans.* Also Draper, *Rediscovery of Black Nationalism.*

24. Horton and Horton, *In Hope of Liberty,* 201.

25. Aptheker, *Documentary History,* vol. 1, p. 71.

26. Ibid., 109. Also *Liberator,* February 12, 1831.

27. Foner and Walker, *Proceedings of the Black State Convention, 1840–1865,* vol. 1, pp. 193–94.

28. Ibid., 45; also vol. 2.

29. Ibid., 45–46.

30. Adeleke, *UnAfrican Americans*. Also, Williams, "Black American Attitudes Toward Africa."

31. Foner and Walker, *Proceedings*, vol. 2, p. 208.

32. Ibid., 211.

33. Wilson, *Falsification of Afrikan Consciousness*, 40–41.

34. Campbell, *Middle Passages*, xxiv.

35. Adeleke, "Constructing a Dual Cultural Space."

36. Hine and McLeod, *Crossing Boundaries*.

37. Gomez, *Exchanging Our Country Marks*, 154.

38. Wright, *Black Intellectuals, Black Cognition*, 40.

## Chapter 5

1. Asante, *Painful Demise of Eurocentrism*, "Preface," 1–8. M Ani, *Yurugu*.

2. Shujaa, *Too Much Schooling*, 31.

3. Asante, "Where Is the White Professor Located?"

4. Holt, *Problem of Race in the 21st Century*; Barndt, *Understanding and Dismantling Racism*.

5. Holloway, *Change the World Without Taking Power*; Stiglitz, *Globalization and Its Discontents*; Held and McGrew, *Globalization/Anti-Globalization*.

6. Cohen, *Global Diasporas*, 155, 157.

7. Ibid., 174–75.

8. Adeleke, *UnAfrican Americans*. See also his "Constructing a Dual Cultural Space."

9. Delany, "Political Destiny of the Colored People on the American Continent"; "International Policy of the World Towards the African Race"; "Political Events"; "Political Aspect of the Colored Race of the United States."

10. Clarke, *Marcus Garvey and the Vision of Africa*; Cronon, *Black Moses*.

11. Williams, *Destruction of Black Civilization*, 362, 381.

12. Asante, *Afrocentric Idea*; *Afrocentricity*; *Kemet, Afrocentricity and Knowledge*.

13. Madhubuti, *Enemies*, 187, 186, 190.

14. Ani, *Yurugu*.

15. Richards, *Let the Circle Be Unbroken*.

16. Ani, *Yurugu*.

17. Ibid., 528–70, 4.

18. Cohen, *Global Diasporas*, 174.

19. Ani, *Yurugu*.

20. Asante, *Painful Demise of Eurocentrism*, vii.

21. Ibid., vii, 7.

22. Gilroy, *Black Atlantic*; Hall, "What Is 'Black' in Black Popular Culture?"; Ackah, *Pan-Africanism*; Segal, *Black Diaspora*; Hall, *In the Vineyard*; Walker, *We Can't Go Home Again*.

23. Hall, *In the Vineyard*.

24. Martusewicz, *Seeking Passage*, 108.

25. Ibid., 28.

26. Williams, "Rethinking the African Diaspora," 109.

27. Lewis, "To Turn as on a Pivot," 5.

28. Hall, "Cultural Identity and Diaspora," 235.

29. Greene, "Beyond Power," 332.

30. Manger and Assal, *Diasporas Within and Without Africa*, 10.

31. Conrad, "'We Are the Warsay of Eritrea in Diaspora'"; Abusharaf, "Southern Sudanese," 140–64; Assal, "Somalis and Sudanese in Norway."

32. Hamilton, "Rethinking the Diaspora: Global Dynamics," 12, 7, 8.

33. Ibid., 1–40.

34. Smith, "Toward a Global Culture?" 178, 179, 180.

35. Tsehloane, Keto, *Vision, Identity and Time*, 64, 22.

36. Ibid.

37. Ibid., 22.

38. Ibid., 23.

39. Intall, "Renovating Australian Citizenship."

40. Ackah, *Pan-Africanism*, 91.

41. Ibid., 93, 97.

42. Cohen, *Global Diasporas*, 174.

43. Intall, "Renovating Australian Citizenship."

## Conclusion

1. Mboya, "Africa and Afro-America," 256.

2. Anise, "African Redefined," 446.

3. Watkins, "Black Is Back, and It's Bound to Sell."

4. Ibid., 448.

5. Hamilton, "Rethinking the African Diaspora: Global Dynamics," 32.

6. Cabral, "National Liberation and Culture," 141, 149. See also Opoku, "Cabral and the African Revolution."

7. Liyong, "Negroes Are Not Africans," 260–61.

8. Mboya, "American Negro Cannot Look to Africa for an Escape," 409–14.

9. Hacker, *Two Nations*.

10. D'Souza, *End of Racism*.

11. Kincheloe and Steinberg, *Changing Multiculturalism*, 29–30,

12. Picca and Feagin, *Two-Faced Racism*.

13. Feagin and Vera, *White Racism*, ix.

14. Feagin, *Racist America*, 2.

15. Chideya, *Color of Our Future*, 7, 25–26.

16. Chideya, *Don't Believe the Hype*, xiii.

17. Payne, *Getting Beyond Race*, 193–200.

18. Steinhorn and Diggs-Brown, *By the Color of the Skin*, 24.

19. Ibid., 30.

20. Ibid., 236.

21. Bonilla-Silva, "New Racism," 271–85. See also, Bonilla-Silva, *Racism Without Racists*; Brown et al., *Whitewashing Race*; Feagin, *Systemic Racism*.

# Bibliography

## Books

Ackah, William B. *Pan-Africanism: Exploring the Contradictions: Politics, Identity and Development in Africa and the African Diaspora.* London: Ashgate, 1999.

Adeleke, Tunde. *UnAfrican Americans: Nineteenth-Century Black Nationalists and the Civilizing Mission.* Lexington: University Press of Kentucky, 1998.

Akbar, N. *Chains and Images of Psychological Slavery.* Jersey City, N.J.: New Mind Productions, 1984.

Alkalimat, Abdul, ed. *Perspectives on Black Nationalism and Social Revolution.* Chicago: Twenty-First Century Books, 1990.

Alpers, Edward A., and Pierre-Michael Fontaine, eds. *Walter Rodney: Revolutionary and Scholar, A Tribute.* Los Angeles: Center for Afro-American Studies and African Studies Center, University of California, Los Angeles, 1982.

Ani, Marimba. *Yurugu: An African-Centered Critique of European Cultural Thought and Behavior.* Trenton, N.J.: Africa World Press, 1996.

Apraku, Kofi K. *Outside Looking In: An African Perspectives on American Pluralistic Society.* Westport, Conn.: Praeger, 1996.

Aptheker, Herbert. *American Negro Slave Revolts.* New York: International Publishers, 1952.

———. *A Documentary History of the Negro in the United States*, vol. 1. New York: Citadel Press, 1965.

Asante, Molefi K. *The Afrocentric Idea.* Philadelphia: Temple University Press, 1987.

———. *Afrocentricity.* Trenton, N.J.: Africa World Press, 1988.

———. *Kemet, Afrocentricity and Knowledge.* Trenton, N.J.: Africa World Press, 1990.

———. *Malcolm X as Cultural Hero and Other Afrocentric Essays.* Trenton, N.J.: Africa World Press, 1993.

———. *The Painful Demise of Eurocentrism: An Afrocentric Response to Critics.* Trenton, N.J.: Africa World Press, 1999.

Austin, Algernon. *Achieving Blackness: Race, Black Nationalism and Afrocentrism in the Twentieth Century.* New York: New York University Press, 2006.

Awolowo, O. *Awo: The Autobiography of Chief Obafemi Awolowo.* London: Cambridge University Press, 1960.

Ayittey, George B. N. *Africa Betrayed.* New York: St. Martin's Press, 1992.

Azevedo, Mario, ed. *A Survey of Africa and the African Diaspora.* Durham, N.C.: Carolina Academic Press, 2005.

Barndt, Joseph. *Understanding and Dismantling Racism: The Twenty-First Century Challenge to White America.* Minneapolis: Fortress Press, 2007.

Bell, Howard H. *A Survey of the Negro Convention Movement, 1830–1861.* New York: Arno Press and *The New York Times*, 1969.

Bernal, Martin, *Black Athena: The Afroasiatic Roots of Classical Civilization, vol. 1. The Fabrication of Ancient Greece, 1785–1985*. New Brunswick, N.J.: Rutgers University Press, 1987.

———. *Black Athena: The Afroasiatic Roots of Classical Civilization, vol. 2. The Archaeological and Documentary Evidence*. New Brunswick, N.J.: Rutgers University Press, 1991.

———. *Black Athena Writes Back: Martin Bernal Responds to His Critics*. Durham, N.C.: Duke University Press, 2001.

Bell, Howard H. *Minutes of the Proceedings of the National Negro Convention Movement, 1830–1864*. New York: Arno Press and *New York Times*, 1969.

———. *A Survey of the Negro Convention Movement, 1830–1861*. New York: Arno Press and *New York Times*, 1969.

Bethel, Elizabeth R. *The Roots of African-American Identity: Memory and History in the Antebellum Free Communities*. New York: St. Martin's Press, 1997.

Blassingame, John. *The Slave Community: Plantation Life in the Antebellum South*. New York: Oxford University Press, 1979.

Blaut, J. M. *The Colonizers Model of the World: Geographical Diffusionism and Eurocentric History*. New York: Gilford Press, 1993.

Bonilla-Silva, Eduardo. *Racism Without Racists: Color-Blind Racism and the Persistence of Racial Inequality in the United States*. New York: Rowman & Littlefield, 2003.

Bracey, John, August Meier, and Elliot Rudwick, eds. *The Afro-Americans: Selected Documents*. Boston: Allyn & Bacon, 1972.

Breitman, George, ed. *Malcolm X: By Any Means Necessary: Speeches, Interviews and a Letter by Malcolm X*. New York: Pathfinder Press, 1970.

Brown, Michael K., et al. *Whitewashing Race: The Myth of a Color-Blind Society*. Berkley and Los Angeles: The University of California Press, 2005.

Campbell, James. *Middle Passages: African American Journeys to Africa, 1787–2005*. New York: Penguin, 2006.

Carmichael, Stokely. *Stokely Speaks: Black Power to Pan-Africanism*. New York: Vintage, 1971.

Chideya, Farai. *The Color of Our Future: Race for the 21st Century*. New York: William Morrow, 1999.

———. *Don't Believe the Hype: Fighting Cultural Misinformation about African-Americans*. New York: Penguin, 1995.

Clarke, John H, ed. *Marcus Garvey and the Vision of Africa*. New York: Vintage, 1973.

Cohen, Robin, *Global Diasporas: An Introduction. Seattle*: University of Washington Press, 1997.

Connolly, William E. *Identity/Difference: Democratic Negotiations and Political Paradox*. Ithaca, N.Y.: Cornell University Press, 1991.

Cronon, Edmund David. *Black Moses: The Study of Marcus Garvey and the Universal Negro Improvement Association*. Madison: University of Wisconsin Press, 1969.

Crouch, Stanley. *The All-American Skin Game; or the Decoy of Race: The Long and the Short of It, 1990–1994*. New York: Pantheon, 1995

Crowder, Ralph L. *John Edward Bruce: Politician, Journalist and Self-Trained Historian of the African Diaspora.* New York: New York University Press, 2006.

Crummell, Alexander. *Addresses and Proceedings of the Congress on Africa Held Under the Auspices of the Stewart Missionary Foundation for Africa.* Atlanta: Gammon Theological Seminary, 1896.

———. *Africa and America: Addresses and Discourses.* New York: Negro University Press, 1969.

———. *The Future of Africa: Being Addresses, Sermons, Delivered in the Republic of Liberia.* New York: Charles Scriber, 1862.

Curry, Leonard P. *The Free Black in Urban America, 1800–1850: The Shadow of the Dream.* Chicago: University of Chicago Press, 1981.

Dalton, Harlon L. *Racial Healing: Confronting the Fear Between Blacks and Whites.* New York: Doubleday, 1995.

Davis, David Brion. *Inhuman Bondage: The Rise and Fall of Slavery in the New World.* New York: New York University Press, 2006.

Delany, Martin R., and Robert Campbell, eds. *Search for a Place: Black Separatism and Africa.* Ann Arbor: University of Michigan Press, 1971.

Delany, Martin R. *The Condition, Elevation, Emigration and Destiny of the Colored People of the United States.* 1852; Baltimore: Black Classic Press, 1993.

Dent, Gina, ed. *Black Popular Culture.* Seattle: Bay Press, 1992.

Dickerson, Debra. *The End of Blackness: Returning the Souls of Black Folk to Their Rightful Owners.* New York: Anchor Books, 2004.

Diop, Cheikh Anta. *The African Origin of Civilization: Myth or Reality.* Chicago: Lawrence Hill, 1974.

———. *Civilization and Barbarism: An Authentic Anthropology.* New York, 1991.

Doane, Ashley W., and Eduardo Bonilla-Silva, eds., *White Out: The Continuing Significance of Race.* London: Routledge, 2003.

Draper, Theodore. *The Rediscovery of Black Nationalism.* New York: Viking, 1970.

D'Souza, Dinesh. *The End of Racism.* New York: Free Press, 1995.

Du Bois, W. E. B. *The Souls of Black Folk.* Chicago: A. C. McClurg, 1903.

Early, Gerald, ed. *Lure and Loathing: Essays on Race, Ideology, and the Ambivalence of Assimilation.* New York: Penguin, 1994.

Edwards, Paul, ed. *Equiano's Travels: The Interesting Narrative of the Life of Olaudah Equiano or Gustavus Vassa the African.* 1789; Long Grove, Ill.: Waveland Press, 2006.

Elkins, Stanley. *Slavery: A Problem in American Institutional and Intellectual Life.* Chicago: University of Chicago Press, 1976.

Erim, O. E., and Okon Uya, eds. *Perspectives and Methods of Studying African History.* Enugu, Nigeria: Fourth Dimension Publishers, 1984.

Ernest, John. *Liberation Historiography: African American Writers and the Challenge of History, 1794–1861.* Chapel Hill: University of North Carolina Press, 2004.

Esedebe, Olisanwuche P. *Pan-Africanism: The Idea and Movement, 1776–1991.* Washington, D.C.: Howard University Press, 1994.

Eure, Joseph D., and Richard M. Jerome, eds. *Back Where We Belong: Selected Speeches of Minister Louis Farrakhan*. Philadelphia: P.C. International, 1989.

Eyerman, Ron. *Cultural Trauma: Slavery and the Formation of African American Identity*. New York: Cambridge University Press, 2001.

Eze, Emmanuel C. *Race and Enlightenment: A Reader*. London: Blackwell, 1997.

Feagin, Joe. *Racist America: Roots, Current Realities, and Future Reparations*. New York: Routledge, 2001.

————. *Systemic Racism: A Theory of Oppression*. New York: Routledge, 2006.

Feagin, Joe, and Hernan Vera. *White Racism: The Basics*. New York: Routledge, 1995.

Foner, Philip S. *The Life and Writings of Frederick Douglass*, vol. 5 (supplementary). New York: International Publishers, 1975.

————. *The Voice of Black America: Major Speeches by Blacks in the United States, 1797–1973*, vol. 1. New York: Capricorn, 1975.

Foner, Philip S., and George E. Walker, eds. *Proceedings of the Black State Conventions, 1840–1865*, vols. 1 and 2. Philadelphia: Temple University Press, 1980.

Frederickson, George. *The Black Image in the White Mind: The Debate on Afro-American Character and Destiny, 1817–1914*. New York: Harper and Row, 1971.

Gaines, Kevin K. *African Americans in Ghana: Black Expatriates and the Civil Rights Era*. Chapel Hill: University of North Carolina Press, 2006.

Genovese, E. *The World the Slaveholders Made: Two Essays in Interpretation*. New York: Pantheon, 1969.

Gilroy, Paul. *The Black Atlantic: Modernity and Double Consciousness*. London: Verso, 1993.

Goldberg, Whoopi, *Book*. New York: William Morrow, 1997.

Gomez, Michael. *Exchanging Our Country Marks: The Transformation of African American Identities in the Colonial and Antebellum South*. Chapel Hill: University of North Carolina Press, 1998.

Gordon, Vivian. *Black Women, Feminism and Black Liberation: Which Way?* Chicago: Third World Press, 1991.

Graves, Joseph L. *The Race Myth: Why We Pretend Race Exists in America*. New York: Penguin Group, 2004.

Griffith, Cyril E. *The African Dream: Martin R. Delany and the Emergence of Pan-African Thought*. University Park: Pennsylvania State University Press, 1975.

Hacker, Andrew. *Two Nations: Black and White, Separate, Hostile, Unequal*. New York: Ballantine, 1992.

Hall, Perry. *In the Vineyard: Working in African American Studies*. Knoxville: University of Tennessee Press 1999.

Harris, Joseph E. *Global Dimensions of the African Diaspora*. Washington, D.C.: Howard University Press, 1993.

Held, David, and Anthony McGrew. *Globalization/Anti-Globalization*. Malden, Mass.: Blackwell Publishers, 2002.

Hickey, Dennis, and Kenneth C. Wylie. *An Enchanting Darkness: The American Vision of Africa in the Twentieth Century*. East Lansing: Michigan State University Press, 1993.

Hine, Darlene C. *The State of Afro-American History: Past, Present, Future.* Baton Rouge: Louisiana State University Press, 1986.

Hine, Darlene C., and Jacqueline McLeod, eds. *Crossing Boundaries: Comparative History of Black People in Diaspora.* Bloomington: Indiana University Press, 1997.

Holloway, John. *Change the World Without Taking Power: The Meaning of Revolution Today.* London: Pluto, 2002.

Holt, Thomas C. *The Problem of Race in the Twenty-First Century.* Cambridge, Mass.: Harvard University Press, 2002.

Horton, James O. *Free People of Color: Inside the African American Community.* Washington, D.C.: Smithsonian Institution Press, 1993.

Horton, James, and Lois E. Horton. *In Hope of Liberty: Culture, Community, and Protest Among Northern Free Blacks, 1700–1860.* New York: Oxford University Press, 1997.

Howe, Stephen. *Afrocentrism: Mythical Pasts and Imagined Homes.* London: Verso, 1998.

Huggins, Nathan I. *Key Issues in the Afro-American Experience*, vols. 1 and 2. New York: Harcourt Brace, 1971.

Jacobs, Donald M. ed. *Courage and Conscience: Black and White Abolitionists in Boston.* Bloomington: Indiana University Press, 1993.

Jacques-Garvey, Amy. *Philosophy and Opinions of Marcus Garvey.* New York: Atheneun, 1970.

James, G. G. M. *Stolen Legacy: The Greeks Were Not the Authors of Greek Philosophy, but the People of North Africa, Commonly Called the Egyptians.* 1954; New York, 1989.

Johnson, Robert. *Why Blacks Left America for Africa: Interviews With Black Repatriates, 1971–1999.* Westport, Conn.: Praeger, 1999.

Johnson, Sterling. *Black Globalism: The International Politics of a Non-State Nation.* London: Ashgate, 1998.

Jones, Norese T. *Born a Child of Freedom, Yet a Slave: Mechanisms of Control and Strategies of Resistance in Antebellum South Carolina.* London: Wesleyan University Press, 1990.

Karenga, M. *Introduction to Black Studies.* Los Angeles: Sankore University Press, 1993.

———. *Kawaida Theory: An Introductory Outline.* Los Angeles, 1980.

———. *Kwanza: Origins, Concepts, Practice.* Los Angeles, 1977.

Keto, Tsehloane C. *Vision, Identity and Time: The Afrocentric Paradigm and the Study of the Past.* Dubuque, Iowa: Kendall-Hunt, 1995.

Kincheloe, J. L., and Shirley Steinberg. *Changing Multiculturalism.* Philadelphia: Open University Press, 2001.

Kinshasa, Kwando M. *Emigration vs. Assimilation: The Debate in the African American Press, 1827–1861.* Jefferson, N.C.: McFarland & Co., 1988.

Kolchin, Peter. *American Slavery, 1619–1877.* New York: Hill and Wang, 1993.

Langley, Ayodele J. *Pan-Africanism and Nationalism in West Africa, 1900–1945.* Oxford: Clarendon Press, 1973.

Laurie, Bruce. *Working People of Philadelphia, 1800–1850.* Philadelphia: Temple University Press, 1980.

Lefkowitz, Mary. *Not Out of Africa: How Afrocentrism Became an Excuse to Teach Myth as History.* New York: Basic Books, 1996.

Lemelle, Sidney L., and Robin D. G. Kelley, eds. *Imagining Home: Class, Culture and Nationalism in the African Diaspora.* New York: Verso, 1994.

Lewis, David Levering, ed. *W. E. B. Du Bois: A Reader.* New York: Henry Holt & Co., 1995.

Lewis, Rupert, and Patrick Beyan, eds. *Garvey: His Work and Impact.* Trenton, N.J.: Africa World Press, 1991.

Lewis, Rupert, and Maureen Warner-Lewis, eds. *Garvey: Africa, Europe, the Americas.* Trenton, N.J.: Africa World Press, 1994.

Lincoln, Eric. *Coming Through the Fire: Surviving Race and Place in America.* Durham, N.C.: Duke University Press, 1996.

Litwack, Leon F. *North of Slavery: The Negro in the Free States, 1790–1860.* Chicago: University of Chicago Press, 1961.

Mabee, Carlton. *Black Freedom: The Nonviolent Abolitionists from 1830 through the Civil War.* London: Macmillan, 1970.

Madhubuti, Haki. *Enemies: The Clash of Races.* Chicago: Third World Press, 1978.

Magubene, Bernard M. *The Ties That Bind: African-American Consciousness of Africa.* Trenton, N.J.: Africa World Press, 1987.

Manger, Leif, and Munzoul A. M. Assal, eds. *Diasporas Within and Without Africa: Dynamism, Heterogeneity, Variation.* Uppsala, Sweden: Nordic Africa Institute, 2006.

Martusewicz, Rebecca. *Seeking Passage: Post-Structuralism, Pedagogy, Ethics.* New York: Teachers College Press, 2001.

McAdoo, Bill. *Pre-Civil War Black Nationalism.* New York: David Walker, 1983.

Meier, August, and Elliott Rudwick. *Black History and the Historical Profession, 1915–1980.* Urbana: University of Illinois Press, 1986.

Meier, August, John H. Bracey, and Elliott Rudwick, eds. *Black Nationalism in America.* New York: Bobbs-Merrill Co., 1970.

Meriwether, James H. *Proudly We Can Be African: Black Americans and Africans, 1935–1961.* Chapel Hill: University of North Carolina Press, 2002.

Miller, Floyd J. *The Search for a Black Nationality: Black Emigration and Colonization, 1787–1863.* Urbana: University of Illinois Press, 1975.

Miller, John T., ed. *Alternatives to Afrocentrism.* Washington, D.C.: Manhattan Institute, 1994.

Mills, Charles W. *The Racial Contract.* Ithaca, N.Y.: Cornell University Press, 1997.

Mohammed, Elijah. *The Fall of America.* Newport News, Va.: *National Newport News & Commentator,* 1993.

Moses, Wilson J. *Afrotopia: The Roots of African American Popular History.* Cambridge: Cambridge University Press, 1998.

———. *Alexander Crummell: A Study of Civilization and Discontent.* New York: Oxford University Press, 1989.

———. *Classical Black Nationalism: From the American Revolution to Marcus Garvey.* New York: New York University Press, 1996.

———. *The Golden Age of Black Nationalism, 1850–1925.* New York: Oxford University Press, 1978.

Mutiso, Gideon-Cyrus M., and S. W. Rohio, eds. *Readings in African Political Thought.* London: Heinemann, 1975

Mwakikagile, Godfrey. *Relations Between Africans, African Americans and Afro-Caribbean: Tensions, Indifference and Harmony.* Pretoria, South Africa: New Africa Press, 2007.

———. *Relations Between Africans and African Americans: Misconceptions, Myths and Realities.* Johannesburg, South Africa: Continental Press, 2005.

Nash, Gary B. *Forging Freedom: The Formation of Philadelphia's Black Community, 1720–1840.* Cambridge, Mass.: Harvard University Press, 1988.

Nkrumah, Kwame. *Some Essential Features of Nkrumaism.* London: Panaf Books, 1975.

Nnoli, O. *Ethnic Politics in Nigeria.* Enugu, Nigeria: Fourth Dimension Publishers, 1978.

Oakes, James. *The Ruling Race: A History of American Slaveholders.* New York: W. W. Norton & Co. 1998.

Ofari, Earl. *Let Your Motto Be RESISTANCE: The Life of Henry H. Garnet.* Boston: Beacon Press, 1972.

Okoye, Felix N. *The American Image of Africa: Myth and Reality.* New York: Black Academy Press, 1971.

Payne, Richard. *Getting Beyond Race: The Changing American Culture.* Boulder: Westview Press, 1998.

Picca, Leslie H., and Joe Feagin. *Two-Faced Racism: Whites in the Backstage and Frontstage.* New York: Routledge, 2007.

Quarles, Benjamin. *Black Abolitionists.* New York: Oxford University Press, 1969.

———. *Black Mosaic: Essays in Afro-American Historiography.* Amherst: University of Massachusetts Press, 1988.

Rawick, George. *From Sundown to Sunup: The Making of the Black Community.* Westport, Conn.: Greenwood Press, 1972.

Redkey, Edwin S. *Black Exodus: Black Nationalism and Back-to- Africa Movement, 1890–1910.* New Haven, Conn.: Yale University Press, 1969.

———. *Respect Black: The Writings and Speeches of Henry McNeal Turner.* New York: Arno Press, 1971.

Reed, Harry. *Platform for Change: The Foundation of the Northern Free Black Community, 1775–1865.* East Lansing: Michigan State University Press, 1994.

Richards, Dona Marimba. *Let the Circle Be Unbroken: The Implications of African Spirituality in the Diaspora.* Trenton, N.J.: Red Sea Press, 1980.

Richards, Leonard. *"Gentlemen of Property and Standing": Anti-Abolitionist Mobs in Jacksonian America.* New York: Oxford University Press, 1970.

Richburg, Keith. *Out of America: A Black Man Confronts Africa.* New York: Basic Books, 1996.

Rigsby, Gregory U. *Alexander Crummell: Pioneer in Nineteenth-Century Pan-African Thought*. Westport, Conn.: Greenwood Press, 1987.

Rodney, Walter. *The Groundings with My Brothers*. London: Bogle L'Ouverture, 1969.

———. *A History of the Upper Guinea Coast, 1540–1800*. Oxford: Clarendon Press, 1970.

———. *How Europe Underdeveloped Africa*. London: Bogle L'Ouverture, 1972.

Rollin, Frank (Frances). *Life and Public Services of Martin R. Delany*. Boston: Lee & Shepard, 1868.

Rutherford, Jonathan, ed. *Identity, Community, Culture, Difference*. London: Lawrence and Wishast, 1990.

Schlesinger, Arthur M., Jr. *The Disuniting of America: Reflections on a Multicultural Society* (revised & enlarged edition). London: W. W. Norton & Co., 1998.

Segal, Ronald. *The Black Diaspora: Five Centuries of the Black Experience Outside Africa*. New York: Farrar, Straus and Gireux, 1995.

Seraile, William. *Bruce Grit: The Black Nationalist Writings of John Edward Bruce*. Knoxville: University of Tennessee Press, 2003.

Shabazz, Betty. *Malcolm X on Afro-American History*. New York: Pathfinder Press, 1970.

Shavit, Yaacov. *History in Black: African-Americans in Search of an Ancient Past*. London: Frank Cass, 2001.

Shujaa, Mwalimu, ed. *Too Much Schooling, Too Little Education: A Paradox of Black Life in White Societies*. Trenton N.J.: Africa World Press, 1995.

Sidbury, James. *Becoming African in America: Race and Nation in the Early Black Atlantic*. Oxford: Oxford University Press, 2007.

Sorin, Gerald. *Abolitionism: A New Perspective*. New York: Praeger Publishers 1972.

Soyinka, Wole. *The Open Sore of a Continent: A Personal Narrative of the Nigerian Crisis*. New York: Oxford University Press, 1996.

Stampp, Kennett. *The Peculiar Institution: Slavery in the Antebellum South*. 1956; New York: Vintage Books.

Steele, Shelby. *The Content of Our Character*. New York: St. Martin's 1990.

Steinhorn, Leonard, and Barbara Diggs-Brown. *By the Color of the Skin: The Illusion of INTEGRATION and the Reality of Race*. New York: Penguin, 2000.

Sterling, Dorothy. *The Making of an Afro-American: Martin R. Delany, 1812–1885*. 1971; New York: DaCapo Press, 1996.

Stewart, James B. *Holy Warriors: The Abolitionists and American Slavery*. New York: Hill and Wang, 1976.

Stiglitz, Joseph E. *Globalization and Its Discontents*. New York: W. W. Norton & Co., Inc., 2003.

Thompson, Vincent B. *Africa and Unity: The Evolution of Pan-Africanism*. London: Longman, 1969.

Thorpe, Earl. *Black Historians: A Critique*. New York: William Morrow & Co., 1971.

Tise, Larry E. *Proslavery: A History of the Defense of Slavery in America, 1701–1840*. Athens: University of Georgia Press, 1987.

T'Shaka, Oba. *The Art of Leadership*. Richmond, Calif.: Pan Afrikan Publishers, 1990.

———. *The Political Legacy of Malcolm X*. Richmond, Calif.: Pan Afrikan Publishers, 1983.

Uya, Okon, ed. *Black Brotherhood: Afro-Americans and Africa*. Lexington, Mass.: D. C. Heath, 1971.

Von Eschen, Penny M. *Race Against Empire: Black Americans and Anti-Colonialism, 1937–1957*. Ithaca, N.Y.: Cornell University Press, 1997.

Walker, Clarence E. *We Can't Go Home Again: An Argument About Afrocentrism*. New York: Oxford University Press, 2001.

Wiltse, Charles M. ed. *David Walker's Appeal*. New York, 1991.

Walvin, James. *Questioning Slavery*. New York: Routledge, 1996.

Wamba, Philippe E. *Kinship: A Family's Journey in Africa and America*. New York: Plume Books, 2000.

William, Seraile. *Bruce Grit: The Black Nationalist Writings of John Edward Bruce*. Knoxville: University of Tennessee Press, 2003.

Williams, C. *The Destruction of Black Civilization*. Chicago: Third World Press, 1976.

Williams, John A, and Charles F. Harris, eds. *Amistad 1: Writings on Black History and Culture*. New York: Vintage Books, 1970.

———. *Amistad 2: Writings on Black History and Culture*. New York: Vintage Books, 1971.

Williams, Lorraine A. ed. *Africa and the Afro-American Experience*. Washington, D.C.: Howard University Press, 1977.

Wilson, Amos N. *The Falsification of Afrikan Consciousness: Eurocentric History, Psychiatry and the Politics of White Supremacy*. New York: Afrikan World InfoSystems, 1993.

Woodson, Carter G. *The Mis-Education of the Negro*. 1933; Trenton, N.J.: Africa World Press, 1990.

Wright, Bobby E. *The Psychopathic Racial Personality and Other Essays*. Chicago: Third World Press, 1994.

Wright, Richard. *White Man Listen!* New York: Doubleday & Co, 1964.

Wright, W. D. *Black Intellectuals, Black Cognitions, and a Black Aesthetic*. Westport, Conn.: Praeger, 1997.

———. *Crisis of the Black Intellectual*. Chicago: Third World Press, 2007.

X, Malcolm. *Malcolm X on Afro-American History*. New York: Pathfinder, 1970.

Ziegler, Dhyana, ed. *Molefi Kete Asante and Afrocentricity: In Praise and in Criticism*. Nashville, Tenn.: James C. Winston Publishing Co., 1995

## Articles and Essays

Abusharaf, Roqaia. "Southern Sudanese—A Community in Exile." In *Diasporas Within and Without Africa: Dynamism, Heterogeneity, Variation*, edited by Leif Manger and Munzoul A. M. Assal. Uppsala, Sweden: Nordic Africa Institute, 2006.

Adeleke, Tunde. "Afro-Americans and Moral Suasion: The Debate in the 1830s." *Journal of Negro History* 83, no. 2 (Spring 1998). 127–41.

———. "Black Americans and Africa: The Racial Hermeneutics of Popular response to Keith Richburg." *UFAHAMU: Journal of the African Activist Association* 25, no. 3 (1997): 86–109.

———. "The Color Line as a Confining and Restraining Paradigm: Keith Richburg and His Critics Analyzed." *Western Journal of Black Studies* 23, no. 2 (1999): 97–110.

———. "Constructing a Dual Cultural Space: Protests and Adaptations in Nineteenth Century Black American Nationalism." *Anglophonia: French Journal of English Studies* 19 (2006): 235–42.

———. "Gloracialization: The Responses of Pan-Blackists to Globalization." *Globalization* 5, no. 1 (2005).

———. "Guerilla Intellectualism: Walter A. Rodney and the Weapon of Knowledge in the Black Liberation Struggle." *Journal of Thought* 35, no. 1: 37–59 (Spring 2000): 37–59.

———. "Primacy of Condition: The Moral Suasion Debate among African-Americans in the 1830s." *Journal of American and Canadian Studies* 12 (1994): 25–46.

———. "Race and Ethnicity in Martin R. Delany's Struggles." *Journal of Thought* 29, no. 1 (Spring 1994): 19–49.

———. "Religion in Martin R. Delany's Liberation Thought." *Religious Humanism* 27, no. 2 (Spring 1993): 80–92.

Ajayi, Jacob F. A. "The Black Heritage Summit." Unpublished internet circulation of the USA-Africa Dialogue, January 2007.

Akbar, Na'im. "Africentric Social Sciences for Human Liberation." *Journal of Black Studies* 14, no. 4 (June 1984).

Allegritti, Inta. "Renovating Australian Citizenship: A Post-Liberal Approach to Citizenship." Keynote Address at the International Conference on 'Cultural Citizenship: Challenges of Globalization' Deakin University, Melbourne, Australia, December 6, 2002.

Anise, Laduna. "The African Redefined: The Problems of Collective Identity." *Pan-African Journal* 6, no. 4 (Winter 1973).

Aptheker, Herbert. "Consciousness of Negro Nationality to 1900," In *Toward Negro Freedom*, by Herbert Aptheker, 104–11. New York: New Century Publishers, 1956.

Asante, Molefi K. "Racism, Consciousness and Afrocentricity." In *Lure and Loathing: Essays on Race, Ideology and the Ambivalence of Assimilation*, edited by Gerald Early, 127–43. New York: Penguin, 1994.

———. "The Afrocentric Idea in Education." *Journal of Negro Education* 60, no. 2 (1991): 170–79.

———. "Where Is the White Professor Located?" *Perspectives* 31, no. 6 (1993): 19.

———. "On Historical Interpretations." In *Malcolm X as Cultural Hero and Other Afrocentric Essays*, by Molefi K. Asante. Trenton, N.J.: Africa World Press, 1993.

———. "On Afrocentric Metatheory." In *Malcolm X as Cultural Hero and Other Afrocentric Essays*. Trenton, N.J.: Africa World Press, 1993.

Assal, Munzoul A. M. "Somalis and Sudanese in Norway—Religion, Ethnicity/Clan and Politics in the Diaspora." in *Diasporas Within and Without Africa*, edited by

Leif Manger and Munzoul A. M. Assal, 165–96. Uppsala, Sweden: Nordic Africa Institute, 2006.

Bell, Howard H. "The American Moral Reform Society, 1836–1841." *Journal of Negro Education* 27 (Winter 1958): 34–40.

Berger, Joseph. "Professor's Theories on Race Stir Turmoil at City College." *New York Times*, April 20, 1990.

Berlin, Ira. "From Creole to Africa: Atlantic Creoles and the Origins of African-American Society in Mainland North America." In *How Did American Slavery Begin?* edited by Edward Countryman. New York: St. Martin's Press, 1999.

"Black Scholar Interviews: Walter Rodney." *The Black Scholar*, November 1974.

Blyden, Edward W. "The African Problem and the Methods of Its Solution." *The Voice of Black America: Major Speeches by Blacks in the United States, 1797–1973*, edited by Philip Foner, 570–86. New York: Capricorn Books, 1975.

Bonilla-Silva, Eduardo. "New Racism: Color-Blind Racism and the future of Whiteness in America." In *White Out: The Continuing Significance of Racism*, edited by Ashley Doane and Eduardo Bonilla-Silva. New York: Routledge, 2003.

Bruce, John E. "Reasons Why the Colored American Should Go to Africa." Philip Foner, ed., *The Voice of Black America: Major Speeches by Blacks in the United States, 1797–1973*, vol. 1, 489–91. New York: Capricorn, 1975.

Cabral, Amilcar. "National Liberation and Culture." In *Cabral: Unity and Struggle (Speeches and Writings)* by Amilcar Cabral, 128–56. London: Heinemann, 1980.

Conrad, Bettina. "We Are the Warsay of Eritrea in Diaspora: Contested Identities and Social Divisions in Cyberspace and in Real Life." In *Diasporas Within and Without*, edited by Leif Manger and Munzoul A. M. Assal, 104–39. Uppsala, Sweden: Nordic Africa Institute, 2006.

Cook, Samuel DuBois. "A Tragic Conception of Negro History." *Journal of Negro History* 45 (October 1960).

Coulter, Merton E. "Henry M. Turner: Georgia's Negro Preacher-Nationalist During the Reconstruction." *Georgia Historical Quarterly* 48, no. 4 (December 1964): 371–409.

Crouch, Stanley. "Who Are We? Where Did We Come From? Where Are We Going?" In *Lure and Loathing: Essays on Race, Ideology, and the Ambivalence of Assimilation*, edited by Gerald Early, ed., 80–94. New York: Penguin, 1994.

Crummell, Alexander. "Address Before the American Geographical Society." In *Africa and America: Addresses and Discourses*, by Alexander Crummell, 316–23. New York: Negro University Press, 1969.

———. "Civilization as a Collateral and Indispensable Instrumentality in Planting the Christian Church in Africa." In *Addresses and Proceedings of the Congress on Africa Held Under the Auspices of the Stewart Missionary Foundation for Africa*, by Alexander Crummell, 119–24. Atlanta: Gammon Theological Seminary.

———. "The Duty of a Rising Christian State to Contribute to the World's Well-Being and Civilization." In *The Future of Africa: Being Addresses, Sermons, Delivered in the Republic of Liberia*, by Alexander Crummell. New York: Charles Scribner, 1862.

——. "The English Language in Liberia." In *The Future of Africa: Being Addresses, Sermons, Delivered in the Republic of Liberia*, by Alexander Crummell, 32–36. New York: Charles Scriber, 1862.

——. "Our National Mistakes, and the Remedy for Them." In *Africa and America*, 181–87. Originally published in 1891.

——. "Progress of Civilization Along the West Coast of Africa." In *The Future of Africa: Being Addresses, Sermons, Delivered in the Republic of Liberia*, by Alexander Crummell. New York: Charles Scribner, 1862.

——. "The Relations and Duty of the Free Colored Men in America to Africa." In *The Future of Africa: Being Addresses, Sermons, Delivered in the Republic of Liberia*, by Alexander Crummell. New York: Charles Scribner, 1862.

Delany, Martin R. Delany letter to Dr. James McCune Smith. *Weekly Anglo-African*, January 4, 1862.

——. Delany to Professor M. H. Freeman. *Weekly Anglo-African*, February 1, 1862.

——. "Important Movement (Delany to Dr. James McCune Smith)." *Weekly Anglo-African*, January 4, 1862.

——. "The International Policy of the World towards the African Race." In *Life and Public Services of Martin R. Delany*, by Frank Rollin, 313–27. Boston: Lee & Shepard, 1868.

——. "The Moral and Social Aspect of Africa." In *The Voice of Black America: Major Speeches by Blacks in the United States, 1797–1973*, vol. 1, edited by Philip Foner, 288–94. New York: Capricorn, 1975.

——. "Official Report of the Niger Valley Exploring Party (1860)." In *Search for a Place: Black Separatism and Africa*, edited by Martin Delany and Robert Campbell, 26–148. Ann Arbor: University of Michigan Press, 1971.

——. "Political Aspect of the Colored People of the United States." *Provincial Freeman*, October 13, 1855.

——. "Political Destiny of the Colored Race on the American Continent." (1854.) In Frank Rollin, *Life and Public Services of Martin R. Delany*, 327–67. Boston: Lee & Shepard, 1868.

——. "Political Events." *Provincial Freeman*, July 5, 1856.

Diop, Cheikh Anta. "Africa: Cradle of Civilization." *Nile Valley Civilization (Journal of African Civilization)* 6, no. 2 (1984).

——. "Origins of the Ancient Egyptians." In *UNESCO General History of Africa, vol. 2: Ancient Civilizations of Africa*, edited by G. Mokhtar. Berkeley, Calif.: 1981.

Drake, St. Claire. "Diaspora Studies and Pan-Africanism." In *Global Dimensions of the African Diaspora*, edited by Joseph E. Harris, 341–402. Washington, D.C.: Howard University Press, 1993.

Draper, Theodore. "The Father of Black American Nationalism." *New York Times Review of Books*, March 12, 1970.

Du Bois, W. E. B. "To the Nations of the World." In *W. E. B. Du Bois: A Reader*, edited by David Levering Lewis, 639–41. New York: Henry Holt & Co., 1995.

Egbo, Chinyere E. "Self-Denial and Retribution: Richburg and His African Past." *African Profiles USA*, July–August, 1997.

Fisher, Miles M. "Lott Cary: The Colonizing Missionary." *Journal of Negro History* 7, no. 4 (December 1922).

Franklin, John H. "On the Evolution of Scholarship in Afro-American History." In *The State of Afro-American History: Past, Present, Future*, edited by Darlene Clark Hine, 13–22. Baton Rouge: Louisiana State University.

Friedman, Neil. "Africa and the Afro-American: The Changing Negro Identity." *Psychiatry*, May 1969, 127–36.

Gienapp, William E. "Abolitionism and the Nature of Ante-Bellum Reform." *Courage and Conscience: Black and White Abolitionists in Boston*, edited by Donald M. Jacobs, 21–46. Bloomington: Indiana University Press, 1993.

Greene, Jack P. "Beyond Power: Paradigm Subversion and Reformulation and the Re-Creation of the Early Modern Atlantic World." In *Crossing Boundaries: Comparative History of Black People in Diaspora*, edited by Darlene Clark Hine and Jacqueline McLeod, 319–42. Bloomington: Indiana University Press, 1997.

Grisham, G. N. "The Functions of the Negro Scholar." In *The Voice of Black America: Major Speeches by Blacks in the United States, 1797–1973*, vol. 1, edited by Philip S. Foner, 629–33. New York: Capricorn, 1975.

Hall, Stuart. "Cultural Ideology and Diaspora." In *Identity, Community, Culture, Difference*, edited by Jonathan Rutherford, 222–37. London: Lawrence & Wishart, 1990.

———. "What is 'Black' in Black Popular Culture?" In *Black Popular Culture*, edited by Gina Dent, 21–33. Seattle: Bay Press, 1992.

Hamilton, Ruth S. "Rethinking the African Diaspora: Global Dynamics." In *Routes of Passage: Rethinking the African Diaspora, vol. 1, Part 1*, edited by Ruth Simms Hamilton, 1–39. East Lansing: Michigan State University Press, 2007.

Harding, Vincent. "Beyond Chaos: Black History and the Search for the New Land." In *Amistad 1: Writings on Black History and Culture*, edited by John A. Williams and Charles F. Harris, 269–92. New York: Vintage Books, 1970.

Harris, Mene-lik, P. D. "Jamaica Pre-Summit Calls for an African Diaspora Union." Unpublished internet circulation of the *Nigernet* Discussion Group, May 2007.

Harris, Robert L. "Coming of Age: The Transformation of Afro-American Historiography." *Journal of Negro History* 67, no. 2 (Summer 1982): 107–21.

Hill, Robert A. "Walter Rodney and the Restatement of Pan-Africanism in Theory and Practice." In *Walter Rodney; Revolutionary and Scholar, A Tribute*, edited by Edward A. Alpers and Pierre-Michael Fontaine, 77–97. Los Angeles: Center for Afro-American Studies and African Studies Center, University of California, Los Angeles, 1982.

Isaacs, Harold L. "The American Negro and Africa: Some Notes." *Phylon Quarterly* 20, no. 3 (Fall 1959): 219–33.

Jones, Rhett S. "Why Pan-Africanism Failed: Blackness and International Relations." *Griot: The Journal of African American Studies* 14, no. 1 (1995).

Karenga, M. "Corrective History: Rewriting the Black Past." *The First World* 1, no. 3 (May-June 1977).

Lefkowitz, Mary. "Origins of the 'Stolen Legacy.'" In *Alternatives to Afrocentrism*, edited by John Miller, 27–31. Washington, D.C.: Manhattan Institute, 1994.

Lemelle, Sidney J. "The Politics of Cultural Existence: Pan-Africanism, Historical Materialism and Afrocentricity." In *Imagining Home: Class, Culture and Nationalism in the African Diaspora*, edited by Sidney Lemelle and Robin Kelly. New York: Verso, 1994.

Lewis, Earl. "To Turn As on A Pivot: Writing African Americans into a History of Overlapping Diasporas." In *Crossing Boundaries: Comparative History of Black People in Diaspora*, edited by Darlene Clark Hine and Jacqueline McLeod, 3–32. Bloomington: Indiana University Press, 1997.

Liyong, Taban L. "Negroes are not Africans." In *Black Homeland, Black Diaspora: Cross-Currents of the African Relationship*, edited by Jacob Drachler. New York: Kennikat Press, 1975.

Loury, Glen. "Free At Last? A Personal Perspective on Race and Identity in America." In *Lure and Loathing: Essays on Race, Ideology, and the Ambivalence of Assimilation, edited by* Gerald Early, 1–12. New York: Penguin, 1994.

Mazrui, Ali. "On the Concept 'We're all Africans.'" *American Political Science Review* 1, no. 57 (March 1963).

Mboya, Tom. "Africa and Afro-Americans." In *Black Homeland, Black Diaspora: Cross-Currents of the African Relationship*, edited by Jacob Drachler. New York: Kennikat Press, 1975.

———. "The American Negro Cannot Look To Africa for an Escape." In *Americans from Africa: Old Memories, New Moods*, edited by Peter I. Rose. New York: Atherton Press, 1970.

McCormick, Richard P. "William Whipper: Moral Reformer." *Pennsylvania History* 43 (January 1976).

Morris, Aldon, and Naomi Braine. "Social Movement and Oppositional Consciousness." In *Oppositional Consciousness: The Subjective Roots of Social Protest*, edited by Jane Mansbridge and Aldon Morris, 20–37. London: University of Chicago Press, 2001.

Ohaegbulam, Festus U. "Continental Africans and Africans in America: The Progression of a Relationship." In *A Survey of Africa and the African Diaspora*, edited by Mario Azevedo, 225–52. Durham, N.C.: Carolina Academic Press, 2005.

Olusanya, Gabriel O. "African Historians and the Pan-Africanist Tradition." In *Perspectives and Methods of Studying African History*, edited by Erim O. Erim and Okon Uya, 10–16. Enugu, Nigeria: Fourth Dimension Publishers, 1984.

Opoku, Kwame. "Cabral and the African Revolution." *Presence Africaine* 105/106 (1978): 45–60.

Pease, William H., and Jane H. Pease. "The Negro Convention Movement." In *Key Issues in the Afro-American Experience*, vol. 1, edited by Nathan Huggins, 191–205. New York: Harcourt Brace, 1971.

Rael, Patrick. "Black Theodicy: African Americans and Nationalism in the Antebellum North." *The North Star* 3, no. 2 (Spring 2000): 1–19.

Redkey, Edwin S. "Bishop Turner's African Dream." *Journal of American History* 54, no. 2 (September 1967).

———. "The Flowering of Black Nationalism: Henry McNeal Turner and Marcus Garvey." In *Key Issues in the Afro-American Experience*, vol. 2, edited by Nathan Huggins, 107–24. New York: Harcourt Brace, 1971.

"Resist Recolonization!: General Declaration by the Delegates and Participants at the Seventh Pan-African Congress." In *Imagining Home: Class, Culture and Nationalism in the African Diaspora*, edited by Sidney L. Lemelle and Robin D. G. Kelley. New York: Verso, 1994.

"The Richburg Firestorm." *African Profiles USA*, July-August 1997.

Rodney, Walter. "African History in the Service of Black Revolution." In *The Groundings With My Brothers*, by Walter Rodney, 51–59. London: Bogle L'Ouverture, 1969.

Sackeyitio, Aba. "For a Self-Denying 'African'-American Journalist." *African Profiles USA*, July-August 1997.

Scruggs, Ottey M. "We the Children of Africa in this Land: Alexander Crummell." *Africa and the Afro-Americans Experience*, edited by Lorraine A. Williams, 77–96. Washington, D.C.: Howard University Press, 1977.

Sherwood, Henry N. "Paul Cuffee." *Journal of Negro History*, April 8, 1928.

———. "Paul Cuffee and his Contributions to the American Colonization Society." *Proceedings of the Mississippi Valley History Association, 1912–1913*, vol. 6, 1913.

Simmons, Adam, D. "Ideologies and Programs of the Negro Anti-Slavery Movement, 1830–1861." Ph.D. dissertation, Northwestern University, 1983.

Smith, Anthony D. "Towards a Global Culture?" In *Global Culture: Nationalism, Globalization and Modernity*, edited by Mike Featherstone, 170–91. London: Sage Publications, 1990.

Stuckey, Sterling. "Twilight of Our Past: Reflections on the Origins of Black History." *Amistad 2: Writings on Black History and Culture*, edited by John A. Williams and Charles F. Harris, 261–95. New York: Vintage Books, 1971.

Turner, Henry M. "The Afro-American Future."

———. "The American Colonization Society."

———. "An Emigration Convention."

———. "Emigration to Africa."

———. "The Question of Race." In *Respect Black: The Writings and Speeches of Henry McNeal Turner*, edited by Edwin Redkey, 73–75. New York: Arno Press, 1971.

Walker, Clarence E. "The Distortions of Afrocentric History." In *Alternatives to Afrocentrism*, edited by John T. Miller, 32–36. Washington, D.C.: Manhattan Institute, 1994.

———. "The Virtuoso Illusionists: Marcus Garvey." In *Deromanticizing Black History: Critical Essays and Reappraisals*, by Clarence E. Walker, 34–55. Knoxville: University of Tennessee Press, 1991.

Watkins, Craig S. "Black Is Back, and It's Bound to Sell: Nationalist Desire and the Production of Black Popular Culture." In *IS IT NATION TIME?: Contemporary Essays on Black Power and Black Nationalism*, edited by Eddie S. Glaude Jr., 189–214. Chicago: University of Chicago Press, 2002.

Whipper, William. "An Address on Non-Resistance to Offensive Aggression 1 & 2." *The Colored American*, September 16, 30, 1837.

————. "Eulogy on William Wilberforce." In *The Voice of Black America: Major Speeches by Blacks in the United States, 1797–1973*, vol. 1, edited by Philip S. Foner, 71–77. New York: Capricorn, 1975.

Williams, Dwayne. "Rethinking the African Diaspora: A Comparative Look at Race and Ideology in a Transatlantic Community, 1878–1921." *Crossing Boundaries: Comparative History of Black People in Diaspora*. edited by Darlene C. Hine and Jacqueline McLeod, 105–20. Bloomington: Indiana University Press, 1997.

Williams, Peter. "Slavery and Colonization." In *The Voice of Black America: Major Speeches by Blacks in the United States, 1797–1973*, vol. 1, edited by Philip S. Foner, 57–60. New York: Capricorn, 1975.

Williams, Walter. "Black American Attitudes Toward Africa, 1877–1900." *Pan-African Journal* 4, no. 2 (Spring 1971).

Woodson, Lewis. "The West." *The Colored American*, February 17, May 3, 1838; January 15, February 5, March 2, 16, July 15, August 31, 1839.

# Index

www.ingramcontent.com/pod-product-compliance
Lightning Source LLC
Chambersburg PA
CBHW030648270326
41929CB00007B/262